I0621818

To my wife, Marie, truly a gift from God,
and to our children, and our children's children.
May you be blessed with every blessing under heaven.

DEMYSTIFYING
SPIRIT
BAPTISM

UNVEILING THE GATEWAY
TO CHRISTIAN LIFE

JEFFREY D. CHAMBERLAIN

Five Lamps
PRESS

© 2024 by Jeffrey D. Chamberlain
Published by Five Lamps Press LLC
P.O Box 22, Lovettsville, VA 20180

Printed in the United States of America

All rights reserved. No part of this publication may be reproduced, stored in a retrieval system, or transmitted in any form or by any means, electronic, mechanical, photocopying, recording, or otherwise, without the publisher's prior written permission. The only exception is brief quotations in printed reviews.

ISBN 979-8-9911775-0-4 (softcover)
ISBN 979-8-9911775-1-1 (ebook)
ISBN 979-8-9911775-2-8 (hardcover)

Library of Congress Control Number: 2024916463

Scripture quotations are from The ESV° Bible (The Holy Bible, English Standard Version°), © 2001 by Crossway, a publishing ministry of Good News Publishers. Used by permission. All rights reserved.

Excerpts from the English translation of the Catechism of the Catholic Church for use in the United States of America Copyright © 1994, United States Catholic Conference, Inc. -- Libreria Editrice Vaticana. Used with Permission. English translation of the Catechism of the Catholic Church: Modifications from the Editio Typica copyright © 1997, United States Conference of Catholic Bishops—Libreria Editrice Vaticana.

References to Internet websites (URLs) were accurate at the time of writing and are offered as a resource. They are not intended to be or imply an endorsement by Five Lamps Press, nor does Five Lamps Press vouch for the content of these sites for the life of this book.

Permission was granted for use of materials from the following sources:

Illustration, page 20: JOHNNY MILANO/The New York Times/Redux

Lyrics: **I Still Haven't Found What I'm Looking For**
Words and Music by U2
Copyright © 1987 UNIVERSAL MUSIC PUBLISHING INTERNATIONAL B.V.
All Rights in the United States and Canada Controlled and Administered by UNIVERSAL –
POLYGRAM INTERNATIONAL PUBLISHING, INC.
All Rights Reserved   Used by Permission
Reprinted by Permission of Hal Leonard LLC

Cover and interior design: Enterline Design Services

CONTENTS

Part Three - Practical Considerations

PRELUDE

Here are a few thoughts before we dive in. This book is about possibilities, abundance, and generosity, not limitations, lack, or selfishness. Many will tell you what you must believe and what you must then do, but offered here is how you might understand to spur thought, conversation, and even action.

The book begins with a chapter on risk, as risk management was my career for nearly thirty years, and its principles can help us understand our spiritual journey. Risk managers evaluate potential adverse events and their related risks. We think about the likelihood of events occurring, the possible severity of loss, and how to accept, manage, or reduce risk. Our desire is to increase the chance of success while reducing the risk of loss. That is my heart in writing—to increase our chance of success as the body of Christ, to improve our chance of growing in intimacy with God, and to reduce the risk of falling short of our calling as disciples of Christ.

Why Write?

When we believe we have exhausted all there is to know about something or someone, we turn a corner, and we're face-to-face with the undiscovered. This discovery occurs regularly in science, from finding new species to understanding the inner workings of our bodies to glimpsing the farthest reaches of the universe. In a similar way, God continually expands our understanding of his infinite wisdom and love.

For some, the subject matter of this book is familiar, and for others, it covers uncharted territory. The book's primary focus is Spirit baptism, or "baptism with/in the Holy Spirit." In the 20th century, this was a central feature of a renewal that spread to almost every part of the body of Christ. Thirty-one years ago, a friend took the time to share with me about Spirit baptism, and my life was changed forever.

This work is intended to pay it forward, sharing what I have experienced, contemplated, and learned. I hope these words will stir up your passion for a deeper relationship with God in some small or significant way.

Many books on Spirit baptism are available from pastoral and academic authors, and each shares unique perspectives with various emphases that may speak to each of us differently. When we share our understanding and processing of our life in Christ (an integral part of our testimony), we often help others see different facets of a relationship with God that might otherwise be hidden. I hope that type of discovery happens here too.

Who Is This For?

According to the Center for Global Christianity, nearly three out of every four Christians[1] are not considered in any way Pentecostal or charismatic.[2] (They likely have not experienced Spirit baptism.) This book is aimed at that group and also speaks to the remainder who

---

[1]   Center for Global Christianity, Annual Statistics: "Status of Global Christianity, 2024, in the Context of 1900-2050." *GordonConwell.edu: https://www.gordonconwell.edu/wp-content/uploads/sites/13/2024/01/Status-of-Global-Christianity-2024.pdf* (February 27, 2024).

[2]   Includes Pentecostals, charismatics, and independent charismatics, collectively referred to herein as "Pentecostal-charismatic." (See "The 20th-Century Outpouring" in chapter 6 for more detail on these three types.) Other similar terms include "Renewalist" and "Spirit-empowered Christians."

have experienced Spirit baptism and anyone else who wants to enter into a personal, experiential relationship with God. For clarity, the God I am referring to is the One who made the heavens and the earth, the God of Abraham, Isaac, and Jacob, the God of the Hebrew Bible (the term used throughout for the Old Testament), and of the New Testament.

One of the modern rules of writing is to have an ideal reader in mind. My ideal reader is you because you have decided to read (or at least begin to read) this book. "He who has an ear, let him hear" (Revelation 2:7).

If you have experienced Spirit baptism, I hope this will encourage you in your walk, provide perspectives that may enhance your understanding, and help you to disciple others. For Christians who have not heard of or experienced this aspect of a relationship with God, I hope it sheds some helpful light on the subject. For those curious about God and Christianity who may only see a shadow of authentic Christianity as they peer into the church today, I'm hoping you'll learn something you didn't know and deepen your desire to look more closely.

Two Guiding Principles

Two principles should drive our thinking as we evaluate our beliefs about the Scriptures and our relationship with God. The first principle is *biblical grounding*, particularly that we should not arbitrarily limit God to something less than what we read in the Bible. If God did anything with any individual or community in the Bible, he could do it with us. The New Testament, in particular, allows us to see how God worked in the lives of others in the early church.

I agree with theologian Craig Keener, who aptly notes, "We are interested in biblical texts … because we expect to share the kind of spiritual experience and relationship with God that we discover in Scripture."[3] I am not suggesting that God cannot do something new that is not documented in Scripture. Still, it at least allows him to reveal himself in similar ways (Malachi 3:6; Hebrews 13:8). Although some things may not be repeated, such as Christ's atoning sacrifice and perhaps the parting of the Red Sea, God continues to reveal himself in many ways, including miracles.

Coupled with biblical grounding is a principle of *relational focus*. That is, God desires that we draw near to him (James 4:8), to be one with him (John 17:21-23), and to be his beloved (John 17:26; Romans 1:7; 1 John 3:1; Revelation 21:2). Any view that violates or lessens that perspective should be scrutinized. Any view that prevents us from deepening our relationship with God should be rejected.

By applying these two principles—biblical grounding and relational focus—we can evaluate if what we believe is potentially limiting God's work in our lives.

How This Book Is Organized

This book is organized into four parts. Part 1 lays a foundation of understanding about risk, ourselves, and God's heart for us. Based on that foundation, part 2, the core of this book, explores the new covenant, the Holy Spirit, and Spirit baptism from a biblical and experiential perspective. Part 3 provides guidance for individuals desiring Spirit baptism,

---

3   Craig S. Keener, *Spirit Hermeneutics: Reading Scripture in Light of Pentecost*, (Grand Rapids, MI: William. B. Eerdmans Publishing Co, 2016), 5.

the individual and corporate use of vocal spiritual gifts, and thoughts on corporate gatherings. Part 4 looks at renewal-related dynamics in play in the body of Christ, with thoughts on the current state, challenges, and future trajectory.

Footnotes are included within the chapters for easier reference. Some footnotes expand thoughts or include quotes or views from other authors. I encourage you to read those. Although the Bible is our primary text, how others have processed the scriptures, theology, doctrines, and experiences is often helpful and enriching.

On a Personal Note

Before we set sail, you should know I'm a recovering perfectionist. As much as I would like to have conquered all of the possible failings that an individual can have in life, I have found myself testing many of them out over the years, often making choices based on pride, fear, intellectual reasoning, the opinion of others, and thankfully at times because of God's leading. My journey is not unlike yours and continues to be a work in progress. I have found it helpful to know that despite my weaknesses, God remains the Perfect One, the Perfect Shepherd and Father, perfectly forgiving, and perfectly "able to do far more abundantly than all that we ask or think, according to the power at work within us" (Ephesians 3:20).

I hope any good seed for your soul contained here would take root and grow, stirring up your passion for him. Let's get started.

PART ONE

FOUNDATIONS FOR UNDERSTANDING

1

What's the Risk?

Resilience in the Storm

> "Everyone then who hears these words of mine and does them will be like a wise man who built his house on the rock. And the rain fell, and the floods came, and the winds blew and beat on that house, but it did not fall, because it had been founded on the rock. And everyone who hears these words of mine and does not do them will be like a foolish man who built his house on the sand. And the rain fell, and the floods came, and the winds blew and beat against that house, and it fell, and great was the fall of it." (Matthew 7:24-27)

Hurricane Michael made landfall in the Florida panhandle on October 10, 2018, as the fourth Category 5 storm to come ashore in the United States since the early 1900s.[4] Maximum sustained wind speeds reached 161 miles per hour, just above the Category 5 threshold.[5] While not the most powerful, destructive, or deadliest

4   Noreen O'Donnell, "'Catastrophic Damage': Category 5 Hurricanes That Have Made Landfall in the US," September 28, 2022. 5 Chicago: *https://www.nbcchicago.com/news/national-international/catastrophic-damage-category-5-hurricanes-that-have-made-landfall-in-the-us/2953096/* (February 29, 2024).

5   John L. Beven II, Robbie Berg, and Andrew Hagen, "Hurricane Michael," *National Hurricane Center Tropical Cyclone Report, May 17, 2019. National Hurricane Center: https://www.nhc.noaa.gov/data/tcr/AL142018_Michael.pdf* (February 29, 2024).

hurricane in recent history, it provides a stark reminder of the power of preparedness.

Two months after Michael hit, our family traveled to Florida to spend winter break with my father and stepmother. During our visit, we saw the impact of the storm. As we drove east through Tyndall Air Force base on our way to Mexico Beach, we saw buildings badly damaged and pine forests flattened. At Mexico Beach, we saw a wasteland with rubble everywhere. All that remained of many homes were ground-level slabs of concrete. Seeing only tile floors where there once had been a kitchen or bathroom was eerie. But this was not true for all of the homes. If you've seen photos of the aftermath, you might recall one house standing nearly unscathed. While there was some damage, the Sand Palace, as the owners called it, stood defiantly in the destruction that surrounded it.

Sand Palace, Mexico Beach, Florida. JOHNNY MILANO/The New York Times/Redux

The owners, a man and his nephew from Tennessee, had completed the construction of their home in April 2018, just six months before Michael hit. They noted in retrospect, "Just like you put on your seat belt every day when you get in the car to get you ready for something that hopefully never happens, we built a house for something we hoped would never happen. We built it for the big one, but we had no idea that the big one would come so soon and come barreling right down on Mexico Beach like it did." Building code had called for new homes to withstand 120-130 mile per hour winds, but the owners were not satisfied with the minimum. They added features to fortify their home against 240-250 mile per hour winds, increasing building costs by 15 to 20 percent.[6] Few would argue that this was not money well spent.

The owners of the Sand Palace exhibited wisdom and action that resulted in resilience in the face of disaster—epitomizing wise risk management. I suggest we also wisely consider risk in our decisions about how we relate to God in this life. Life's storms will undoubtedly come, and we may face devastating events. (See John 16:33; 2 Timothy 3:12; 1 Peter 4:12; Revelation 2:10; James 1:2-4, 12; Psalm 34:19.) How will we cope? Will we be utterly cast down, or will we walk in peace and joy in the midst of life's trials? And how do we fortify our minds and hearts to enable us to stand in the storm and not be overcome?

Here's a softball question: Given the devastation that Hurricane Michael caused at Mexico Beach, which home would you prefer to have owned?

---

6   Amanda Schmidt, "'We built it for the big one': How this Mexico Beach house survived Hurricane Michael," October 18, 2018. *AccuWeather: https://www.accuweather.com/en/weather-news/we-built-it-for-the-big-one-how-this-mexico-beach-house-survived-hurricane-michael/342440* (February 29, 2024).

Have you gone the extra mile to fortify against any loss in your life as these two men did? Can you think of times when your extra effort or expense paid off? Do you think about the impacts of your decisions with potential risks and rewards in mind?

A Risk Management Worldview

At the heart of the human experience, most of us are risk managers. Our risk appetite is seen in the life choices we make. We often apply our intellect and knowledge to chart our course through life, seeking the best outcomes for ourselves and those we care for. The risk averse may choose a career or life path that is relatively stable and certain, to the degree that life can be stable or certain. Others may choose a high-risk path, even one that involves a heightened risk of death. Many of our military and first responders are among these. And as the owners of the Sand Palace showed us, there are actions we can take to influence our outcomes. Our military and first responders train rigorously and use protective gear and equipment to shield them from potentially fatal injury. While not all of us are on the front lines, we all face risk, and we should prepare by seeking counsel, researching, praying for wisdom, and taking appropriate actions.

As mentioned in the Prelude, professional risk managers seek to understand the risks of choices and events. They consider the likelihood of an event and how severe the loss will be. They may also consider various outcome paths—from the most likely to the most extreme—and determine actions that can help minimize losses.

Using a risk assessment approach has direct application not only to financial and material risks but also to our faith journey. Personal and even eternal risks are associated with our doctrines, beliefs, and practices. Observing the breadth of Christian denominations and faith streams, it is evident that there are many interpretations of the Bible and many versions of how one can live out their faith. While different emphases and understandings may be reasonable, certain beliefs that are direct opposites or differ in material ways raise the probability that some of these practices and beliefs do not align with God's intent. The possibility also exists that some of our doctrines and practices—however well intentioned—may be detrimental to our walk with him, creating spiritual risk.

Cat Risk

In our home, one of our two cats, affectionately called "G," developed a habit of knocking over cups of water, typically at night after we've all gone to bed. There's always a sinking feeling when I hear a thud and splash in the kitchen downstairs. The result of this cat event is usually only a wet counter, but the damage can be worse if something valuable or meaningful gets wet or the water soaks into the wood floor below. Being conscientious risk managers, we have trained ourselves to leave these "toys" out far less often. But sometimes we forget. And when a cup is left out, G will invariably knock it over.

These somewhat frequent but low-cost risk events were outdone a couple of years ago after a Thanksgiving break away. My heart sank when I entered the kitchen and saw the wood floor saturated in a ten-foot section in front of the sink. It spiraled even further after I went to our basement and found that water had made its way into a finished room below and was leaking through the ceiling and wall. The damage ultimately resulted in tens of thousands of dollars of work to repair.

From a tiny leak in our dishwasher, a small whirlwind of damage was done. Thankfully, what some might consider a moderate loss (our home didn't burn down after all) was covered by our homeowner's insurance policy, minus our deductible, of course. Praise God!

The damage from our dishwasher leak or G's waterfalls is inconsequential compared to the insurance industry's version of cat (short for catastrophe) risk. These are typically low-frequency but very high-cost events. They include earthquakes, tornadoes, hurricanes, and even large-scale terrorist attacks (such as September 11, 2001), which damage or destroy buildings, homes, infrastructure (roads, bridges, power grid), vehicles, air and watercraft, revenue streams, and sadly people's lives. For cat events, prudent risk managers use varied approaches to manage potential exposure to loss, including fortifying construction to withstand severe events (as with the Sand Palace), increasing surveillance and deterrence, and purchasing various types of insurance.

But how do these minor, moderate, and catastrophic risk events relate to our spiritual walk? Some of our doctrines and practices present us with a low risk of loss, such as using juice or wine for communion or dressing formally or casually for corporate worship. Still, ultimately, these do not usually present a high risk of going astray from God (assuming that we are seeking him). But what about spiritual cat risk? Let's turn to the New Testament, where several verses illustrate a risk of catastrophic loss.

Spiritual Cat Risk

In the Gospel of Matthew, Jesus speaks of entering through the narrow gate that leads to life, noting that few find it (Matthew 7:13-14). Jesus says hearing his words and not doing them is akin to building a house on sand, and unlike the Sand Palace "the rain fell, and the floods came, and the winds blew and beat against that house, and it fell, and great was the fall of it" (Matthew 7:26-27). The plight of those who come to Christ only to return to the entanglements of this world are described in the two passages below:

> For if, *after they have escaped the defilements of the world through the knowledge of our Lord and Savior Jesus Christ*, they are *again entangled in them and overcome*, the last state has become worse for them than the first. For it would have been better for them never to have *known the way of righteousness* than *after knowing it to turn back* from the holy commandment delivered to them. What the true proverb says has happened to them: "The dog returns to its own vomit, and the sow, after washing herself, returns to wallow in the mire." (2 Peter 2:20-22, emphasis added)

> For it is impossible, in the case of *those who have once been enlightened*, who have *tasted the heavenly gift*, and have *shared in the Holy Spirit*, and have *tasted the goodness of the word of God and the powers of the age to come*, and then have fallen away, to restore them again to repentance, since they are crucifying once again the Son of God to their own harm and holding him up to contempt. (Hebrews 6:4-6, emphasis added)

The individuals described above had gone well beyond a verbal profession of faith and had known Christ and the way of righteousness, shared in the Holy Spirit and his power, and escaped the world's defilements. However, based on their actions, it appears that they are no longer committed to the covenant they once enjoyed. As a risk manager, given these descriptions, it seems more than a slight possibility that those who think they can make a profession of faith at one point in time and never lose their relationship with God are mistaken. Would you agree that losing a relationship with God is a catastrophic event?

Some of Jesus' sayings and parables also emphasize the priority of knowing God, doing his will, and preparing for his return:

"*Not everyone who says to me, 'Lord, Lord,' will enter the kingdom of heaven*, but the one who does the will of my Father who is in heaven. On that day many will say to me, 'Lord, Lord, did we not *prophesy* in your name, and *cast out demons* in your name, and *do many mighty works* in your name?' And then will I declare to them, '*I never knew you; depart from me*, you workers of lawlessness.' (Matthew 7:21-23, emphasis added)

"Then the kingdom of heaven will be like ten virgins who took their lamps and went to meet the bridegroom. Five of them were foolish, and five were wise. For when the *foolish took their lamps, they took no oil with them*, but *the wise took flasks of oil with their lamps*. As the bridegroom was delayed, they all became drowsy and slept. But at midnight there was a cry, 'Here is the bridegroom! Come out to meet him.' Then all those virgins rose and trimmed their lamps. And the foolish said to the wise, 'Give us some of your oil, for our lamps are going out.' But the wise answered, saying, 'Since there will not be enough for us and for you, go rather to the dealers and buy for yourselves.' And while they were going to buy, *the bridegroom came, and those who were ready went in with him to the marriage feast*, and the door was shut. *Afterward the other virgins came also, saying, 'Lord, lord, open to us.' But he answered, 'Truly, I say to you, I do not know you.'* Watch therefore, for you know neither the day nor the hour. (Matthew 25:1-13, emphasis added)

Have you ever wondered what the oil represents in the Matthew 25 passage above and how we are to know God? In Scripture, oil often represents the Holy Spirit, the Spirit of God. Isaiah 61:1, as recounted in Luke 4:18, speaks of God's anointing Jesus with the Spirit. The Hebrew root of the title "Messiah" (*Moshiach*) means "anointed one." Further, the title "Christ" is from the Greek *Christos*, also meaning "anointed one," identified as Jesus of Nazareth in Acts 10:38. In his letter to the Romans, Paul equates *not* having the Spirit of Christ with *not* belonging to Christ:

Those who are in the flesh cannot please God. *You, however, are not in the flesh but in the Spirit, if in fact the Spirit of God dwells in you. Anyone who does not have the Spirit of Christ does not belong to him.* But if Christ is in you, although the body is dead because of sin, the Spirit is life because of righteousness. *If the Spirit of him who raised Jesus from the dead dwells in you,* he who raised Christ Jesus from the dead will also give life to your mortal bodies through his Spirit who dwells in you. (Romans 8:8-11, emphasis added)

Given Paul's words, is there a risk that we are in the flesh, potentially as nominal (in name only) Christians, possibly even trying to walk out our faith in our own strength? And might it be that, because of our doctrines and possibly our fears, or perhaps due to the twisted witness of others, we reject the work and presence of the Spirit in our lives? Might we be giving him less of ourselves than he desires? If so, do we risk missing out because of our predispositions?

In your faith walk, could you be discounting beliefs and behaviors that might lead to a catastrophic event? At the extreme, do you ever wonder whether you are genuinely saved, have the Holy Spirit in you, or are truly living the Christian life described in the Bible? Do you wish you could remove some of the uncertainty?

The Odds

Based on statistics from the US Fire Administration and the 2020 US census, approximately one in every 378 homes (0.26 percent) experienced some form of house fire in 2020. That means that roughly 99.7 percent of homes did not. In 2020, residential fire losses were $8.6 billion, or an average of nearly $23,000 loss per event.[7] A much smaller percentage of homes had fires that resulted in a total loss. Most households would not be able to bear an unexpected $23,000 repair expense, let alone the cost to replace an entire home, so homeowners purchase insurance. It is relatively unlikely that a house will have a fire, but we insure it nonetheless. A bank or lender often requires a homeowner's policy because they often have the most to lose financially if the home is destroyed.

How likely do you think it is that your theology is 100 percent correct? And if we spend money to buy coverage for the unlikely event that our homes will suffer damage, should we not also ensure that we have fortified our understanding of the biblical new covenant that we live under today?

---

7 "Residential Building Fire Trends (2012-2020)," Residential Fire Estimate Summaries. *U.S. Fire Administration:* *https://www.usfa.fema.gov/statistics/residential-fires/* (March 14, 2023); Total Housing Units in United States, *United States Census Bureau: https://data.census.gov/profile/United_States?g=010XX00US* (August 15, 2024).

Are there any areas of your faith that you have not sought to understand more deeply and simply taken what others have said as true? I am not saying we should discount or challenge the historical accounts recorded in the Bible, nor the words of the Bible, but do we understand how we arrived at our doctrines (our interpretations) and how our doctrines might negatively impact our relationship with God?

What Is True?

Many of our "truths" started as the thoughts or interpretations of one person or a few "experts" but in time gained widespread support. For centuries people were afraid to explore the world because they thought it was flat. Of course, they were wrong. The filters of our minds, flesh (sinful nature), experiences, and cultures can all negatively impact how we translate truth into understanding. Our understanding is not inconsequential because it influences our actions.

If I believe that God is impersonal and distant, I will be much less likely to pursue dialogue with him and much less likely to listen for his voice. Similarly, if I believe he does *not* heal people physically today, I will be much less likely to pray for healing. This *belief-leads-to-practice* dynamic amplifies the importance of considering the process we use to arrive at our beliefs.

The issue of evaluating and correcting beliefs was present even in the early church. Both Jesus and the New Testament authors were wary of aberrant thinking and teaching leading people astray.

> I am astonished that you are so quickly deserting him who called you in the grace of Christ and are turning to a different gospel— not that there is

another one, but *there are some who trouble you and want to distort the gospel of Christ.* But even if we or an angel from heaven should preach to you a gospel contrary to the one we preached to you, let him be accursed. As we have said before, so now I say again: *If anyone is preaching to you a gospel contrary to the one you received, let him be accursed.* (Galatians 1:6-9, emphasis added)

I appeal to you, brothers, to watch out for *those who cause divisions and create obstacles contrary to the doctrine that you have been taught;* avoid them. For such persons do not serve our Lord Christ, but their own appetites, and by smooth talk and flattery they deceive the hearts of the naive. (Romans 16:17-18, emphasis added)

Many of the epistles and gospels were written to clarify what was true and desirable for Christian life. These letters often included correction and teaching for the immature or misguided, and at times, they countered errant views introduced by outsiders and interlopers.[8]

The Book of Revelation does precisely that. Jesus calls out false apostles (2:2), abandonment of their first love (2:4), holding to false teaching (2:14-15), following a seductress (2:20), being dead, asleep (3:1-2), and resting in their riches (3:16-17). If those in the body of Christ were straying when John was alive, is it possible that we have strayed, too? Is it possible that the understanding passed down through the generations has in any way fallen short of the faith walk of the first disciples of Christ?

I am not suggesting that we cannot know anything to be 100 percent true. Facts are all around us. I have ten fingers and ten toes. This is

---

8   See other examples in Matthew 7:15; 2 Corinthians 11:12-15; Ephesians 4:14; Colossians 2:8; 1 Timothy 1:3-4, 6:3-5; 2 Timothy 3:2-9, 4:3-4; 2 John 1:7-11; Jude v. 4.

a fact. My heart is beating, sending blood throughout my body. This is a fact. I love my wife. This is a fact, although I'm still learning to love as Christ loves.

Turning to the Bible, Paul tells us that "All Scripture is breathed out by God and profitable for teaching, for reproof, for correction, and for training in righteousness" (2 Timothy 3:16). Peter commends people to Paul's writings and highlights that it is possible to twist the Scriptures to our destruction.

> And count the patience of our Lord as salvation, just as our beloved brother *Paul also wrote to you according to the wisdom given him, as he does in all his letters when he speaks in them of these matters.* There are some things in them that are hard to understand, which *the ignorant and unstable twist to their own destruction, as they do the other Scriptures.* (2 Peter 3:15-16, emphasis added)

So, there is a testimony that the Bible is a work of the Spirit through man and is something we can rely on. We must decide if we agree on this point. We might explore how the church arrived at the canon of Scripture (the books that are recognized as being divinely inspired and are part of our Bibles today, which differs slightly for Protestants, Roman Catholics, and Orthodox), but this will leave us still having to decide if we trust that God worked through men to make this selection.

Paul tempers our expectation of being able to know everything, declaring that "we know in part and we prophesy in part, but when the perfect comes, the partial will pass away" (1 Corinthians 13:9-10). While there are some things we will not know fully, Jesus tells us that we will know conclusively when he has made his home in us:

> "I will not leave you as orphans; I will come to you. Yet a little while and the world will see me no more, but you will see me. Because I live, you also will live. *In that day you will know that I am in my Father, and you in me, and I in you.*" (John 14:18-20, emphasis added)

Experiencing the presence of Christ *in us* radically changes us and enables us to testify as eyewitnesses of his presence in our lives and on the earth. He transforms us daily to be more like him (2 Corinthians 3:17-18), so our posture should allow room for growth and maturation. We should expect that our understanding of God, and thus our comprehension of Scripture, will deepen and broaden over time. We can see this transformation lived out in the experiences of Abraham, Samuel, Moses, and Saul of Tarsus, among many others. When they encountered God, their understanding and the path of their lives was forever changed.

Can you identify any examples of your perspectives or beliefs that have changed due to new experiences, information, or insights? What prompted these changes? Awareness of this dynamic is essential when pursuing a relationship with God and seeking truth.

Jesus calls himself the Truth (John 14:6) and tells us that the Spirit of Truth would teach us all things (John 14:26). So, we are not without a resource to encounter and understand God. Often, though, in our human nature and learned behavior, we tend to neglect asking, seeking, and knocking for understanding. We rely on the viewpoints of others or the cultural norm rather than applying our God-given intellect and curiosity to verify what others label as truth.

Have you engaged all your faculties and resources to know our Father and his ways? Have you sought the Spirit of Truth to discover what he wants you to know? Would you wager your life—indeed your eternal life—on your current conclusions about your faith walk?

Pascal raised this very question.

Pascal's Wager

In the 17th century, the French philosopher, scientist, and theologian Blaise Pascal attempted to describe and suggest a reasonable choice for one of the most foundational questions that man might pose. In what is known as "Pascal's Wager," he highlights a risk of enormous proportions. Pascal proposed that each person is given the opportunity to believe that either the God of the Bible exists or he does not. Either answer would result in massive consequences for the individual's life.

In this wager, if you choose to believe there is no God, you get to keep your freedom to live how you desire now, but if your choice is wrong, you forfeit infinite blessings in a life with God both now and in eternity. If you choose to believe there is a God and you are right, you win everything, but if you are wrong and there is no God, you will have needlessly forfeited living as you please, which is almost nothing compared with the infinite riches in a relationship with God. Pascal argued that the rational person would choose to believe in God and find that they had "wagered for something certain and infinite, for which you have given nothing."[9]

Pascal's wager is not only about winning or losing. It makes us think more deeply about the question: What will happen if I am wrong?"

---

9   Blaise Pascal, *Pensées*, (Grand Rapids: Christian Classics Ethereal Library), Section 3.233, accessed at *https://www.ccel.org/ccel/pascal/pensees.html* (August 20, 2024). Some might also argue that giving up our freedom to do as we please in this life is a heavy cost to pay for following God.

Have you taken any doctrinal stances that could significantly impact your life? Do you understand what other Christians believe and practice and why, and have you weighed these things against your beliefs? In Pascal's Wager, the fundamental question is whether God exists. I believe a similar wager is in play regarding what it means to know God (Father, Son, and Spirit) experientially in the new covenant.

Pascal's Wager 2.0

This similar wager—Pascal's Wager 2.0—relates to the role of Holy Spirit baptism in a Christian's life and how it impacts our relationship with God. Some believe that Spirit baptism happens with water baptism or the profession of faith in Christ. Others think it can occur as a separate, distinct event or even a series of events in the life of a Christian. Some have no view, having never been exposed to the topic, while others ignore Spirit baptism to avoid divisiveness.

If "belief in God" in Pascal's original wager came with a minimal cost and infinite potential gain, then so does this second version. You can either believe that Spirit baptism is a distinct event or you do not. In a sense, these two wagers are connected, as version 2.0 proposes an actualization, bringing to full fruition the positive answer to Pascal's original wager. If I believe God exists in response to the original wager, how do I experience him now (v2.0) in this new covenant that he is offering, a covenant where the Holy Spirit will live in us?

Based on many scriptures, examples of Spirit baptism in the Book of Acts, my personal experience and that of many others, Spirit baptism is a distinct life-altering event. Further, I believe it is highly likely that Spirit baptism is the biblical event where the Holy Spirit first indwells the Christian, actualizing God's desire to put his Spirit in man. This view embraces an experiential reality that union with God is something we can know through direct experience. Spirit baptism is the gateway to intimate and personal knowledge of God as Father, Son, and Spirit.

As a betting person, I can ignore Spirit baptism as a distinct event, or I can believe it warrants investigation and pursuit. There are risks and rewards with either position. The rest of this book is intended to provide context and deepen understanding for those trying to decide if Spirit baptism is something they should embrace. It also speaks to those seeking further understanding about the Spirit baptism they have already experienced.

Let's look next at us, God's creation, who have been given the task of discerning and choosing a path in life.

2

Who Are We?

Our Common Experience

> For you formed my inward parts; you knitted me together in my mother's
> womb. I praise you, for I am fearfully and wonderfully made. Wonderful
> are your works; my soul knows it very well. (Psalm 139:13-14)

As much as we can be separated and categorized into recognizable people groups and cultures, some fundamental aspects of our experiences
bind us together. In all cultures, each of us is the product of a birth,
which resulted from conception, development in our mother's womb,
and an exit from that womb. To reach adulthood, we were sufficiently
nourished and protected from mortal harm. Most of us acquired the
ability to communicate and engage in relationships and essential skills
to help us navigate life and meet our daily needs.

We all have to make a conscious effort to meet our physical needs.
We purchase, grow, raise, or hunt and forage for food and obtain clean
water sources. In most climates, we need shelter for our safety and
well-being. Our senses and sensations aid in identifying and signaling
these universal needs. For all of us, some sensations are more challenging than others to ignore, with hunger and thirst being among the
strongest.

The Human Hunger

> As a deer pants for flowing streams, so pants my soul for you, O God. My soul thirsts for God, for the living God. (Psalm 42:1-2)

We've all experienced the sensation of hunger or desire for something in our lives. If we haven't eaten for some time, our bodies tell us there is a deficiency. We typically feel this sensation multiple times daily. And assuming we have access to food, we respond by satisfying that physical hunger with a snack or meal. We can also discipline our bodies to ignore our hunger. During extended fasting, our bodies can enter a resting state where there is no hunger signal. In a sense, our bodies stop expecting food to come, so they stop asking for it.

People also experience relational hunger, the need or desire to be with and connected to others. To satisfy our hunger, we spend time with family, establish friendships, seek out life partners, gather in groups, and participate in community. Relationships, if healthy, give us satisfaction, a sense of belonging and being, and encouragement for life's journey. Lack of relationships can leave us without personal fulfillment, despondent, and disengaged. A stark example was documented in the work of Rene Spitz, who showed that orphan babies' bodies shut down, stopped growing, and many died when deprived of loving care, touch, and interaction.[10]

---

10 "London's Foundling Museum documents in depth these harsh realities. In the 1940s, the work of psychoanalyst Rene Spitz further documented high infant death rates (one out of three) and, among the babies who didn't die, high percentages of cognitive, behavioural and psychological disfunction. Most of these deaths were not due to starvation or disease, but to severe emotional and sensorial deprivation – in other words, a lack of love. These babies were fed and medically treated, but they were absolutely deprived of important stimulation, especially touch and affection." Inês Varela-Silva, "Can a lack of love be deadly?" May 19, 2016. *The Conversation: https://theconversation.com/can-a-lack-of-love-be-deadly-58659* (February 29, 2024).

When we engage in relationships and activities and find they don't fully satisfy our hunger, we may also become aware of a spiritual hunger, a desire to connect with God or find meaning in life and the purpose of our existence. Our communities and cultures often attempt to provide understanding, and sometimes, we may see the answer lacking. Crises, life events, and nagging dissatisfaction can cause us to look deeper—beyond what is "known." Just like physical pangs of hunger and thirst, our spiritual hunger demands satisfaction.

Have you thought about where these hungers came from? Have you considered hunger as a call to action by the God who made us? From a physical perspective, ignoring thirst can quickly put us in peril. In desert climates, extreme heat can quickly overwhelm even the fittest. Just as drinking water involves a voluntary action, spiritual thirst requires an intentional pursuit of God.

Do you find yourself wondering if there may be more to life? Do you wonder why you're here? Do you question the reality of your relationship with God? Do you lack peace, joy, and a sense of God's presence with you? Do you regularly run to other distractions to make you feel at ease or help you escape? If you answered yes to any of these questions, it might point to a more profound need, a spiritual hunger in your soul that may not be fully satisfied. Our hunger or lack signifies our need for deeper relationships, particularly one that only God can fill. But is our hunger satisfied by simply believing, or does this require the experience of another?

Belief versus Experience

> On the last day of the feast, the great day, Jesus stood up and cried out, "If anyone thirsts, let him come to me and drink. (John 7:37)

There is a significant difference between believing that water exists and can satisfy thirst and the experience of actually drinking water. Drinking water has a tangible effect: quenching thirst, hydrating cells, and enabling bodily functions. This principle of belief versus experience is also at play regarding spiritual hunger. Pascal makes a reasonable case for why we might want to believe in God, yet a question remains. How is this belief actualized? How do we "drink" of God?

For many of us, belief is an entry point to an engagement with God in a relationship. But we cannot stop there. For relationships to flourish, there must be rapport, conversation, and quantity and quality time spent together. To have intimacy with another, we must share our inner selves through dialogue, listening, and speaking with the intent to know and be known.

What we say comes from what is within us (Matthew 12:34-35). When we share with others our desires, fears, and how we process life, we enter a deeper dimension of connectedness. In marriage, this connectedness is to surpass all other earthly relationships, baring our whole selves to one another in complete vulnerability. We are to be the same way with God.

That is how it was initially in the Garden of Eden. Adam and Eve were naked before each other physically, and they had nothing inward to hide from God or each other before sin was present. But after their sin, they hid and covered themselves (Genesis 3:7-8). God desires to reverse the curse of Eden and bring us to the place of complete vulnerability with him, to experience his presence unhindered by our brokenness. We are to experience this unhindered presence in the new covenant by having God *in* us.

It is not only through the words of the heart that we can experience or drink of one another, but also through actions. How we give our time, emotional and physical attention, resources, and help, as well as our demeanor, all speak much about who we are. Over time and across various situations, we see how others deal with life, their strengths and weaknesses, and how much they care. We become more aware of how they process emotions and what pleases and upsets them. Whether with a person or with God, time and experience are integral to growing in knowledge and trust with one another. Trust is the foundation of relationships, and building relationships is a primary feature of our lives.

A People Equipped for Relationship

Have you ever considered how many aspects of your body and mind are oriented to interacting with others and how responsive they are to relationships? With our ears, we can hear the words another speaks, the tone, pitch, volume, timbre, and emotion of a voice, helping us to know what is in the mind and soul of another. With our eyes, we can see the expression on the face of another, where their attention is directed, and the subtleties of their body language. We can see if they are withdrawn, open and engaged, angry or joyful. We can discern when someone needs help, guidance, or reassurance and whether they invite us to relax and come close. With our hands and faces, we can feel a heartbeat and the warmth of another's skin. Our senses combine to tell us someone is approaching or nearby.

With our feet and legs, we can approach or withdraw from another. On our knees, we can work, serve, plead, and pray. With our noses, we can smell the scent of another or the gifts they bring (flowers, food, fragrances). With our tongues, we can taste, and combined with our vocal cords and breath, we can communicate in the simplest or most complex speech and song. Our heart races, rests at peace, or leaps within us in anticipation of being with another. And our minds store memories and enable us to process thoughts that help us to decide if we should be vulnerable or protect ourselves.

With all of this "equipment," it would be difficult to conclude that we were not made for relationships. And it is no wonder that Scripture says we are "fearfully and wonderfully made" (Psalm 139:14) in the image of God (Genesis 1:27). It is not only how we are made that is part of our shared experience but also how we perceive the world around us. And our perception often influences our choices. Sharing ourselves in a relationship is *not* automatic; we must choose to be vulnerable.

A Life of Choices

For each of us, life begins in an instant, a moment in time. Have you ever considered that our lives are the sum of the instants, the moments in time that have led to today? We have been making daily choices that create our history and legacy while setting a course for our present and future. By exercising our minds and will, we have contributed to the tapestry that is our life. Many of the events of our lives were *not* determined solely by our actions but also by the choices of others and our circumstances. Some of those choices and circumstances caused us to regress or to be injured, while others caused us to mature and heal. Many of us make choices that we believe will result in the best outcome for us at a moment in time, and still others think about how they will impact the future. And depending on our risk profile, some choices are well-informed or heavily researched, and others are made purely on emotion, intuition, or a whim.

Regarding spirituality, we wrestle with questions about our place in the world, the origins of man and the cosmos, and what it means to be human. Do we decide to believe in a creator or chance? Is this creator benevolent or tyrannical? Can I know this creator, and how should this knowledge impact my life? Depending on what we believe about God, the Creator, the path of our lives can be radically altered. Our choices can help us draw near to God or keep him at a distance. But who is this God, and why would we want to know Him experientially?

3

The God of Relationship

How Do We Perceive God?

When you think of the God who made heaven and earth, what comes to mind first? Is it his majesty, power, judgment, wisdom, holiness, all-knowing and ever-presence, glory, splendor, and love? Or is it his holy anger, wrath, severity, and rebuke? Is it easy to believe he loves us, created a world for us to live in, and gave his Son to forgive our sins, but much more difficult to see him desiring to engage with us as his bride in the here and now? Is it easier to think of being with God one day on the "other side of glory," on "heaven's shores"? Or do you view God as a very close and personal friend? Are you aware of where your view came from, and have you considered how that view is validated or challenged by your relationship with God? Have you considered God both being love and defining love?

God's Love in the Hebrew Bible

God's enduring love is expressed in words and actions throughout the Bible. The three passages below provide insight into his heart for his people.

When Israel was a child, I loved him, and out of Egypt I called my son. The more they were called, the more they went away; they kept sacrificing to the Baals and burning offerings to idols. Yet *it was I who taught Ephraim to walk*; I took them up by their arms, but *they did not know that I healed them. I led them with cords of kindness, with the bands of love, and I became to them as one who eases the yoke on their jaws, and I bent down to them and fed them.* (Hosea 11:1-4, emphasis added)

"Fear not, for you will not be ashamed; be not confounded, for you will not be disgraced; for you will forget the shame of your youth, and the reproach of your widowhood you will remember no more. *For your Maker is your husband*, the Lord of hosts is his name; and *the Holy One of Israel is your Redeemer*, the God of the whole earth he is called. For the *Lord has called you like a wife* deserted and grieved in spirit, like a wife of youth when she is cast off, says your God. For a brief moment I deserted you, but with great compassion I will gather you. In overflowing anger for a moment I hid my face from you, but *with everlasting love I will have compassion on you*," says the Lord, your Redeemer. "This is like the days of Noah to me: as I swore that the waters of Noah should no more go over the earth, so I have sworn that I will not be angry with you, and will not rebuke you. For the mountains may depart and the hills be removed, but *my steadfast love shall not depart from you, and my covenant of peace shall not be removed*," says the Lord, who has compassion on you. (Isaiah 54:4-10, emphasis added)

I have loved you with an everlasting love; therefore I have continued my faithfulness to you. Again I will build you, and you shall be built, O virgin Israel! Again you shall adorn yourself with tambourines and shall go forth in the dance of the merrymakers. (Jeremiah 31:3-4, emphasis added)

In addition to revealing his enduring love, Scripture tells us that God does not change (Malachi 3:6; Hebrews 13:8; James 1:17), so looking back helps us understand his heart today. When we read the Hebrew Bible, we hear God expressing himself in relational terms.

In Genesis, he is present in the Garden, talking with and teaching Adam and Eve (Genesis 1:28-30; 2:16-17; 3:8-13, 16-19). As a Husband to Israel, God speaks of his great love for her and his promise to redeem her (Deuteronomy 4:37; 7:6-9; 10:15; 33:3; Isaiah 54:5; 62:4-5; Jeremiah 31:3, 32; Ezekiel 16:8; Hosea 2:16, 19-20, among others). He repeatedly says that Israel will be his and he will be their God, language of marriage (Genesis 17:8; Exodus 6:7; 29:45; Leviticus 26:45; Jeremiah 7:23; 31:33; 32:38; Ezekiel 11:20; 14:11; 37:23; Zechariah 8:8; among others). He tells of his desire to dwell within his people (Ezekiel 37:26-28), and as we will explore in chapter 4, he speaks of his desire to put his Spirit in man, his beloved, in a new covenant.

God initiated a relationship with man when he created Adam and Eve. Before Christ's arrival, God made covenants with Noah, Abraham, Jacob, Moses, David, and the Jewish people. These covenants expressed his care and love. In his covenant with Noah (Genesis 9:8-17), God promised to never again cut off life from the earth through a flood. To Abraham, he promised to give land to his descendants and to give him a multitude of offspring (Genesis 15:4-21), to make him a father of nations, to be his God and the God of his offspring, and to establish his covenant with his son Isaac (Genesis 17:1-21). Through his covenant with Israel at Sinai, delivered through Moses, God pledged to be their God and expressed his desire that Israel be consecrated to him, living as a faithful spouse (Exodus 19:3-6; 20-24). God's covenant with David included his promise to maintain a king on David's throne forever and plant Israel in their own land (2 Samuel 7:8-16).

God was the initiator and is the keeper of these covenants that promise a blessing to the participants. Why would God, who is greater than all, choose to interact with man and to covenant with him? Why does any prospective spouse enter a covenant with a desired life partner? God desires *union* with his beloved, his Bride.

God's Love in the New Testament

That same desire for union is found in the New Testament, where Christ is revealed as the bridegroom for his people (Mark 2:18-20; Luke 5:34-35; 2 Corinthians 11:2; Revelation 19:7). The Shepherd of shepherds, Jesus the Messiah, fully God and fully man, is revealed in veiled glory (Philippians 2:6-8). But even in veiled glory, his appearing was magnificent. He brought a quality and quantity of love the world had never experienced in human form. His words and deeds beckoned man to draw near.

> Come to me, all who labor and are heavy laden, and I will give you rest. Take my yoke upon you, and learn from me, for I am gentle and lowly in heart, and you will find rest for your souls. (Matthew 11:28-29)

> So his fame spread throughout all Syria, and they brought him all the sick, those afflicted with various diseases and pains, those oppressed by demons, those having seizures, and paralytics, and he healed them. (Matthew 4:24)

When we see the love of the Son, we see the love of the Father (John 14:8-11). We see it in the compassion of Christ for those in need. We see it in the testimony of those who were with Christ and how John, the beloved friend of Jesus, tells us plainly that "God is Love," a love that was with us (1 John 4:9-10) and would be in us (John 14:17, 20).

We see Jesus' love in his interactions with his disciples and those he encountered, patiently leading and teaching them (Matthew 4:17-22; 5-7; Luke 5:3-10, 31-39; 15:11-32, among many others). He came as the one who would heal the brokenhearted and bind their wounds (Psalm 147:3; Isaiah 61:1; Luke 4:18-21). Through his words and actions, Jesus showed his compassion for the sick, the disabled, the deaf, the dumb, the demon-possessed, and the outcasts (Matthew 4:24; 14:14; Luke 5:12-14, etc.). He called those burdened to come to him and find rest (Matthew 11:28-29), even when they rejected him.

> "O Jerusalem, Jerusalem, the city that kills the prophets and stones those who are sent to it! How often would I have gathered your children together as a hen gathers her brood under her wings, and you were not willing! (Matthew 23:37)

The same Spirit in Jesus as he spoke the above lament over Jerusalem enabled David to prophetically exclaim what only Jesus could bring to ultimate fulfillment:

> *Your steadfast love, O Lord, extends to the heavens*, your faithfulness to the clouds. Your righteousness is like the mountains of God; your judgments are like the great deep; man and beast you save, O Lord. *How precious is your steadfast love, O God! The children of mankind take refuge in the*

> *shadow of your wings. They feast on the abundance of your house, and you give them drink from the river of your delights. For with you is the fountain of life; in your light do we see light. Oh, continue your steadfast love to those who know you,* and your righteousness to the upright of heart! (Psalm 36:5-10, emphasis added)

It is through his Spirit that God's love is poured out (Romans 5:5), and through his Spirit we experience his love (Ephesians 3:16-19; Jude vv. 20-21). We see love in the gift of his Son (John 15:9; Romans 5:8). In his love, he adopts us as his children (Romans 8:15; 1 John 3:1). Our capacity to love comes from him (1 John 4:19) and walking in his love is our calling (John 13:34-35; 1 Corinthians 13:1-8).

The ultimate picture of his love is in the sacrifice of Christ, the perfect sacrificial lamb, that we might be saved (John 3:16-18; Galatians 2:20; Ephesians 2:4-8; Colossians 2:13; Hebrews 9:12, 14). Through this loving sacrifice, he made a way for us into the presence of God (Hebrews 10:19-20), the only way to the Father (John 14:6). And we now *all* have the potential for this access to God. If access is granted, what are we to do with this open door?

The Most Important Thing

> But seek first the kingdom of God *[the place where the King is present, ruling]* and his righteousness *[a right relationship with him]* and all these things will be added to you. (Matthew 6:33, italicized text added)

If you ask someone in the real estate business what the most important considerations are when buying a property, you will often hear the adage "Location! Location! Location!" For example, a home near shopping, schools, workplaces, public transportation, and in a safe and pleasant neighborhood would be more desirable than a similar home built in the flight path of a busy airport.

Similarly, we might ask what the most critical consideration about God and faith is. A wise friend once suggested that our reply should be "Relationship! Relationship! Relationship!" Living as closely as possible to God is the highest value among all possible pursuits. God made us to know him and to be known by him (John 10:14, 17:3; Ephesians 3:19; Hebrews 8:11). He is to be closer to us than anyone else, even *in* us, and we are to become *one* with him (John 17:21-23, 26).

The Bible is filled with examples of men and women God sought for relationships. We mentioned Adam and Eve in the garden (Genesis 2:16-17; 3:8-9). God called Abraham (Genesis 12:1-3), visiting and interacting with him (Genesis 15, 17, 18, 22, etc.). It is little wonder that he is called the father of the faithful (Romans 4:16-22; Galatians 3:29). Abraham experienced God and trusted him.

God first appeared to Moses in the burning bush (Exodus 3) and began a dialogue with him, the beginning of a mutual relationship that would ultimately result in Moses leading the Hebrews out of captivity. God spoke through Moses (and his brother Aaron) on behalf of the Israelites at Sinai (Exodus 19-34), and he continued to talk to his people through the prophets that followed. And the same God who visited with man as recorded in the Hebrew Scriptures, who spoke through the prophets (Hebrews 1:1; 1 Peter 1:10-12), ultimately came speaking in physical form through Christ (Hebrews 1:2). He came to reveal himself to Israel, to teach and shepherd them, and to lay down his life in a desire to make his love known, that we "should not perish, but have eternal life," (John 3:16), knowing God experientially: "And this is eternal life, that they know you, the only true God, and Jesus Christ whom you have sent" (John 17:3).

Who Are We to Be?

In the book of Acts, Luke tells us of the interrogation of Peter and John by the Jewish rulers, elders, and scribes in Jerusalem and that "when they saw the boldness of Peter and John, and perceived that they were uneducated, common men, they were astonished. And they recognized that they had been with Jesus" (Acts 4:13). When rebuked by the elders and leaders with a warning to no longer speak of Jesus, Peter, and John responded: "Whether it is right in the sight of God to listen to you rather than to God, you must judge, for we cannot but speak of what we have seen and heard" (Acts 4:19-20). Peter and John were recognized as having been with Jesus, eyewitnesses to his ministry.

We, too, are called to be people known as being with God and witnesses of what we have experienced. Our direct relationship with God and our eyewitness account should be the mark upon our lives, expressed in all we say and do as we bear his peace and joy on the earth—even a supernatural peace and joy in the face of trials and suffering. As we come to know him, we become a people who implicitly trust the One who lives inside us (John 14:17-20, 23). All else flows from our knowledge of the King of Kings (Matthew 6:33).

The example of Mary and Martha (Luke 10:38-42) is almost a cliche, but many of us can relate to Martha's desire to serve rather than sit at her master's feet. We often ask, "What can I do, build, and impact," but less frequently, "How do I know God more deeply?" Our calling is to be a people who bear the presence of God, our bodies the dwelling place for his Spirit (1 Corinthians 6:19), closer than any other person can be. And out of that lived reality, we are to impact the world with the witness of his love in and through us (John 13:34-35; Acts 1:8; James 2:17, 26). It is the role of the Holy Spirit to reveal Christ and the Father personally, to share God's presence with us. As we noted earlier, in his presence, we are transformed to become like him, to walk in his ways.

> Now the Lord is the Spirit, and where the Spirit of the Lord is, there is freedom. And we all, with unveiled face, beholding the glory of the Lord, are being transformed into the same image from one degree of glory to another. For this comes from the Lord who is the Spirit. (2 Corinthians 3:17-18)

If we see our foundational role as growing closer to God, pursuing intimacy with him, and spending time in his presence, and if we walk in this calling, we will be transformed and be known as ones who know him. Only through knowing him personally can we fully know his love experientially (1 John 4:8, 19). We receive his love (Jude vv. 20-21) and then return that love to him and those around us (Luke 10:27; 1 John 3:16). He reveals himself in us, and as we mature, everything we do is more and more grounded in our connection to him. We increasingly surrender to him, laying down our lives as a living sacrifice (John 15:13; Romans 12:1). For this to occur, we must abide in him, the True Vine (John 15:1-5). We are to be fruit bearers who abide in his love (John 15:8-9). And this abiding is through the indwelling Spirit. The Spirit gives life (John 6:63), the life-giving flow that comes through the vine and nurtures the branches.

In his letter to the Philippians, Paul beautifully expresses his journey toward perfection in Christ and righteousness—a right relationship with God. This right relationship is founded on faith (trust), knowing him, and the transformative power of his love (Philippians 3:8-14). Just as Christ as our elder brother (Romans 8:29; Hebrews 2:11-12) set the example of how to love and do his Father's will (John 8:28; 12:49), we are transformed by him to walk more and more in his ways, doing the things he leads us to do and speaking what he gives us to speak. God's abiding love, through his indwelling Spirit, enables us to truly love one another (1 John 4:12-13).

Experiencing His Presence

> You will call upon me and come and pray to me, and I will hear you. You will seek me and find me, when you seek me with all your heart. I will be found by you, declares the Lord. (Jeremiah 29:12-14)

To be known as being with Jesus, we must be present to Jesus as an integral part of our lives. Jeremiah tells us that if we are seeking after God, we will find him. At times, even those who are not seeking him encounter him. Jesus came to Paul on the Damascus Road (Acts 9:3-9; 26:12-18) as Paul was on his way to persecute Christians. If it had not been for Jesus' initiative, Paul would have remained unaware of his presence. For those with an openness or desire to know him and those who know him well, he makes himself available by being with and even within. If we have received his Spirit, God the Father and Son are in us through the Spirit (John 14:17, 20, 23). We don't have to wait until Sunday morning to be with him, as he is ever with us.

There are many different views across the various streams of Christianity of how we are to experience God's presence. Some might say it is through the sacraments, often in the Eucharist (Holy Communion). Some say we experience him in prayer or reading his Word. Some may encounter him in nature, art, worship, and study. We might hear his voice in a sermon, a movie, a choir's musical offering, or the nightingale's song. We may experience his presence and glory as we sing praises with others or stand before a snow-capped mountain that towers majestically over us. Some encounter him as the one who lives in them continually. Each of these can be true, for God is unlimited in his capacity to reveal himself to us. But being present to God also takes awareness on our part.

The book, *The Practice of the Presence of God*, captures recollections and letters of Brother Lawrence, a 17th-century monk who learned to be present to God even in the most mundane tasks. Lawrence recounts that "The time of business does not with me differ from the time of prayer: and in the noise and clatter of my kitchen, while several persons are at the same time calling for different things, I possess God in as great tranquility as if I were upon my knees at blessed sacrament." He made it his aim to remain continually aware of God's presence throughout all of his waking hours, engaging in inward conversation that "often causes me joys and raptures inwardly, and sometimes also outwardly, so great that I am forced to use means to moderate them and prevent their appearance to others."[11]

After reading Brother Lawrence's short book, I found that adopting his approach, being present to God throughout the day, talking with

---

11   Brother Lawrence, *The Practice of the Presence of God*, (Westwood, NJ: Fleming H. Revell Company, 1958), 30-31, 33, 35, 37-38.

him, and listening as I came and went or amid the tasks of the day brought a more profound sense of ongoing connectedness. This change in perspective was transformative in my relationship with God. And rightly so. Everything we do is to be infused with the presence of God, and we are to be ever and always conscious of him with and in us. In this practice, we recognize and engage our ultimate Friend who is closer than a brother (Proverbs 18:24).

Do you regularly experience God's presence in your life? Does Brother Lawrence's approach seem realistic to you? If it were possible to practice consistently, would it transform how you live?

The Currency of Relationship

In chapter 2, we mentioned getting to know one another through conversation, where people share the innermost issues of their hearts. God made us in his image and gave us the ability to communicate with him. Some speak of "saying a prayer," but that phrase may sometimes limit our understanding and the depth of our relationship with him. Prayer is not only a one-way petition or request, just something we say, and it is not simply a religious obligation, a tool, or something super-spiritual that is only used on certain occasions of need. God intends to engage in a two-way conversation with us, which means we are to speak *and* listen.

God's conversations with and God's words to individuals, communities, and nations are recorded throughout the Bible. Again, God does not change, and he desires to continue dialogue with his sons and daughters in our current day. The Lover longs to engage with his beloved and share his heart with us, and his desire has not lessened with time.

Jesus made time to talk with his Father (Matthew 14:23; Mark 1:35; Luke 5:16; 6:12; 9:18, 28-29; 11:1, among others). The apostle Paul speaks of his prayer (Acts 22:17; 1 Corinthians 14:18) and that we are built up as we pray in the Spirit (1 Corinthians 14:4). As we have noted, Jude also speaks of being strengthened in faith and keeping ourselves immersed in God's love through Spirit-borne prayer (Jude vv. 20-21).

In his letter to the Ephesians, Paul prays that the Father would give us "the Spirit of wisdom and of revelation in the knowledge of him … and what is the immeasurable greatness of his power toward us who believe" (Ephesians 1:17, 19). Just as the power of the love of a parent comes through the way they interact with their children, so it is with our heavenly Father, who speaks to us and cares for us through his Spirit both now (John 14:26; 15:26; 16:7-8) and in the past.

How do you see prayer? Is it difficult for you to talk with or connect with God? Does your theology allow for a God who will interact with you in the here and now, to both listen and speak and to be with you throughout your busy day? Is anything stopping you from pursuing an ongoing, daily interactive dialogue with him?

The Bible Speaks

Prayer is but one means of communicating with God. God has given a priceless gift to his children in the Hebrew Bible and the New Testament. These books contain a record of his relationship with man in the past, his instructions for how to live, and even a glimpse into the future. The books of the Bible are far more than a biography or memoir. They are life-giving, as the Spirit uses them to guide, encourage, and correct us.

However, there is also a risk related to the Scriptures. Some live as if the Holy Trinity includes the Father, the Son, and the Holy Scriptures, looking to the Bible as their primary or even sole source for hearing from and understanding God while de-emphasizing the direct role of the Holy Spirit. While the Scriptures contain many good things, they are not more significant than the One they point to, the One whose heart and thoughts they express. They record God's words, helping us understand him and his will, but should not replace a direct relationship with him.

If you asked the greatest author who ever lived to write your spouse's biography, the book would not be a substitute for the real person. Similarly, our time in Scripture should not be at the neglect of spending time with him in conversation, in prayer and worship, and listening for his voice directly spoken to our hearts. As we ask questions, God often uses the Bible to answer, but it is not the only way he speaks. If we have not heard his response, we are to keep asking, keep seeking, keep knocking, and keep searching.

Still Searching

In 1987, the band U2 released the single "I Still Haven't Found What I'm Looking For," and in 2021, it was reprised for a much younger generation in the animated movie *Sing 2*. I wasn't expecting what would happen when I took some of my children and their cousins to see a "kid's movie." A scene near the end had me in tears. It was a healing moment experienced by the lion character, Clay Calloway (voiced by Bono), as he and the porcupine named Ash (voiced by Scarlet Johansson) sang portions of the U2 song to a shocked crowd. Calloway had to press through years of isolation, pain, and loss to return to the stage. He emerges, playing the opening guitar riff, and begins singing:

I believe in a Kingdom come
And all the colors will bleed into one, bleed into one
Yes, I'm still runnin'

You broke the bonds and you loosed the chains
You carried the cross of my shame, of my shame
You know I believe it

But I still haven't found what I'm looking for
But I still haven't found what I'm looking for
I still haven't found what I'm looking for. [12]

Could these be the words of one who intellectually believes and has pursued God but has not found the fullness of love in an experiential relationship with him? Is it one who has encountered God but still has something missing? And what might it be that is still missing?

As mentioned earlier, Jesus calls us to himself, the One whose yoke is easy (Matthew 11:28-30). St. Augustine's famous words speak of the restlessness that comes with not knowing Christ: "Thou hast prompted him, that he should delight to praise thee, for thou hast made us for thyself and restless is our heart until it comes to rest in thee."[13] Similarly,

---

12   U2, "I Still Haven't Found What I'm Looking For," *The Joshua Tree*, (London: 1987, Island Records, Ltd.).

13   Augustine of Hippo, *Confessions*, (Grand Rapids: Christian Classics Ethereal Library), 1.1, accessed at *https://ccel. org/ccel/augustine/confess/confess.i.html* (August 15, 2024).

Isaiah 26:3 declares: "You keep him in perfect peace whose mind is stayed on you, because he trusts in you."

How, then, does one find this place of rest? How does one come to him and fully allow him to care for us as the Good Shepherd? How do we "lie down in green pastures" (Psalm 23:2)? We will seek to answer that question, at least in part, in Part Two.

Are You Relationally Satisfied?

What comes to mind when you think about your current relationship with God? Would you sing with Bono, even half-heartedly, that you still haven't found what you are looking for? Are you satisfied, complete, and peace-filled, or are you aware of a lack and desire for more? When is the last time you recall experiencing absolute peace? Do you see your relationship with God primarily as a matter of commands and obligations, obedience and punishment, or legal certainties? If so, does this make you want to get to know him better? Have you considered God's passionate love for you, his desire to be closer than any other to you, and to not just share his love but to pour it into you so it overflows limitlessly? Do you see him only as Lord, King, and Savior, Shelter and Strong Tower, or also as Husband and Lover of your soul?

Are you close to God, or do you feel there is a barrier to knowing God better? If there is a barrier, do you think it is possible to break through it? Do you want to break through it? Have you encountered His Spirit in your life?

PART TWO

THE PROMISED
HOLY SPIRIT

4

The Holy Spirit
and the New Covenant

Who Is the Holy Spirit?

> And behold, I am sending the promise of my Father upon you. But stay in
> the city until you are clothed with power from on high." (Luke 24:49)

Since our target topic in this journey is Spirit baptism, let's first talk
about who the Holy Spirit is. For many, describing the Holy Spirit causes
a slight tension, eyes glazing over, and a puzzled look. Some are quick to
say "the third person of the Trinity," and others might say the invisible
God. Some might call him a force, a weapon, a source of power. Some
call him the Holy Ghost (many thanks to the King James Version of
the Bible), possibly bringing to mind ghoulish apparitions or whisps of
former men and women.

Let us see how Jesus speaks of the Holy Spirit:

> And I will ask the Father, and he will give you another Helper, to be with
> you forever ... But the Helper, the Holy Spirit, whom the Father will send in
> my name, he will teach you all things and bring to your remembrance all
> that I have said to you. (John 14:16, 26)

> But when the Helper comes, whom I will send to you from the Father, the Spirit of truth, who proceeds from the Father, he will bear witness about me. (John 15:26)

> Nevertheless, I tell you the truth: it is to your advantage that I go away, for if I do not go away, the Helper will not come to you. But if I go, I will send him to you. And when he comes, he will convict the world concerning sin and righteousness and judgment ... When the Spirit of truth comes, he will guide you into all the truth, for he will not speak on his own authority, but whatever he hears he will speak, and he will declare to you the things that are to come. He will glorify me, for he will take what is mine and declare it to you. All that the Father has is mine; therefore I said that he will take what is mine and declare it to you. (John 16:7-8, 13-15)

Jesus refers to the Holy Spirit as our helper (counselor, advocate, paraclete), one who is "another Helper" (John 14:16), the same kind as Jesus.[14] Scripture also refers to the Lord, God as helper (Psalm 54:4; 118:7; Hosea 13:9; Hebrews 13:6) and Savior (Isaiah 43:11; 45:15, 21; 49:26; 60:16; Hosea 13:4; Luke 1:47, etc.), the same title given to Jesus the Messiah (Luke 2:11; Acts 5:31, etc.). As noted earlier, Jesus tells his disciples that the Spirit is the giver of life (John 6:63).[15]

The Spirit is the One who will cause rivers of living water to flow from within us (John 7:38-39). As the giver of life, the Spirit is inherently a deliverer from death. He is the same God who delivered the Israelites

---

14   Raymond E. Brown, *The Gospel According to John XIII-XXI*, (New Haven: Yale University Press, 2008), 645, 1139-1141.

15   Clark Pinnock notes that "Spirit is Lord and giver of life, in creation and new creation. Spirit gives us creaturely vitality and resurrection newness." Clark H. Pinnock, *Flame of Love: A Theology of the Holy Spirit*, 2d ed. (Downers Grove: InterVarsity Press, 2022), 187.

from the Egyptian army at the Red Sea and Daniel from the lions' den. And just as Jesus tells us that he spoke what the Father told him and did what he saw the Father doing (John 5:19; 12:49-50), he says the same of the Spirit, who will not speak of his own authority (John 16:13).

The Holy Spirit appears in the Hebrew Bible (Psalm 51:11; Isaiah 63:10-11, etc.). He is called the Spirit of God in Genesis (Gen 1:2, among others) and the Spirit of the Lord (Isaiah 11:2), working and speaking through prophets, leaders, artisans, and judges, who were men and women just like us. The angel Gabriel calls him the Holy Spirit, who bears the power of the Most High that will cause Mary to conceive Jesus, the Son of God (Luke 1:35). He is the one who guides and gives revelation to Simeon of the baby Jesus as the Savior (Luke 2:25-35). He descends like a dove upon Jesus at his baptism in the Jordan (Matthew 3:16).

Paul connects the Spirit to both the Father and Son:

> You, however, are not in the flesh but in the Spirit, if in fact the *Spirit of God dwells in you.* Anyone who does not have *the Spirit of Christ* does not belong to him. But *if Christ is in you,* although the body is dead because of sin, the Spirit is life because of righteousness. If the *Spirit of him who raised Jesus from the dead dwells in you,* he who raised Christ Jesus from the dead *will also give life* to your mortal bodies *through his Spirit who dwells in you.* (Romans 8:9-11, emphasis added)

To Paul, the Spirit of God is the "Spirit of him who raised Jesus from the dead" (Romans 8:11). Paul confirms that it is the Father who accomplished the work of resurrection (Galatians 1:1; 1 Thessalonians 1:9-10; Hebrews 5:7). It is by this very Spirit, the Spirit of God the Father, the Spirit of Christ, that we come to have life, are adopted, and we cry "Abba," (the affectionate term children use for their father in Hebrew).

> For you did not receive the spirit of slavery to fall back into fear, but you have received the Spirit of adoption as sons, by whom we cry, "Abba! Father!" The Spirit himself bears witness with our spirit that we are children of God. (Romans 8:15-16)

So, the Spirit is both the Spirit of God (Romans 8:9, 11, 14; 15:19; 1 Corinthians 2:11-14; 3:16; 6:11; 7:40; 12:3; Ephesians 4:30; Philippians 3:3; 1 Peter 4:14; 1 John 4:2) and the Spirit of Christ (Romans 8:9; Galatians 4:6; Philippians 1:19). Put plainly, the Holy Spirit is how we experience God the Father and Son in the present time.[16] The Spirit is how the love of God is poured out into our hearts (Romans 5:5).

He Has Been with You and Will Be in You

> And I will ask the Father, and he will give you another Helper, to be with you forever, even the Spirit of truth, whom the world cannot receive, because it neither sees him nor knows him. You know him, for *he dwells with you and will be in you*.... "I will not leave you as orphans; I will come to you. Yet a little while and the world will see me no more, but you will

---

16   Gordon Fee summarizes: "For Paul, the Spirit is not merely an impersonal force of influence or power. The Spirit is none other than the fulfillment of the promise that God himself would once again be present with his people." Gordon D. Fee, *Paul, the Spirit, and the People of God*, (Peabody, MA: Hendrickson Publishers, 1996), 22. Fee further notes: "The Spirit is thus "the Holy Spirit of God" and "The Spirit of Jesus Christ" – the way God is currently present with and among his people." Gordon D. Fee, *God's Empowering Presence: The Holy Spirit in the Letters of Paul*, (Peabody, MA: Hendrickson Publishers, 1994), 898. David Coffey affirms regarding the Spirit that "the content of our experience is Christ and the Father." David Coffey, *The Pere Marquette Lecture in Theology 2005, "Did You Receive the Holy Spirit When You Believed?": Some Basic Questions for Pneumatology*, (Milwaukee: Marquette University Press, 2005), 89.

> see me. Because I live, you also will live. *In that day you will know that I am in my Father, and you in me, and I in you....* Jesus answered him, "If anyone loves me, he will keep my word, and my Father will love him, and *we will come to him and make our home with him.* (John 14:16-17, 18-20, 23)

Let's consider together more closely what Jesus says in the verses above. We recall that after he was baptized in the Jordan River, the Holy Spirit descended on Jesus and remained (Matthew 3:16; Mark 1:10; Luke 3:22; John 1:32). By the Holy Spirit, Jesus cast out demons, healed the sick, and raised the dead (Matthew 12:28; Luke 8:40-56; John 11:38-44; Acts 10:38; etc.). By the Holy Spirit, the disciples also performed miracles (Matthew 10:8; Mark 6:13; Luke 9:6) when Jesus sent them out to minister (Matthew 10:1; Mark 6:7; Luke 9:1-2; 10:1, 9, 17). That is, the same Holy Spirit that was *with* them in Christ and when they ministered in Jesus' name was the same Holy Spirit that would soon take up permanent residence *in* them (John 14:17).

They would know not only the Holy Spirit in them but also that Jesus and the Father were there as well (John 14:20, 23). The implications of these words are life-transforming: God the Father and Son, through the Spirit, make their home in mortal man.[17] The risen Christ in us!

Might such a fantastic thing be true?

If so, should this not cause a massive shift in our ability to know both Father and Son? It is not only in the "sweet by and by" that we

---

17 Craig Keener agrees. "Through the Spirit, Jesus and the Father will come and make their dwelling within each disciple (John 14:23), thus making them temples of the Lord (the Father's house).... Jesus gave his followers the Spirit so that they could continue to develop their relationship with him." Craig Keener, *Gift & Giver: The Holy Spirit for Today,* (Grand Rapids, MI: Baker Academic, 2001), 29, 40. See also: Brown, *The Gospel According to John XIII-XXI,* 643.

are to experience the personal presence of God, but our experience of heaven begins now, his presence in us.

Paul also speaks of our being "in Christ" (Romans 8:1; 2 Corinthians 5:17), having Christ in us (Romans 8:10), and that we must have the Spirit of Christ to belong to him (Romans 8:9). Jesus tells us of his mutual indwelling with his Father and with us (John 14:10, 20; 17:21, 23). Might it be that the goal of Christ's coming, of his atonement for our sin, of the tearing of the veil (Matthew 27:51), giving us access to the Holy of Holies (Hebrews 10:19-20), is fulfilled in his making our bodies his dwelling place through the Spirit (1 Corinthians 3:16-17; 6:19)? And if we, as many do, stop at the atonement, death and resurrection of Christ as the totality of the gospel, have we missed the remarkable revelation that God the Father and Son desire to indwell us? If we, as many do, stop at our repentance and receiving forgiveness of sin, do we risk falling short of what God wants for us?

What are some practical implications of understanding the Father and Son are to be in us through the Spirit? Should it not be easier to be a witness (Acts 1:8) to the reality of Jesus' resurrection and the fulfillment of his words to his disciples of the coming of the Spirit?[18] Jesus said, "You will receive power when the Holy Spirit has come upon you, and you will be my witnesses in Jerusalem and in all Judea and Samaria, and to the end of the earth."

Is he not only speaking of those in Jerusalem at the time of Pentecost but to all who would eventually receive the Holy Spirit? Christ in us continues his work on the earth, not only through his one body,

---

18   Ralph Martin shares that "The Holy Spirit brought the disciples after Pentecost into an intimate experience of union with the risen Lord himself, enabling them to share in the fervor of Jesus' love for his Father, and Jesus' love for the human race." Excerpt from Ralph Martin, "Prophecy: How do we strengthen the prophetic dimension of the Catholic Charismatic Renewal," *Pentecost Today*, Issue 2, (2023): 15, National Service Committee of the Catholic Charismatic Renewal of the US @ www.PentecostTodayUSA.org.

as when he walked the earth, but through the body of Christ, which contains many members.[19]

> For just as the body is one and has many members, and all the members of the body, though many, are one body, so it is with Christ. For in one Spirit we were all baptized into one body—Jews or Greeks, slaves or free—and all were made to drink of one Spirit. (1 Corinthians 12:12-13)

Have you ever considered that the Spirit is the personal presence of the Father and Son? Do you believe it is possible to experientially know that Jesus is in you, or must it be taken on blind faith? The prophets envisioned a day when we would each know God experientially, which we will look at next.

The New Covenant Foretold

As discussed in chapter 3, the Hebrew Bible records covenants God made with man. God initiated each of these covenants, and each came with promises. The prophet Jeremiah speaks of a new covenant in which God will forgive Israel's sins and put his law within them. In this new covenant, they would all know him.

> "Behold, the days are coming, declares the Lord, when I will make a *new covenant* with the house of Israel and the house of Judah, not like the covenant that I made with their fathers on the day when I took them by the

---

19   Pinnock concludes that "He transferred Spirit to them so that his actions could continue through their agency. The bearer of the Spirit now baptizes others with the Spirit, that there might be a continuation of his testimony in word and deed and a continuation of his prophetic and charismatic ministry." *Flame of Love*, 133.

hand to bring them out of the land of Egypt, *my covenant that they broke, though I was their husband*, declares the Lord. For this is the covenant that I will make with the house of Israel after those days, declares the Lord: *I will put my law within them, and I will write it on their hearts. And I will be their God, and they shall be my people.* And no longer shall each one teach his neighbor and each his brother, saying, 'Know the Lord,' for *they shall all know me, from the least of them to the greatest,* declares the Lord. For I will forgive their iniquity, and I will remember their sin no more." (Jeremiah 31:31-34, emphasis added)

This knowing, "they shall all know me" (Hebrew *yada*) in verse 34, speaks of experiential understanding. The same verb is used in Genesis to describe Adam knowing Eve intimately (Genesis 4:1, 25). Ezekiel also foretells the new covenant when he speaks of God putting his Spirit within the Israelites, giving them life and the ability to walk in his commandments, fulfilling the requirements of the law:

I will take you from the nations and gather you from all the countries and bring you into your own land. I will sprinkle clean water on you, and you shall be clean from all your uncleannesses, and from all your idols I will cleanse you. And *I will give you a new heart, and a new spirit I will put within you. And I will remove the heart of stone from your flesh and give you a heart of flesh. And I will put my Spirit within you, and cause you to walk in my statutes and be careful to obey my rules.* You shall dwell in the land that I gave to your fathers, and you shall be my people, and I will be your God. (Ezekiel 36:24-28, emphasis added; also see 11:19-20)

And *I will put my Spirit within you, and you shall live,* and I will place you in

> your own land. Then you shall know that I am the Lord; I have spoken, and
> I will do it, declares the Lord." (Ezekiel 37:14, emphasis added)

This giving of the Spirit goes beyond God's giving of the physical breath of life (Hebrew *neshamah*) that is described when God breathes life into Adam (Genesis 2:7). It is God himself, coming to dwell in man (John 14:17, 20, 23; 17:23, 26). This new covenant reality is foreshadowed when God puts his Spirit on seventy elders to help Moses govern the Israelites (Numbers 11:16-17, 24-28). To Joshua's inquiry about that event, Moses prophetically replies, "Would that all the Lord's people were prophets, that the Lord would put his Spirit on them!" (Numbers 11:29).

The prophet Joel, speaking by the Holy Spirit, talks of the fulfillment of Moses' desire:

> "And it shall come to pass afterward, that I will pour out my Spirit on all
> flesh; your sons and your daughters shall prophesy, your old men shall
> dream dreams, and your young men shall see visions. Even on the male
> and female servants in those days I will pour out my Spirit. (Joel 2:28-29)

On the day of Pentecost, the fulfillment of Joel's prophecy began in earnest, as Peter attests (Acts 2:14-18, 33). By the Spirit, the Law was now written on believers' hearts (Jeremiah 31:33; Ezekiel 36:27). By the love of the Spirit poured out (Romans 5:5), believers were now empowered to fulfill the Law by truly loving God and neighbor (Matthew 22:36-40; Romans 13:8-10; Galatians 5:14).

Isaiah, writing over 700 years before Christ was born, compared water being poured out with the pouring out of the Holy Spirit, water that will save us and cause us to rejoice.

> For I will pour water on the thirsty land, and streams on the dry ground; I will pour my Spirit upon your offspring, and my blessing on your descendants. (Isaiah 44:3)

> You will say in that day: "I will give thanks to you, O Lord, for though you were angry with me, your anger turned away, that you might comfort me. "Behold, God is my salvation; I will trust, and will not be afraid; for the Lord God is my strength and my song, and *he has become my salvation.*" With joy you will *draw water from the wells of salvation.* (Isaiah 12:1-3, emphasis added)

Jesus also uses the imagery of water when he speaks of the new birth and the role of the Holy Spirit. On the final day of Sukkot (also known as the Feast of Tabernacles or Booths), he stood up in the Temple and cried out to the people:

> "*If anyone thirsts, let him come to me and drink.* Whoever believes in me, as the Scripture has said, '*Out of his heart will flow rivers of living water.*" *Now this he said about the Spirit,* whom those who believed in him were to receive, for as yet the Spirit had not been given, because Jesus was not yet glorified. (John 7:37-39, emphasis added)

Isaiah likens the arrival of the Lord to a rushing stream. This covenant of the Spirit upon man will draw the nations.

> So they shall fear the name of the Lord from the west, and his glory from the rising of the sun; for *he will come like a rushing stream*, which the wind of the Lord drives. "And *a Redeemer will come to Zion*, to those in

Jacob who turn from transgression," declares the Lord. "And as for me, this is my covenant with them," says the Lord: "*My Spirit that is upon you, and my words that I have put in your mouth, shall not depart out of your mouth, or out of the mouth of your offspring, or out of the mouth of your children's offspring,*" says the Lord, "from this time forth and forevermore." Arise, shine, for *your light has come*, and *the glory of the Lord has risen upon you.* For behold, darkness shall cover the earth, and thick darkness the peoples; but the *Lord will arise upon you, and his glory will be seen upon you. And nations shall come to your light, and kings to the brightness of your rising.* (Isaiah 59:19-60:3, emphasis added)

And God who comes will live with them (John 14:23).

I will make a covenant of peace with them. It shall be an everlasting covenant with them. And I will set them in their land and multiply them, and will *set my sanctuary in their midst* forevermore. My *dwelling place shall be with them*, and I will be their God, and they shall be my people. Then the nations will know that I am the Lord who sanctifies Israel, when *my sanctuary is in their midst* forevermore." (Ezekiel 37:26-28, emphasis added)

God's dwelling in our midst is not only a future hope (Revelation 21:3), but it is for now, as we are to be the temple of his Holy Spirit (again, 1 Corinthians 3:16-17; 6:19). Paul summarizes this for us in his Second Letter to the Corinthians:

For we are the temple of the living God; as God said, "I will make my dwelling among them and walk among them, and I will be their God, and they shall be my people." (2 Corinthians 6:16)

So, this new covenant is one where God forgives sin and comes to make his home in man, restoring the relationship that was broken in the Garden. The new covenant not only restores but also surpasses the relationship with God in the Garden and during the visitation of Christ over two thousand years ago. God fulfills his desire to be in us, and we in him, one with him (John 17:21-23).

How does this description match or differ from your understanding? Is there anything here that troubles you or contradicts what you have been taught? When compared to your own perspective, does this understanding favor a closer or more distant relationship with God the Father and Son?

What Then Is Salvation?

A woman from Samaria came to draw water. Jesus said to her, "Give me a drink." (For his disciples had gone away into the city to buy food.) The Samaritan woman said to him, "How is it that you, a Jew, ask for a drink from me, a woman of Samaria?" (For Jews have no dealings with Samaritans.) Jesus answered her, *"If you knew the gift of God, and who it is that is saying to you, 'Give me a drink,' you would have asked him, and he would have given you living water."* The woman said to him, "Sir, you have nothing to draw water with, and the well is deep. Where do you get that living water? Are you greater than our father Jacob? He gave us the well and drank from it himself, as did his sons and his livestock." Jesus said to her, "Everyone who drinks of this water will be thirsty again, but *whoever drinks of the water that I will give him will never be thirsty again. The water that I will give him will become in him a spring of water welling up to eternal life."* The woman said to him, "Sir, give me this

water, so that I will not be thirsty or have to come here to draw water."
(John 4:7-15, emphasis added)

If the trajectory of the new covenant is God in man, what does this mean for our understanding of salvation? We are to drink from the wells of salvation (Isaiah 12:3) and drink from Christ (John 7:37). Jesus equates the water that he will give with eternal life (John 4:14). He also tells us that it is the Spirit who gives life (John 6:63; Romans 8:6, 10-11). As we noted earlier, in his prayer to his Father not long before the crucifixion, Jesus defines eternal life as knowing God and Christ experientially (John 17:3). To make this possible, he provides us with access to him that exceeds our access to any other person on this earth, the Spirit of God in man. The writer of Hebrews tells us that it is because we are cleansed and forgiven through Christ's sacrifice, his atoning death, that we can now freely be in the personal presence of God (Hebrews 10:19-22), the true Holy of Holies.

To understand more deeply what we are being saved from, let's look again at the fall of man in the Garden. Before Adam and Eve sinned, they were tempted by the serpent who told them they would not die if they ate the fruit of the tree of knowledge of good and evil (Genesis 3:4). The serpent contradicted God, seeking to break their trust in God. Due to their disobedience, their once unhindered relationship became clouded by shame, fear, and guilt (Genesis 3:8-10) and their newfound *experiential* knowledge of evil. Their sin created a dividing wall between the hearts of man, woman, and their Father. They hid themselves. Adam blamed Eve, and Eve blamed the serpent (Genesis 3:12-13). Being disconnected from their source of life, God himself, they experienced spiritual death. Their death was the agony of life apart from God's care and abiding presence. Physical death would come later.

Thankfully, God is long-suffering, patient, and the one who is Love (1 John 4:8). He had a plan to redeem his lost children and restore the relationship he had with them before their sin in the Garden. But he would not only restore that relationship. It would one day become what he had always intended. He would become one with his created ones—the highest and most profound expression of intimacy and love in all creation.

God made us for oneness with him, and it is the advent of the in-you relationship that I am suggesting brings the fullness of "salvation." It is not merely a legal decree that absolves us of our sins and wrongdoing but also makes available a source of new life in a relationship with the One we were made for.[20]

We can see this new life exemplified in a restored marriage, where adultery had caused a break between husband and wife. Restoring a marriage involves repentance and forgiveness. Having the humility and facing the risk of retribution by baring one's heart and sin to another and asking for forgiveness opens the door of hope for a restored relationship. When met with divinely inspired genuine forgiveness, complete restoration can proceed. There may be time and evidence needed to rebuild trust and heal the underlying issues of brokenness. With proper help and commitment from both parties, a relationship can emerge from the ashes that is stronger than ever before. It is no coincidence that when a marriage is restored, we commonly say it has been saved.

---

20 Pinnock aptly notes, "Union with God is not peripheral to salvation but the goal.... Spirit is leading us to union- to transforming, personal, intimate relationship with the triune God.... Since we have been forgiven, our eyes are on the goal of union with the love of God.... Being saved is more like falling in love with God." Pinnock, *Flame of Love*, 174, 171, 179. Salvation can also be seen in a broader context, as in the ultimate consummation of God's plan to restore his creation and the resurrection of the dead, worshiping and living under the care of the King of Kings (1 Corinthians 15:42-57, Revelation 21-22, among others).

Jeremiah, inspired by the Holy Spirit, describes Israel as an adulterous wife who forsakes her husband (Jeremiah 2:13, 20; 3:1-2, 8-9). Despite her transgression, God desires to restore her to her rightful place with him (Jeremiah 3:14-17). These verses portray a picture of salvation, a relationship restored, and the potential to grow together in union and love. God's desire is not just to forgive us and then allow us to experience him only after we leave our physical bodies. We are to walk in intimacy with him now, characterized by an overflow of peace, joy, and hope that plants seeds and bears fruit on the earth. God's healing and saving glory is the manifestation of his presence revealed within and through us by his indwelling Spirit.[21]

From a risk management perspective, if I assert that salvation is merely a "decision for Christ," a transaction that guarantees my place in heaven when I leave this earth, do I not risk missing out on the richness of life with God on the earth through his indwelling Spirit? How might you view a situation where a spouse vows to remain faithful after breaking his or her marriage vows but remains emotionally distant and does not engage in a growing and maturing relationship with his or her partner? Is such a marriage truly saved?

---

21 Fee concludes, "Whatever else, the newly formed people of God are Spirit people. They have come to life by the life-giving Spirit (Gal 5:25; 2 Cor 3:3, 6); they walk by the Spirit, and they are led by the Spirit. For Paul, therefore, to "get saved" means first of all to "receive the Spirit." Fee, *Paul, the Spirit, and the People of God*, 89. William Atkinson notes that "Christian life could only be experienced in any meaningful ongoing sense through receiving the gift of the Spirit for oneself. As salvation in Luke was more than crossing some line from "unforgiven" to "forgiven," but was incorporation into a community that was existentially experiencing the life of the kingdom of God." William P. Atkinson, *Baptism in the Spirit: Luke-Acts and the Dunn Debate*, (Cambridge: Lutterworth Press, 2012), 60. Max Turner notes that "Experience of 'salvation' might *commence* in assurance of God's forgiveness, but this was understood as the beginning of an on-going experience of God's inbreaking reign." Max Turner, *Power from on High: The Spirit in Israel's Restoration and Witness in Luke-Acts*, (Sheffield, UK: Sheffield Academic Press, 2000), 346.

Is Salvation a Process?

In the book of Acts, Peter tells the Pentecost onlookers that "it shall come to pass that everyone who calls upon the name of the Lord shall be saved" (Acts 2:21, quoting Joel 2:32). But what does it mean to call upon the name of the Lord? Is this calling instantaneous? Is it a one-time event or the beginning of a process?

Paul speaks of repentance that leads to salvation (2 Corinthians 7:10). If we repent, turn around, and go in the opposite direction toward life with God, we should ultimately find belonging, safety, and security in knowing him.[22] We are to work out our salvation with fear and trembling (Philippians 2:12). That is, we are to pursue a relationship with God, walking as his disciples and allowing him to live and love through us as an awe-filled response to his presence in our life. And as we do, we are delivered from our imprisonments, the things that keep us from him, both in a moment and over time.

Our journey to freedom often begins as the words of the Spirit through man (directly through others, the church, as some would say, or through the Scriptures), leading us to this restored relationship (Acts 11:14). Mark tells us that those who believe and are baptized will be saved (Mark 16:16). In the passage below, Paul seems to say that our words and belief bring justification and salvation.

---

22 Bruce Malina shares that "in the Mediterranean, currently and especially in the past, the focal institution of the various societies has been and is kinship. The family is truly everything.... When the family is the highlighted institution of concern, then the organizing principle is belongingness. Success consists in having and making the right interpersonal connections, in being related to the right people.... A person's identity depends on belonging to and being accepted by the family." Bruce J. Malina, *The New Testament World: Insights from Cultural Anthropology,* (Louisville, KY: Westminster John Knox Press, 2001), 29.

"If you confess with your mouth that Jesus is Lord and believe in your heart that God raised him from the dead, you will be saved. For with the heart one believes and is justified, and with the mouth one confesses and is saved" (Romans 10:9-10).

Similarly, in the book of Acts, Luke records a statement by Paul and Silas: "Believe in the Lord Jesus, and you will be saved, you and your household" (Acts 16:31). In his parable of the sower, Jesus associates unbelief with being kept from salvation (Luke 8:12).

The statement "you will be saved" (Greek *sōthēsē*) above in Acts 16:31 and Romans 10:9 is in the future tense. From a risk management perspective, is it possible that it is not only our profession and belief that constitute salvation but also our reception of the Spirit and engagement in an ongoing relationship that make this a reality? Paul alludes to an ongoing process, that we are *being* saved:

For the word of the cross is folly to those who are perishing, but to us who are being saved it is the power of God. (1 Corinthians 1:18)

Now I would remind you, brothers, of the gospel I preached to you, which you received, in which you stand, and by which you are being saved, if you hold fast to the word I preached to you—unless you believed in vain. (1 Corinthians 15:1-2).

For we are the aroma of Christ to God among those who are being saved and among those who are perishing. (2 Corinthians 2:15)

The early disciples seem to equate Peter's testimony of the giving of the Holy Spirit to the Gentiles at Cornelius's household with life:

> And I remembered the word of the Lord, how he said, 'John baptized with water, but you will be baptized with the Holy Spirit.' If then *God gave the same gift to them as he gave to us when we believed in the Lord Jesus Christ,* who was I that I could stand in God's way?" When they heard these things, they fell silent. And they glorified God, saying, "Then to the Gentiles also *God has granted repentance that leads to life."* (Acts 11:16-18, emphasis added)

Repentance in the passage above is not life but *leads to* life. Through Christ's sacrifice, the way to God is made open, and we are cleansed and can enter his presence. We must walk through the door, receive his forgiveness, and come to him, the true Savior and Shepherd of our souls.

> I am the door. If anyone enters by me, he will be saved and will go in and out and find pasture. The thief comes only to steal and kill and destroy. I came that they may have life and have it abundantly. (John 10:9-10)

Jesus makes the way and is the way to the Father's presence. Paul notes that it is "by grace you have been saved through faith. And this is not your own doing; it is the gift of God" (Ephesians 2:8). The goal of this faith, though, as we have noted, is not just to believe, but to receive life that comes from union with the Holy Spirit. In this union and the outworkings of the Spirit in our lives, God is glorified.

Most agree that salvation is impossible without the Holy Spirit's presence and action in an individual's life. Paul describes our salvation by both the "washing of regeneration and renewal of the Holy Spirit."

> *He saved us*, not because of works done by us in righteousness, but according to his own mercy, *by the washing of regeneration and renewal of the Holy Spirit.* (Titus 3:5, emphasis added).

Washing comes through the forgiveness offered through the Cross and received by the believer. Life, "renewal," comes by the "new heart" described in Ezekiel 36:26-27, God's Spirit within us. [23]

Peter proclaims that salvation is only in Christ (Acts 4:12). For it is Christ, through his atonement for our sin *and* his indwelling Spirit, who makes it possible for us to be one with our Father (John 14:6; 17:21-23). As we partake in this relationship, we are not to allow anything, even persecution, to cause us to withdraw from God. We are to stay close to him and endure to the end for salvation (Matthew 10:22).

In summary, salvation is a work of the Holy Spirit and involves knowing God in a restored relationship with him. How better to foster this relationship than God putting his Spirit within us and giving us unhindered access to his presence in this new covenant—the same Spirit within that Jesus had when he walked the earth?

What Is a Christian?

If God had not yet poured out his Spirit, the events leading up to the out-pouring that began in Acts 2 might still be considered under the Hebrew Bible's prior covenants. But Jesus' presence among the people inaugurated

---

23   Keener notes that "The Essenes and some other Jewish people associated the Spirit with purification, especially based on Ezekiel 36:25-27, where God cleanses his people from their idolatry." He also points out in reference to being born again in John 3:5, "Whereas Jewish teachers generally spoke of converts to Judaism as 'newborn,' only in the sense that they were legally severed from old relationships, an actual rebirth by the Spirit would produce a new heart (Ezek 36:26)." Craig S. Keener, *The IVP Bible Background Commentary* (Downers Grove, IL: IVP Academic, 2014) 255, 630.

a new way. Jesus walked filled with the Spirit and in perfect communion and obedience to his Father. Nothing stood between them, and there was no sin. Again, nothing he did or said was apart from his Father's will (John 5:19; 8:38; 12:49-50), including laying down his life (Luke 22:42). His obedience, borne out of Spirit-oneness, was pleasing to his Father.

> Now when all the people were baptized, and when Jesus also had been baptized and was praying, the heavens were opened, and the Holy Spirit descended on him in bodily form, like a dove; and a voice came from heaven, "You are my beloved Son; with you I am well pleased." (Luke 3:21-22, see also Matthew 17:5)

With God's Spirit in us, as it was in Christ, we can have a relationship with Father and Son and participate in the world's redemption.[24] Just as God took of the Spirit that was upon Moses and placed it on the seventy elders (Numbers 11:24-27) and as Jesus similarly empowered the twelve and seventy-two disciples with his authority (Luke 9:1-6; 10:1-11, 17-20), we too are to carry on his mission, having received new life by the Spirit that was upon him (Acts 1:8). A Christian then, is one who has repented, received forgiveness, *and* who lives by the same indwelling Spirit that was in Christ, in the same type of relationship that Jesus had with his Father.[25]

---

24 Amos Yong notes "That the baptism of Love in the Spirit is now unconditionally and eschatologically available to all … those of us who have been baptized into that love are in a position of heralding its accessibility and embodying its reality." Amos Yong, Spirit of Love: *A Trinitarian Theology of Grace*, (Waco, TX: Baylor University Press, 2012), 163-164.

25 Pinnock asserts that "To be a real Christian is to be alive in the Spirit in a life-transforming manner." *Flame of Love*, 189. Dunn notes that "It was only at Pentecost that the 120 became Christians…. As the 120 received the benefits of the death and resurrection of Christ at Pentecost through receiving the outpoured Spirit, so do all now become Christians by receiving the same Spirit." James D.G. Dunn, *Baptism in the Holy Spirit*, (Philadelphia: Westminster Press, 1970), 53-54. Veli-Matti Kärkkäinen, in describing Schleiermacher's pneumatology, states that "the basis for Christian life is the union of the human with the divine Spirit." Veli-Matti Kärkkäinen, *Pneumatology: The Holy Spirit in Ecumenical, International, and Contextual Perspective*, (Grand Rapids: Baker Academic, 2018), 92.

Born Again of the Spirit?

> Now there was a man of the Pharisees named Nicodemus, a ruler of the
> Jews. This man came to Jesus by night and said to him, "Rabbi, we know
> that you are a teacher come from God, for no one can do these signs that
> you do unless God is with him." Jesus answered him, "Truly, truly, I say to
> you, *unless one is born again he cannot see the kingdom of God.*" Nicode-
> mus said to him, "How can a man be born when he is old? Can he enter
> a second time into his mother's womb and be born?" Jesus answered,
> "Truly, truly, I say to you, *unless one is born of water and the Spirit*, he
> cannot enter the kingdom of God. That which is born of the flesh is flesh,
> and *that which is born of the Spirit is spirit.* Do not marvel that I said to you,
> 'You must be born again.' The wind blows where it wishes, and you hear
> its sound, but you do not know where it comes from or where it goes. So
> it is with everyone who is born of the Spirit." (John 3:1-8, emphasis added)

Being "born again" is another way of describing entering into a new
life in Christ. As noted earlier, some Christian streams understand entering into this new life as the result of sacramental grace (a gift of God
given as part of the enactment of a sacrament, such as water baptism),
where one is incorporated into the church, the body of Christ. Others
understand new birth to happen at the moment of belief or confession/
profession of faith in Christ, asking him to be their Lord, or perhaps the
reception of the forgiveness of Christ. Indeed, these can be a work of the
Spirit, but do they confer a fullness of new life, a new birth?

And again, were the 120 disciples (Acts 1:15), and perhaps Cornelius the Roman centurion (Acts 10), as believers in Christ the Messiah
and followers of God, already born again before the crucifixion and

resurrection of Christ? If the Spirit had not yet been given (John 7:39) and it is the Spirit that gives life (John 6:63), was it even possible that these were already born again of the Spirit (John 3:5-8)?[26]

Physical birth connotes entry into a new stage of life, and in our earthly experience, it is most certainly an observable event. Is it possible that new life, the life of the Spirit in them, begins for Cornelius and the 120 disciples upon receiving the Holy Spirit as described in Acts chapters 10 and 2, their Spirit baptism?

In John 3:8, the word "wind" is the Greek *pneuma*, which can be translated as either wind or spirit, and Jesus says that it "blows where it wishes, and you hear its sound." Is it possible that Jesus was hinting at the coming day of Pentecost where "there came from heaven a sound like a mighty rushing wind, and it filled the entire house where they were sitting" (Acts 2:2)? And from a risk management perspective, I wonder if it is within the realm of possibility that the spiritual birth described by Jesus to Nicodemus in the passage above is the Spirit baptism of the Book of Acts?[27] This possibility raises the potential importance of understanding our main topic, Spirit baptism, which we will turn to next.

---

26 Dunn makes the argument that "for the writers of the NT the baptism in or gift of the Spirit was part of the event (or process) of becoming a Christian … it was the chief element in conversion-initiation so that only those who had thus received the Spirit could be called Christians … the reception of the Spirit was a very definite and often dramatic experience, the decisive and climactic experience in conversion-initiation." *Baptism in the Holy Spirit*, 4.

27 It is interesting to note Keener's observation that "When Jesus tells Nicodemus to be born from "the water of the Spirit," he is calling Nicodemus to undergo a "spiritual" proselyte baptism, i.e., a baptism in the Holy Spirit." *Gift & Giver*, 151.

5

Holy Spirit Baptism

An Often-Debated Topic

Most Christians agree on the basics of what it means to live as sons and daughters of God. These typically include some type of initiation into the body of Christ, pursuing and communing with God through prayer, reading the Bible, participating in worship individually and in community, partaking of sacraments, serving and evangelizing, laying down our lives (our time, talents, resources, and in exceptional cases, even our bodies) for others. Debate and division continue across various streams and denominations regarding the meaning and priority of some of these activities.

Spirit baptism and its meaning and role in the life of the Christian are among those topics with varied interpretations. As previously noted, some avoid discussing Spirit baptism because they don't understand its importance. Others avoid the topic because they believe it can lead to division. Still others reject it as errant theology. Even those who claim it as a distinctive of their denomination or stream understand Spirit baptism differently.

To ground ourselves in this topic, this chapter will look at the historical evidence of the New Testament and the record of the Spirit upon man in the Hebrew Bible. But first, what is Spirit baptism?

A Baptism of Love

Baptism can be defined as the process of "immersion, submersion and emergence."[28] If water baptism is a water immersion, we might say that Spirit baptism is an immersion in God, the Holy Spirit. Just as a sponge can be in water and filled with water, Spirit baptism is an immersion that results in a saturation (a filling, Acts 2:4) and also a union (John 17:23) and indwelling (John 14:17). Spirit baptism is said to "immerse into the very life of God," where Messiah will "inundate you with the Spirit of God ... plunge you into his own divine life!"[29]

The life of God is a life of love. As Pentecostal theologian Amos Yong eloquently states: "The God who is love works through the unconditional Gift that is the Spirit of Love in order to lavish love upon creatures and draw creation into the loving embrace of the Creator."[30] And from the early 20th century, a man whose comment would be echoed by many stated: "It was a baptism of love. Such abounding love!"[31]

If God is love, to be baptized in His Spirit, immersed in Him, is to be baptized in love. Just as a man and woman give themselves to each other in marriage, to love and serve, to have and hold, so in this new covenant, God pledges to share his love with us without measure, to envelop us in his love. As there is often a preparation for marriage, there is also often a preparation for Spirit baptism. Let's start there.

---

28 W. E. Vine, *Vine's Complete Expository Dictionary of Old and New Testament Words*, (Nashville: Thomas Nelson, Inc., 1996), s.v. "baptism."

29 International Catholic Charismatic Renewal Services Doctrinal Commission (ICCRS) *Baptism in the Holy Spirit*, (Gibsonia, PA: Pentecost Today USA, 2022), 36.

30 Yong, *Spirit of Love*, 19. See also Frank Macchia, who connects Spirit baptism with God's presence and transformative love. *Baptized in the Spirit: A Global Pentecostal Theology*, (Grand Rapids: Zondervan, 2006) 17, 56,

31 *The Apostolic Faith*, Vol 1, No 1, September 1906.

Preparation

> If you turn at my reproof, behold, I will pour out my spirit to you; I will make my words known to you. (Proverbs 1:23)

> And Peter said to them, "Repent and be baptized every one of you in the name of Jesus Christ for the forgiveness of your sins, and you will receive the gift of the Holy Spirit." (Acts 2:38)

John the Baptist testified that he was "the voice of one crying out in the wilderness, 'Make straight the way of the Lord,' as the prophet Isaiah said" (John 1:23). John also fulfilled the role of Elijah that was prophesied by Malachi (Malachi 3:1; 4:5-6; Matthew 11:14), causing the Jews to turn their hearts (in love) toward one another. This turning is a complete change in attitude of heart and mind, after the realization that one is going the wrong way. "Come back home" is John the Baptist's cry, and his baptism is described as a baptism of repentance for forgiveness (Matthew 3:11; Mark 1:4; Luke 3:3; Acts 13:24; 19:4). We renounce and turn from our past sinful ways through an immersion that speaks of the cleansing of heart attitude, preparing us for fellowship with God.

Both ancient and many current Jews practice ritual immersion in a *mikveh* (ritual bath) in preparation for the Sabbath, celebrations, and as a means of removing ritual impurity. Ritual cleansing enables one to enter the presence of God or others (Exodus 29:4; 40:12; Leviticus 14:8; 15; 16:24-28; 17:15; Numbers 19:7-8, 19), and in some Jewish traditions, is required for conversion to Judaism.[32] As those who received John's message were baptized, they were preparing their hearts for a far more profound encounter with God through his Son.

After the resurrection of Christ, we are baptized in Jesus' baptism, also a baptism of forgiveness (Acts 2:38; 22:16) in water. Through Jesus' death and resurrection, he once-for-all made forgiveness and new life possible (Colossians 2:11-14; Hebrews 10:1-18). We are prepared and cleansed by the forgiveness enacted in this mikveh, not only to enter into his presence but also to become the temple of his Holy Spirit. This cleansing, symbolized by water baptism, is not a matter of outward ritual but results from a repentant heart. We can observe that water baptism is not necessarily required before receiving the Holy Spirit, as in the New Testament, it came both before (Acts 8:12-17; 19:5-6) and after (Acts 10:47) reception of the Holy Spirit. Today, as in the book of Acts, the order can vary, but water baptism most often precedes Spirit baptism.

There was a similar preparation for a relationship with God in the construction and consecration of the Tabernacle in the wilderness. By collaborating with the plans God gave Moses, the people of Israel expressed their willingness and desire for God's presence to come. The construction (Exodus 36-40) of the Tabernacle and the consecration of the Tabernacle and its ministers (Leviticus 8 and 9) outwardly demonstrated that willingness. The Israelites desired the life that came from having God with them.

God's presence in the Tabernacle was in the center of the Israelite

---

32   See Maurice Lamm, "The Mikveh's Significance in Traditional Conversion." *My Jewish Learning: https://www. myjewishlearning.com/article/why-immerse-in-the-mikveh/* (March 1, 2024); Rivkah Slonim, "The Mikvah." *Chabad.org: https://www.chabad.org/theJewishWoman/article_cdo/aid/1541/jewish/The-Mikvah.htm.*

camp, within the 12 tribes surrounding him (Numbers 2). When the glory of God filled the Tabernacle (Exodus 40:34), there was an outward and observable manifestation of his presence, and the people knew that God was in their midst. Similarly, in the new covenant, God places his presence within *us*. When the Spirit appeared in the book of Acts, which we will turn to next, there was also an outward manifestation.

Holy Spirit Baptism in the New Testament

There are seven explicit references to the term "baptize with the Holy Spirit" in the New Testament. Four of these passages record the words of John the Baptist (in the four Gospels), two are in the book of Acts (one mentioned by Jesus and another by Peter), and the seventh, debated by some, is found in Paul's First Letter to the Corinthians (1 Corinthians 12:13). Looking at the gospel record, we find that Spirit baptism, coupled with the forgiveness of sin, is at the forefront of John the Baptist's view of Jesus' purpose in coming.

> The next day he saw Jesus coming toward him, and said, "Behold, the Lamb of God, who takes away the sin of the world!... I myself did not know him, but he who sent me to baptize with water said to me, 'He on whom you see the Spirit descend and remain, this is he who baptizes with the Holy Spirit.'" (John 1:29, 33)

God (the "he" who sent John to baptize) tells John the Baptist that Jesus will baptize with the Holy Spirit. In the role of prophet, John (the Baptist) reveals God's purpose, repeating what he has heard. The other three references to Spirit baptism found in the other three Gospels are very similar, also recording John's words (Matthew 3:11; Mark 1:7-8; Luke 3:16).

> "I baptize you with water for repentance, but he who is coming after me is mightier than I, whose sandals I am not worthy to carry. He will baptize you with the Holy Spirit and fire." (Matthew 3:11)

Just before his ascension, Jesus used the term when speaking with his disciples.

> And while staying with them he ordered them not to depart from Jerusalem, but to wait for the *promise of the Father*, which, he said, *"you heard from me*; for John baptized with water, but *you will be baptized with the Holy Spirit not many days from now."* (Acts 1:4-5, emphasis added)

Luke records the same term for the arrival of the Spirit, "the promise of the Father" in Acts 1:4 and at the end of his Gospel (Luke 24:49). These were not the first times Jesus shared about the giving of the Spirit, but it was as "you heard from me."[33] On the day of Pentecost, Jesus' promise is fulfilled.

> When the day of Pentecost arrived, they were all together in one place. And suddenly there came from heaven a sound like a mighty rushing wind, and it filled the entire house where they were sitting. And divided tongues as of fire appeared to them and rested on each one of them. And they were all filled with the Holy Spirit and began to speak in other tongues as

---

33   At least some of these announcements are recorded in John 14:16, 26 and 15:26.

> the Spirit gave them utterance.... And at this sound the multitude came together, and they were bewildered, because each one was hearing them speak in his own language. (Acts 2:1-4, 6)

Peter speaks to the crowds at this event, explaining that what they see is fulfilling Joel's prophecy that God would pour out his Spirit on all flesh (Acts 2:15-21). The final explicit reference to Spirit baptism occurs in Acts 11, as Peter describes what happened to the Gentiles at the Roman centurion Cornelius' home.

> As I began to speak, the Holy Spirit fell on them just as on us at the beginning. And I remembered the word of the Lord, how he said, 'John baptized with water, but you will be baptized with the Holy Spirit.' If then God gave the same gift to them as he gave to us when we believed in the Lord Jesus Christ, who was I that I could stand in God's way?" (Acts 11:15-17)

Peter later recounts to the apostles and elders at Jerusalem:

> Peter stood up and said to them, "Brothers, you know that in the early days God made a choice among you, that by my mouth the Gentiles should hear the word of the gospel and believe. And God, who knows the heart, bore witness to them, by giving them the Holy Spirit just as he did to us, and he made no distinction between us and them, having cleansed their hearts by faith. (Acts 15:7-9)

What Peter witnessed left no doubt that these Gentiles had received the Holy Spirit.

> While Peter was still saying these things, the Holy Spirit fell on all who heard the word. And the believers from among the circumcised who had come with Peter were amazed, because the gift of the Holy Spirit was poured out even on the Gentiles. For they were hearing them speaking in tongues and extolling God. Then Peter declared, "Can anyone withhold water for baptizing these people, who have received the Holy Spirit just as we have." (Acts 10:44-47)

Acts 2 and 10 record the only events where the term "baptize with the Holy Spirit" is used to describe what has occurred. However, if we observe details of what was happening at these events, we can find other events with many common features that likely describe Spirit baptism. In these Acts 2 and 10 events, Luke describes these Holy Spirit encounters in the following ways:

1. Receiving power (1:8).
2. Being filled with the Holy Spirit (2:4).
3. The Holy Spirit being poured out (2:17-18; 10:45), received (10:47), seen and heard (2:33).
4. The Holy Spirit falling on them (10:44; 11:15).
5. Giving them the same gift (11:17), giving them the Holy Spirit (15:8).
6. Speaking in other tongues (languages), praising and extolling God (2:4; 10:46).
7. The sound of rushing wind and divided tongues as of fire appearing and resting on each of them (2:2-3).

When the Gentiles received the Spirit in Acts 10, there is no mention of the sound of rushing wind or tongues as of fire, but it is certain in Acts 11:17 and 15:8 that the Gentiles have received the Holy Spirit just as the disciples had in Acts 2. From these examples, we can say with a high degree of certainty that being baptized with the Holy Spirit is equivalent to receiving the Holy Spirit (Acts 10:47; 11:17; 15:8). Let's look next at other events recorded in Acts.

Other Similar Events

Given the commonality of language with the Acts 2 and 10 events, the receipt of the Spirit by the Samaritans and Ephesians in Acts 8 and 19 also appear to be Spirit baptism events:

> Now when the apostles at Jerusalem heard that Samaria had received the word of God, they sent to them *Peter and John*, who came down and *prayed for them that they might receive the Holy Spirit, for he had not yet fallen on any of them*, but they had only been baptized in the name of the Lord Jesus. Then they *laid their hands on them and they received the Holy Spirit.* Now when Simon *saw that the Spirit was given through the laying on of the apostles' hands*, he offered them money. (Acts 8:14-18, emphasis added)

> And it happened that while Apollos was at Corinth, Paul passed through the inland country and came to Ephesus. There he found some disciples. And he said to them, *"Did you receive the Holy Spirit when you believed?"* And they said, *"No, we have not even heard that there is a Holy Spirit."* And he said, "Into what then were you baptized?" They said, "Into John's baptism." And Paul said, "John baptized with the baptism of repentance, telling the people to believe in the one who was to come after him, that is,

> Jesus." On hearing this, they were baptized in the name of the Lord Jesus. And *when Paul had laid his hands on them, the Holy Spirit came on them, and they began speaking in tongues and prophesying.* There were about twelve men in all. (Acts 19:1-7, emphasis added)

In the Acts 9 passage below, Ananias' ministry to Saul included laying on of hands to regain his sight and be filled with the Holy Spirit. Assuming that Paul received the Spirit on this occasion, this would be yet another Spirit baptism event.

> So Ananias departed and entered the house. And *laying his hands on him* he said, "Brother Saul, the Lord Jesus who appeared to you on the road by which you came has sent me so that you may regain your sight and *be filled with the Holy Spirit.*" And immediately something like scales fell from his eyes, and he regained his sight. Then he rose and was baptized. (Acts 9:17-18, emphasis added)

In Acts 18 we see Priscilla and Aquila explaining to Apollos "the way of God more accurately" (Acts 18:26). Like the Ephesians in Acts 19, Apollos "knew only the baptism of John" (Acts 18:25; 19:3). While some point to Apollos being "fervent in spirit" and that he "had been instructed in the way of the Lord" (Acts 18:25) as evidence that he had already received the Spirit, the similarity to the Ephesian account raises at least some possibility that he had not yet been baptized with the Holy Spirit.

Considering that Paul's ministry to the Ephesians (Acts 19) results in them receiving the Holy Spirit, it seems not a giant leap to think that Priscilla and Aquila's ministry to Apollos could have had the same result. We cannot argue from silence, but we do know that Paul had a fruitful ministry in Corinth (Acts 18:8, 11), and he stayed with Priscilla and Aquila there (Acts 18:3). We also know that the church at Corinth, perhaps all of them (1 Corinthians 12:7; 14:23), were known to use spiritual gifts including spiritual language (speaking in other tongues). It is highly possible that Priscilla and Aquila witnessed and participated in at least some of the ministry with Paul before traveling to Ephesus, where they encountered Apollos (Acts 18:18-19, 24-26). If so, Priscilla and Aquila's ministry certainly could have included teaching and ministering Spirit baptism among the people, as Paul's did in Ephesus.

Finally, in response to Peter's preaching, as recorded in Acts 2, three thousand were added to their number on the day of Pentecost.

> And Peter said to them, "Repent and be baptized every one of you in the name of Jesus Christ for the forgiveness of your sins, and you will receive the gift of the Holy Spirit.... So those who received his word were baptized, and there were added that day about three thousand souls. (Acts 2:38, 41)

From the text, it is not sure whether they became believers in Christ and were water-baptized only or were baptized with the Holy Spirit on that day, but the latter is certainly possible.

Altogether, three instances of Spirit baptism in Acts (Acts 2, 10, and 19) record the outward sign of Spirit-inspired speech in languages unknown to the speakers.[34] We don't know what outward sign Simon

---

34   I use "Spirit-inspired speech" herein to refer to any speech given by the Spirit, including in one's native tongue or a spiritual language. I use "spiritual language," and "Spirit-given language" interchangeably to describe what the Bible calls tongues (languages) that are unknown to the speaker, also known as glossolalia.

saw in Acts 8:18, but given the three other instances, it was very likely the same.[35]

In Saul's experience (Acts 8), there is no mention of a specific outward sign other than "something like scales" falling from his eyes. That omission does not mean there was no other outward sign. We know that Paul (Saul) spoke in Spirit-given languages regularly (1 Corinthians 14:18), and it is certainly possible that this began for him when Ananias ministered to him, similar to the Acts 2, 10, and 19 events. At the very least, it started sometime afterward. And if the three thousand souls received the Holy Spirit on Pentecost (Acts 2:38), it is not unreasonable to expect that many, if not all, would have spoken in Spirit-given languages.

These New Testament events are not the first recorded in the Bible where the Holy Spirit came upon man in an outwardly recognizable way.

The Spirit Upon Man in the Hebrew Bible

Several of our New Testament examples of Spirit baptism include words spoken under the inspiration of the Spirit and witnessed by others. For this discussion, let us call this "Spirit-inspired speech." We also find Spirit-inspired speech throughout the Hebrew Bible, particularly with the prophets upon whom the Spirit of God rested. God describes this process in his interaction with Moses and Aaron before sending them to Pharaoh, as Exodus describes.

---

35 Timothy Laurito notes that "Luke's silence regarding speaking in tongues in the case of the Samaritan believers does nothing to negate its overall importance. Neither does it refute the biblical pattern of speaking in tongues being the initial physical evidence of Spirit baptism throughout Acts (Acts 2, 10, 19).... When taken in the context of the entirety of Luke's narrative, it is not ambiguous what happened to the Samaritans when they received the Holy Spirit. They spoke in other tongues." Timothy Laurito, *Speaking in Tongues: A Multidisciplinary Defense*, (Eugene, OR: Wipf & Stock, 2021), 14.

"You shall speak to him and put the words in his mouth, and I will be with your mouth and with his mouth and will teach you both what to do. He shall speak for you to the people, and he shall be your mouth, and you shall be as God to him." (Exodus 4:15-16)

And the Lord said to Moses, "See, I have made you like God to Pharaoh, and your brother Aaron shall be your prophet. You shall speak all that I command you, and your brother Aaron shall tell Pharaoh to let the people of Israel go out of his land. (Exodus 7:1-2)

Moses becomes like God to Pharaoh (Exodus 7:1) as he speaks words to Aaron, his prophet (7:2). As mentioned earlier, God instructed Moses to call seventy elders to help him shepherd the people. God takes the Spirit that is upon Moses and places it upon them, equipping them to serve (Numbers 11:16-17).

The Lord came down in the cloud and spoke to him, and *took some of the Spirit that was on him and put it on the seventy elders.* And *as soon as the Spirit rested on them, they prophesied.* Now two men remained in the camp, one named Eldad, and the other named Medad, and the Spirit rested on them. They were among those registered, but they had not gone out to the tent, and so *they prophesied in the camp.* (Numbers 11:25-26, emphasis added)

Here, the elders receive of the Spirit, with an accompanying sign of prophecy (Spirit-inspired speech). Other examples demonstrate a similar occurrence. When the prophet Samuel anoints Saul as the first King of Israel, he tells him that he will meet a group of prophets and "the Spirit of the Lord will rush upon you, and you will prophesy with them and be turned into another man" (1 Samuel 10:6). Later we read that God gave Saul a new heart, and the "Spirit of God rushed upon him, and he prophesied," just as Samuel foretold (1 Samuel 10: 9-10).

When the Spirit of God initially made Saul prophesy, it confirmed Samuel's prophetic word and confirmed Saul's ordination. Years later, when Saul was wrongfully pursuing David, the Spirit of God fell on Saul and his three groups of messengers causing them to prophesy (1 Samuel 19:20-24). Among other things, it allowed David to escape Saul's murderous plot against him.

God placed his Spirit in Ezekiel, giving him words to speak to the Israelites (Ezekiel 2:1-2, 7) as he did for many other prophets of the Hebrew Bible. Through the inspiration of the Holy Spirit, man also spoke prophetically about the coming Messiah through his psalmists, particularly King David (various Psalms, including 2, 22, 110). By this same Spirit, Jeremiah, Ezekiel, Isaiah, and Joel spoke about the coming new covenant and the pouring out of God's Spirit upon man. And the same Spirit of God who spoke through them later brought about the fulfillment of his own words.

Some Observations

The God who created heaven and earth with the sound of his voice (Genesis 1) has communicated with man throughout history by sharing his words through his servants. When the Spirit came into or upon man, it was not uncommon for Spirit-given speech to pour forth. So, it would not be unexpected or out of character for God to repeat this speech through man when his Spirit was poured out on the 120 disciples on

Pentecost. Peter confirmed for the onlookers that the Holy Spirit was the source of their words (Acts 2:15-17). As noted, this outpouring of the Spirit also marks the beginning of the fulfillment of Moses' desire that all of God's people would have his Spirit on them (Numbers 11:29). God truly is longsuffering, patient, and faithful to his word. But is the New Testament the last we hear of God pouring out his Spirit upon man?

6

Some Modern Witnesses

Our Practices as Witnesses

> But if he does not listen, take one or two others along with you, that every charge may be established by the evidence of two or three witnesses. (Matthew 18:16; see also Deuteronomy 19:15 and 2 Corinthians 13:1)

While the verse above is taken slightly out of context (we are not bringing a charge against anyone), looking at other witnesses of Spirit baptism, particularly in our practices, can be helpful. After surveying our first witness, the Bible, it is surprising that Spirit baptism remains one of the more divisive topics in the Christian community. However, it becomes easier to fathom the diversity of understanding when we consider a diversity of cultures, experiences, and doctrines and how those influence our understanding.

For someone who has not had a Spirit baptism experience similar to the Acts accounts, the possibility of this occurring today remains uncertain or even a rock-solid impossibility. But God has purposefully given us pliable minds and hearts, and we can seek out and process new information and experiences to update our perspectives. Often, the witness of others, our friends, mentors, parents, family, and even strangers, can be a powerful catalyst. In this quest to understand Spirit baptism, can the witness of current and historical church practices also provide some fuel for our journey?

The Sacrament of Confirmation

If you are familiar with the more liturgical and sacramental streams of the faith, you may be familiar with the sacrament or practice of confirmation, as it is called for Roman Catholics, Lutherans, Anglican, Methodist, and Reformed traditions, or chrismation, as it is known in the Orthodox tradition.

Confirmation in the Roman Catholic Church (RCC) is one of three sacraments of initiation.[36] For those raised from childhood in the RCC, these sacraments typically occur at different life stages. For adult converts, however, often the three are experienced together. The first is the sacrament of baptism, symbolizing and actualizing allegiance with Christ in his death and resurrection and making one a member of the RCC. Water baptism is seen as "the gateway to life in the Spirit."[37] It is followed by Holy Communion (Eucharist), which generally first takes place for elementary-aged children (typically second grade). The RCC teaches that the Eucharist is bread and wine whose substance has been transformed into the body and blood of Christ, the "Real Presence" of Christ.[38]

The final initiatory rite of confirmation, which can occur from ages seven to seventeen, as determined by the diocese,[39] represents

---

36 Catechism of the Catholic Church (CCC) 1212.
37 CCC 1213. Baptism is also seen as "the washing of regeneration and renewal by the Holy Spirit," signifying and bringing about spiritual birth (CCC 1215).
38 This is the doctrine of transubstantiation. See also "The Real Presence" in chapter 14 for more thoughts on the Eucharist in light of Spirit baptism.
39 "Canon 891 - Age for Confirmation" *United States Conference of Catholic Bishops: https://www.usccb.org/beliefs-and-teachings/what-we-believe/canon-law/complementary-norms/canon-891-age-for-confirmation* (February 27, 2024).

receiving the Holy Spirit. The bishop anoints the confirmands with oil and raises his hands over them to impart the seal of the Holy Spirit.[40] The *Catechism of the Catholic Church* (CCC) describes the effects of the sacrament of confirmation as follows:

> 1302 It is evident from its celebration that the effect of the *sacrament of Confirmation is the full outpouring of the Holy Spirit as once granted to the apostles on the day of Pentecost.* 1303 From this fact, Confirmation brings an increase and deepening of baptismal grace: it roots us more deeply in the divine filiation which *makes us cry, "Abba! Father!"*; it unites us more firmly to Christ; it increases the gifts of the Holy Spirit in us; it renders our bond with the Church more perfect; it *gives us a special strength of the Holy Spirit* to spread and defend the faith by word and action as true witnesses of Christ, to confess the name of Christ boldly, and never to be ashamed of the Cross: Recall then that *you have received the spiritual seal,* the spirit of wisdom and understanding, the spirit of right judgment and courage, the spirit of knowledge and reverence, the spirit of holy fear in God's presence. Guard what you have received. God the Father has marked you with his sign; *Christ the Lord has confirmed you and has placed his pledge, the Spirit, in your hearts.* 1304 Like Baptism which it completes, Confirmation is given only once, for it too imprints on the soul an indelible spiritual mark, the "character," which is the sign that Jesus Christ has *marked a Christian with the seal of his Spirit by clothing him with power from on high so that he may be his witness.* (CCC 1302-1304, emphasis added)

---

40 CCC 1299-1300.

The RCC equates confirmation with the receipt of the Spirit on Pentecost (Acts 2:1-4), the "seal of his Spirit" (CCC 1304). And we know the Acts 2 Pentecost event to be the first Spirit baptism (Acts 1:5). Further, the RCC sees confirmation as rooted in the Acts 8 reception of the Spirit by the Samaritans, which takes place after water baptism by Philip and through the laying on of hands by Peter and John.[41]

Orthodox churches administer the sacrament of chrismation together with baptism, similar to the adult RCC initiatory rites. They also see the sacrament as imparting the Holy Spirit to the individual in an experience of the outpouring of Pentecost.

> If baptism is our personal participation in Easter—the death and resurrection of Christ, then chrismation is our personal participation in Pentecost—the coming of the Holy Spirit upon us.... Chrismation, the gift of the Holy Spirit, is performed in the Orthodox Church by anointing all parts of the person's body with the special oil called holy chrism.... In chrismation a person is given the "power from on high" (Acts 1-2), the gift of the Spirit of God, in order to live the new life received in baptism. He is anointed, just as Christ the Messiah is the Anointed One of God. He becomes—as the fathers of the Church dared to put it—a "christ" together with Jesus. Thus, through chrismation we become a "christ," a son of God, a person upon whom the Holy Spirit dwells, a person in whom the Holy Spirit lives and acts—as long as we want him and cooperate with his powerful and holy inspiration.[42]

---

41 CCC 1315.
42 Thomas Hopko, *The Orthodox Faith Volume 2: Worship*, 2nd ed. (Yonkers, NY: St Vladimir's Seminary Press, 2016), chap. 2, The Sacraments, Chrismation.

The Catholic confirmation and Orthodox chrismation point directly back to the Acts 2 receipt of the Spirit at Pentecost, at the very least acknowledging the importance of the historical Spirit baptism event and its priority for individuals. Other Protestant denominations also practice confirmation as a sacrament, rite, or ritual. Most see confirmation as an affirmation of baptismal vows, a commitment to walk in the ways of Christ, to the church, service/vocation, and strengthening by the Spirit. Some also incorporate the laying on of hands and anointing with oil, founded in the laying on of hands in Acts 8, 9, and 19.

A question remains, though: Do these sacraments, rites, and ordinances as practiced actually equate to Spirit baptism, or do they merely point in its direction? I will address this question later near the end of chapter 14.

It is interesting to note that some Protestant denominations typically do not recognize or practice confirmation following baptism. They see the believer's baptism as a response and affirmation of what God has already done in Christ and believe that full receipt of the Holy Spirit is concurrent with one's profession of faith or initial conversion.[43]

It is also interesting to note that Reform Judaism practices confirmation, introduced in the 1800s. This Jewish form of confirmation is also an opportunity for an individual to reaffirm/confirm his or her faith.[44] The rite is typically practiced during the biblical feast of *Shavuot* (Pentecost), which recalls the giving of the Torah on Mt. Sinai—the

---

43 Among many others, Robert Saucy holds this view. See Robert L. Saucy, "An Open But Cautious View," in *Are Miraculous Gifts for Today? Four Views*, ed. Stanley N. Gundry and Wayne A. Grudem, (Grand Rapids, MI: Zondervan, 1996).

44 See "What is Confirmation?" *ReformJudaism.org: https://reformjudaism.org/beliefs-practices/lifecycle-rituals/what-confirmation*, (February 27, 2024), and "What is Confirmation and what is its connection to Shavuot?" *ReformJudaism.org:https://reformjudaism.org/learning/answers-jewish-questions/what-confirmation-and-what-its-connection-shavuot* (February 27, 2024).

same feast where the outpouring of the Holy Spirit occurred in Acts 2. Could this be a work of God's providence that will one day find its fulfillment in the full outpouring of the Spirit of God in the lives of Reform Jews in a new covenant Pentecost? May it be so!

While it is helpful to understand that certain forms of confirmation point to the Acts 2 receipt of the Holy Spirit on Pentecost, there is yet another witness in our quest to understand. Today, in many modern Christian faith expressions, there is a belief, an expectation, and an experience of the Holy Spirit that aligns with the outpouring of the Spirit and Spirit baptism described in the book of Acts. Let's look more closely at a modern version of this outpouring that came at the dawn of the last century, a third witness in the Spirit baptism inquiry.

The 20th-Century Outpouring

Leading up to the 20th century, some remarkable changes in the religious landscape laid the groundwork for an outpouring of the Spirit that has been unmatched in church history. Over the centuries, the church has experienced various reformations and splits. These movements were typically spearheaded by individuals or groups seeking to recover what they believed was a more authentic Christianity and to correct shortcomings that they observed.

In the 17th century, some groups sought to emphasize returning to an experiential relationship with God. The early Pietists emphasized individual devotional life, small group study of the Bible, and a deepening experiential relationship with Jesus Christ as an alternative to the more doctrine-heavy experience of Lutheran orthodoxy. John Wesley witnessed this pietist ethic in the German Herrnhuter community which highlighted the importance of an "intimate and personal relationship" with Christ and a "living faith."[45]

Not long after Wesley visited Herrnnhut, he and his brother Charles had experiential encounters with the Holy Spirit.[46] In England, their ministry of an experiential faith and structured approach to devotion later became known as Methodism. This same heart for experiential faith was evident in the lives of others who followed and was an integral part of the "Great Awakening" in the 18th-century United States.[47]

Leading up to the early 20th century were numerous revivals featuring Spirit baptism and related spiritual gifts. These revivals were observed in India, the United States, Wales, Chile, and Korea, all contributing foundationally to the global Pentecostal-charismatic movement that grew exponentially in the 20th century.[48]

In the US, arising out of the Holiness stream[49] was the ministry of Charles Parham, a former Methodist Pastor. Parham tasked a group of his students in Topeka, Kansas, with searching the Bible to determine what evidence is present at Holy Spirit baptism. They concluded that it was speaking in other languages/tongues. On January 1, 1901, the first of these students, Agnes Ozman, was baptized with the Holy Spirit with the outward biblical sign of speaking in a Spirit-given language. Soon, others followed.[50]

---

45 Alister E. McGrath, *Christian History: An Introduction*, (West Sussex, UK: John Wiley & Sons, 2013), 222. See also E.D. Burns, "Moravian Missionary Piety and the Influence of Count Zinzendorf." *Training Leaders International: https://trainingleadersinternational.org/jgc/27/moravian-missionary-piety-and-the-influence-of-count-zinzendorf*.

46 Joe Iovino, "Holy Spirit moments: Learning from Wesley at Aldersgate." May 18, 2017. *UMC.ORG: https://www.umc.org/en/content/holy-spirit-moments-learning-from-wesley-at-aldersgate* (August 20, 2024).

47 McGrath, *Christian History*, 223, 225.

48 Todd M. Johnson and Gina A. Zurlo, *Introducing Spirit-Empowered Christianity: The Global Pentecostal & Charismatic Movement in the 21st Century*, (Tulsa, OK: ORU Press, 2023), 13-15.

49 The Holiness movement was focused more on morality and the spiritual life, rather than the defense of doctrinal orthodoxy, with "holy living" as its preeminent feature. McGrath, *Christian History*, 258.

50 Cecil M. Robeck, Jr., *The Azusa St Mission and Revival: The Birth of the Global Pentecostal Movement*, (Nashville: Emanate Books, 2006), 42-43 ; *The Latter Rain Evangel*, January 1909, 2, accessed at *https://pentecostalarchives.org/?a=d&d=LRE190901-01.1.2&e=-------en-20--1--img-txIN------------* (8/21/2024).

In 1905, African-American Holiness minister William J. Seymour attended Parham's Texas Bible training school (due to segregation laws at the time, he had to listen from outside the classroom). In 1906, Seymour started the Apostolic Faith Mission on Azusa Street in Los Angeles. There, he and a small group were also baptized in the Holy Spirit, beginning a revival that lasted three years, spread throughout the United States, and was publicized throughout the world.[51]

While there are varying views on the origins of modern Pentecostalism,[52] Parham and Seymour are often credited with the nascent outpouring that resulted in the formation of several of the denominations within Denominational Pentecostalism (Classical and Oneness Pentecostals), our first type of Pentecostal-charismatics.[53] In the United States, this outpouring did not remain a solely Pentecostal experience. During the 1940s and 1950s, individuals outside of Pentecostalism were being baptized in the Holy Spirit. Some left their denominations to join Pentecostal churches, and others remained in their denominations.[54] By the 1960s, this trickle became a river pouring into the broader church body.

Many point to Episcopal priest Dennis Bennett as the beginning of the second type of Pentecostal-charismatics, the modern charismatic (or neo-Pentecostal) movement within mainline denominations

---

51   Robeck, *Azusa St Mission*, 4-6.

52   Glenn Menzies summarizes three perspectives on modern Pentecostalism's origin that include the ministries of Parham, Seymour, or perhaps even multiple origins, recognizing "nearly simultaneous revivals in India, Korea, Great Britain, United States and elsewhere". Glenn W. Menzies, "The First Fifty Years of the Society for Pentecostal Studies: A Brief History" *Pneuma* 42 (December 2020), 364-365. See also the narrative on the origins and precursors of the Pentecostal and charismatic movements in Timothy B. Cremeens, *Marginalized Voices: A History of the Charismatic Movement in the Orthodox Church in North America 1972-1993*, (Eugene, OR: Pickwick Publications, 2018), 5-38, and footnote 134 for additional resources.

53   The three types are described in Johnson and Zurlo, Introducing *Spirit-Empowered Christianity*, 8, 11.

54   Cremeens, *Marginalized Voices*, 41-43.

(Anglican, Catholic, Orthodox, and Protestant streams).[55] In April 1960, Bennett announced to his California church that he had been baptized with the Holy Spirit and spoke in a spiritual language. The news spread within his parish, nationally and internationally, with stories in *Time* and *Newsweek* garnering wide attention. In time, renewal spread to Lutherans, Presbyterians, and other Protestant denominations. [56] In 1967, with the "Duquesne Weekend," the renewal began spreading to the RCC, [57] eventually leading to the single largest component of the worldwide Pentecostal-charismatic community, the Catholic Charismatic Renewal.[58] By the early 1970s, the renewal spread to the Orthodox Church, but it did not flourish there for various reasons.[59]

The third type, independent charismatics (or neo-charismatic) identify neither as Pentecostal nor as charismatics within mainline denominations. These are new groups, those that left the Pentecostal and denominational charismatic churches, and "indigenous and independent church movements," including "movements such as the Vineyard churches.... African Initiated Churches, Chinese house churches, Brazilian megachurches, and thousands of other groups."[60] Additionally, many in the modern Messianic Jewish movement (Jewish believers in Jesus/Yeshua as Messiah who keep their Jewish identity) have roots in

55 Johnson and Zurlo, *Introducing Spirit-Empowered Christianity*, 11.
56 *Marginalized Voices*, 43-47.
57 See *Marginalized Voices*, 48-52; Randy Clark and Mary Healy, *The Spiritual Gifts Handbook: Using Your Gifts to Build the Kingdom*, (Minneapolis: Chosen Books, 2018), 107-110; John and Therese Boucher, *An Introduction to the Catholic Charismatic Renewal*, (Cincinnati: Servant, 2017), 18-19, among many others.
58 Johnson and Zurlo, *Introducing Spirit-Empowered Christianity*, 34.
59 Some of these issues include the view that the RCC was being "Protestantized" by the influence of the renewal, which came not from within, but from the evangelical/Pentecostal stream, and that Orthodoxy was the lone holdout as the only truly authentic church that was begun by Christ. There also were issues with personalities within the Orthodox charismatic movement. Cremeens, *Marginalized Voices*, 157-166.
60 Johnson and Zurlo, *Introducing Spirit-Empowered Christianity*, 75.

the charismatic renewal of the 1960s, notably the Jesus Movement that began in California.[61]

It is remarkable how many individuals worldwide have been impacted by the outpouring of the Holy Spirit in the 20th and 21st centuries. The total global Pentecostal-charismatic population is estimated at 683 million at mid-2024. Those affected by this modern-day Pentecost experience are 26 percent of the more than two and a half billion Christians worldwide and over 8 percent of the estimated 8.1 billion world population.[62] This outpouring is nothing short of miraculous when you consider its small beginnings.

But what could cause such an exponential spread of these experiences? For those who experienced Spirit baptism, most arrived at a belief that it was possible (or at least that it might have been possible) to receive the Holy Spirit in a way similar to those in Acts 2, 8, 10, and 19 based on the testimony or teaching of others.[63] From those earliest days, the first Pentecostals, like many modern Pentecostals and others, expected to receive the Spirit with the same sign of speaking in a spiritual language.[64] Most charismatics also had to hear or be taught and believe (Romans 10:14) before their experience of the Spirit. If we are not taught and don't believe, we are much less likely (but not

---

61 Peter Hocken, *The Challenges of the Pentecostal, Charismatic and Messianic Jewish Movements: The Tensions of the Spirit*, (Burlington, VT: Ashgate Publishing, 2009), 100.

62 Center for Global Christianity, "Status of Global Christianity."

63 Such was Jack Hayford's mindset when seeking the experience of Spirit baptism. He expected to experience something, a verifiable experience. Jack Hayford, *The Beauty of Spiritual Language: Unveiling the Mystery of Speaking in Tongues*, revised and expanded, (Southlake, TX: Gateway Press, 2018), 40.

64 Some point out that we have no empirical proof that our modern-day Spirit baptism is the same as that in the Scriptures. Given the biblical descriptions, the similarities are remarkable. Also, some do not put as much emphasis on spiritual language as an evidence of Spirit baptism, but that other qualities and fruit can evidence the same. See Keener, "Tongues and the Spirit" in *Gift & Giver*, for a discussion on various views. Simon Chan notes that "Glossolalia does not have the status of proof.... but is the most natural and regular concomitant of Spirit-filling involving an invasive or irruptive manifestation of the Spirit in which one's relationship to Jesus Christ is radically and significantly altered." Simon Chan, *Pentecostal Theology and the Christian Spiritual Tradition*, (London: Sheffield Academic Press, 2003), 58.

unable) to experience Spirit baptism. Such is the teaching of most Pentecostal-charismatics today. If we believe and desire, we can each experience the Spirit baptism (or infilling, as some charismatics call it) of the first-century Christians.[65]

Saying that the Spirit baptism of Acts is available to all of us today may seem divisive to some. From a risk management perspective, I would rather err on the side of the generosity of God rather than limit the experience to history or something less than all people. Are you among those impacted by this renewal, or do you know others who have had a Spirit baptism experience? Do you know their story? If not, ask them to share it with you.

Effects of Spirit Baptism

Up to this point, we have primarily discussed events (who, what, where, when, how many) of Spirit baptism in the biblical and historical record. However, an essential aspect of these events is their effect on individuals and communities. Lest I provide an anemic view of the initial impacts of Spirit baptism (as if anything associated with the action of the Holy Spirit could be rightly called anemic), this section will touch on the Spirit's work as recorded in the New Testament, and examine some of the typical impacts that those baptized in the Spirit report in the modern day, beyond the witness of many of the ability to speak in Spirit-given languages.

From the witness of Spirit-baptized disciples in the New Testament, we can see the outward work of the Spirit through generosity,

---

65 Hocken notes that "All participants in the Renewal are agreed that baptism in the Spirit is its foundational spiritual reality from which all its other characteristics derive." Peter Hocken, *Azusa, Rome, and Zion: Pentecostal Faith, Catholic Reform, and Jewish Roots*, (Eugene, OR: Pickwick Publications, 2016), 66.

love, gifts and fruit of the Spirit, signs, wonders, and miracles, as well as a miraculous increase in the number of believers, in a continuation of the ministry of Christ. Responding to God's poured-out love (Romans 5:5), individuals and communities freely share their lives and resources (Acts 2:44-46; 4:32-37), pray and sing in the face of imprisonment (Acts 16:22-25), withstand affliction (2 Corinthians 11:22-27), and experience miracles and healings (Acts 3:1-10; 4:29-31; 5:12; 9:32-41, among others). The Spirit guides with specific instruction (Acts 8:29; 10:19-20; 13:2; 16:6-7; 21:4). He gives spiritual gifts to individuals for the strengthening of the body (Ephesians 4:11-12; 1 Corinthians 12:4-11, 28; 14) and salvation of the lost. Growing in relationship with God through the Spirit brings the fruit of love, joy, peace, patience, kindness, goodness, faithfulness, gentleness, and self-control (Galatians 4:22).

This fruit is often accompanied by radical changes in the trajectory of individuals' lives. Before Pentecost, in fear and weakness, Peter denies Christ (Matthew 26:69-75). On Pentecost, he stands before the crowd, boldly proclaiming the work of Christ through the outpoured Holy Spirit he has just received (Acts 2:14-36). Paul, who was once a persecutor of Christians (Acts 8:3), becomes a champion of Christ, bearing the gift of the Spirit and the message of salvation first to the Jews and, when they would not listen, to the Gentiles also (Acts 13:45-48).

While each individual's experience is intensely personal and subjective, the human soul has not changed, and what occurred in the book of Acts is still relevant to believers today. For many, the experience of Spirit baptism radically alters their perspective and is a starting point for the transformation of their entire lives. Now possessing the same Spirit that was in the New Testament believers, they can more readily appreciate and understand what those in the Bible experienced and expressed of their walk in Christ. The Bible becomes a reality, and the experience of that reality radically alters the horizon from which they view its content and understand its meaning. [66]

As expected, when the Holy Spirit actually touches a person's heart, they become aware of God's presence and love. Studies of Spirit baptism report that people often speak of "an immediate awareness of a compelling connection with God as a doubtless reality" and that it "convinces the recipient of salvation and of deeper realities of God," accompanied by feelings of "abiding love,… peaceful calm,… intoxication," and "exceeding happiness and joy." One study states that Spirit baptism results in "a connectedness with the reality, presence, and action of God," and "feelings of joy, peacefulness and ease," and that the experience "involves a feeling of being truly loved and/or embraced by God, who is sensed as close, present and real."[67]

Some people report having "new eyes to see God and new ears to hear God's Word" and a "new willingness to renounce sin and be faithful to the Gospel."[68] Others experience "an overflowing fullness of the Spirit," "a deepened reverence for God," "an intensified consecration

---

66 Cremeens observes the impact of experience on understanding, noting that St. Symeon the New Theologian's "teachings were based upon his many visions and direct encounters with the Lord…. As is true in Orthodox spirituality, a theologian is one who teaches theology not from the words of others but by his own experience of God." *Marginalized Voices*, 8-9. Cardinal Suenens shares that "In the New Testament communities, the Spirit was a fact of experience before there was a developed doctrine of the Spirit, the doctrine developing in the light of the experience…. The Spirit was poured out on them and was experienced by them individually and communally as a new reality." Léon Joseph Cardinal Suenens, *Theological and Pastoral Orientations on the Catholic Charismatic Renewal*, (Notre Dame, IN: Word of Life, 1974), 19-21.

67 W. Paul Williamson and Ralph W. Hood, "Spirit Baptism: A Phenomenological Study of Religious Experience," *Mental Health, Religion and Culture* (2010): 1, and Gonti Simanullang, "'Baptism in the Holy Spirit': A Phenomenological and Theological Study," (Melbourne College of Divinity, 2011), cited in David Perry, *Spirit Baptism: The Pentecostal Experience in Theological Focus*, (Leiden, Netherlands: Brill, 2017), 112-114.

68 Boucher, *Catholic Charismatic Renewal*, 3.

to God and dedication to His work." and "a more active love for Christ, for His Word and for the lost."[69]

From the Catholic Charismatic Renewal, there are unsurprisingly similar testimonies of people's faith coming alive, believing becoming knowing, the supernatural becoming reality, and experiencing a deeper awareness of Jesus' real and active presence. With Spirit baptism, people often experience a greater love for God that manifests itself in things such as love for Scripture, love for the church, transformed relationships, and the power to witness.[70]

Leaders within the Catholic Charismatic Renewal note that "... the most immediate effect of baptism in the Spirit is a new awareness of and communion with the Father, Son and Holy Spirit." There is power to overcome sin and addiction, revitalized prayer and worship, gifts of the Spirit, healing, deliverance, care for the poor, a zeal for evangelization, and a "new level of spiritual fellowship with other Christians who received this same grace, based on a common experience of deeper conversion to Christ."[71]

These feelings and perceptions all witness to an underlying reality. If Spirit baptism is the Spirit of God the Father and of Christ coming to indwell us, this outpouring makes perfect sense. If those in the first century were impacted by the physical presence of Jesus, of his love, wisdom, and power, how much more when Jesus fulfills his prophetic words in John 14, that the Spirit who is with us will be in us, that he himself would be in us, and that he and his father would make their home with us (John 14:17, 20, 23)? The personal presence of God

---

69   "Assemblies of God 16 Fundamental Truths," *Assemblies of God: https://ag.org/Beliefs/Statement-of-Fundamental-Truths#7* (February 28, 2024).

70   ICCRS, *Baptism in the Holy Spirit*, 17.

71   ICCRS, *Baptism in the Holy Spirit*, 18-27.

indwelling our mortal, fearfully and wonderfully made flesh. By this, we can know him in ways that were previously impossible.

We have heard from four witnesses: Scripture, the sacraments, the 20th-century outpouring, and the Spirit's outward and inward impact on individuals. Let me add a fifth witness. Just as there are no two fingerprints or retinas that are the same across the world's eight billion people, there are no two journeys with God that are exactly the same. In the next chapter, I will share some of my early encounters with the Living God, hoping that he will be glorified and that you will be encouraged.

7

Another Witness

A Reception of Forgiveness

> The Son of Man came not to be served but to serve, and to give his life as a ransom for many (Mark 10:45)

> This is my blood of the covenant, which is poured out for many for the forgiveness of sins. (Matthew 26:28)

As we noted in chapter 5, preparation and consecration were required to usher in God's presence at the Tabernacle in the wilderness. In most cases, the same is true for us. Before God's presence can reside in us, we are called to repent of our sins (Hebrew *teshuva* – to turn around, return) and be cleansed. Forgiveness granted and forgiveness accepted are both necessary to restore a relationship. We understand that Jesus gave his life so that we might be saved; part of that saving was his atonement for our sins.

As a child, I understood and believed that Jesus was God, God's son, and that he was miraculously conceived, performed miracles, died on the cross for our sins, and was resurrected after three days in the tomb. But I had not yet come to know his forgiveness personally. The reality of the ransom that he paid had not entered my mind or heart. His love was not yet real to me until the spring of 1992, at the age of 25. It was then that my eyes were opened.

Without getting into all of the gnarly details, as a young man from a broken home, I carried a heavy burden of unresolved pain and anger that impacted many aspects of my life. I was broken, and my brokenness followed me from high school into college. I could not rightly love myself or those around me. Apart from God, I tried to get my needs met through dating relationships, drinking to excess, and other unhealthy escapes. No matter what I pursued, I could not find true peace. In early 1992, I hit the proverbial wall. The impact of that crash opened my eyes to see how badly I had hurt those around me and made me painfully aware of my emptiness. I was trapped in a cycle of futility. But as I was soon to find out, God had prepared a way out.

God's tangible appeal to me began years earlier. In 1985, during my second year of college, I had a roommate who used to say that religion was for losers and old ladies. I adopted that sentiment, and my choices reflected it. I had even doubted God's existence during this time. Thankfully, God did not leave me in that state. During an Easter 1986 weekend trip to a classmate's home, I had my first memorable encounter with the living God in a lucid dream.

The dream began with me standing in a room, holding my left arm just below the wrist. My hand had been severed and was gone. I was desperate for help. I realized that I was in a hospital, but as I searched hallways and rooms, calling out for help, no one came. I finally entered a large, empty room. Clenching my arm, I yelled, "Someone please help me!!!"

Seconds later, I looked down and saw that my hand was fully restored. I then heard a voice say firmly and clearly, "Never doubt that I exist!"

I was overwhelmed by these few words and knew that God had just spoken to me. In the dream, I told myself that when I awoke, I would not forget what had just happened. This event has never left my memory, and I never again doubted God's existence. Unfortunately, I continued to avoid him and find ways to medicate my emotional pain for six more years, until the spring of 1992.

That spring, it was not just the spring flowers, plants, and trees preparing to blossom, but something was happening in me. I searched my soul, journaled, and read two popular books emphasizing God's love. It became clear that I didn't have the love needed to engage in healthy relationships with others or myself. I also knew I was not equipped to be a husband or father.

I was searching for answers, and God brought a new friend, an opera castmate, who, unknown to me, was praying for my salvation. That June, he invited me to golf with some of his friends. I am not a golfer, but I thought it might be fun. Near the end of our outing, my golf partner (a friend of my friend) asked me about my spiritual journey. I told him I wanted to know God more deeply and thought I could find him through any of the many world religions. He responded, "But Jesus is the only one who forgives our sins." I thought it was an interesting point and tucked it away for further consideration.

The next day, I was on the phone with a friend, updating her on recent events in my life and recounting the prior day's discussion. As I repeated my golf partner's words about Jesus' forgiveness, I was struck to the core. I began sobbing. My blind eyes had been opened to understand the reality of God's redemptive love through the sacrifice of his Son.

After I hung up the phone, I sat alone with God and confessed my sins to him. He miraculously took the burden that had weighed me down for years. I felt lighter, and a joy welled up inside at this newfound freedom received through his forgiveness. I wanted to learn more about him and get to know him more deeply. My desire to escape through alcohol use was replaced by a desire to tell others of this incredible gift I had received. My regular use of expletives was replaced with thankfulness. I sought to make amends for my wrongs and seek forgiveness from those I had hurt and sinned against in my self-centeredness. Jesus forgave me, and God's love was never more apparent. What could be better? Seven months later, in January 1993, I would find out.

An Immersion

Be Thou my Wisdom, and Thou my true Word;
I ever with Thee and Thou with me, Lord;
Thou my great Father, and I Thy true son;
Thou in me dwelling, and I with Thee one.[72]

Have you ever had the experience of seeing something in an entirely new light, even something you may have looked at for decades? A few years ago, I was responding to a friend's e-mail, and my response contained the name of the Beatles, one of my favorite musical groups growing up in the 1970s. As I typed my note, it occurred to me that it was not spelled Beetles, but Beatles, a play on the musical word "beat" (and more likely influenced by the band's ties to the Beat generation[73]). I love wordplay and laughed inwardly at this discovery. But I was more

---

72 "Be Thou My Vision," trans. Mary E. Byrne, versified by Eleanor H. Hull.
73 See "Beat Visions and the Counterculture: The Beatles and the Beats." *University of Delaware: https://exhibitions. lib.udel.edu/beat-visions-and-the-counterculture/the-beatles/* (February 28, 2024).

shocked that at just over fifty years old, I had never noticed the spelling (or at least I didn't recall noticing). And even more surprisingly, most people I've shared that revelation with hadn't seen it either.

So, we often think we know something, but then a new experience or new information radically alters our understanding. This transformation happened to me a couple of months after my experience of God's forgiveness in June of 1992. At the recommendation of a friend, my future wife (Marie) and I decided to visit a Bible study advertised on a local Christian radio station. The radio ad mentioned learning about an experiential relationship with God as Abba, one like the disciples of the first century experienced. When I heard that a former Pentecostal minister was hosting the Bible study, both my curiosity and suspicion were piqued.

At the first study, I came armed with Bible verses and Webster's definitions of tongues and prophecy, thinking I could spot and challenge any false doctrine I might hear. In the study, I encountered God's heart of love for us and scriptural clarity on his desire to live in us through his Holy Spirit. Given my newfound relationship with God, I would have told you that I had the Spirit with me (I was much happier and knew I was his), but as I later read and heard, my experience was not the same as the Acts examples of Spirit baptism. I had no scriptural or experiential understanding of baptism in the Holy Spirit, but I was curious, willing to listen, and had many questions. I also heard for the first time that this first-century experience of the Spirit was meant for and available to us today.

The study met weekly throughout the fall and into the winter, and it didn't take long for me to decide that I was open to this experience in my own life. As a budding risk manager, I reasoned I had nothing to lose and much to gain by seeing if the Acts Spirit-baptism experience was real. For a while, though, Marie was still processing the teaching, and I wanted to wait for her.

One afternoon in January 1993, we decided to read through the book of Ephesians together. We were both struck by Paul's words and God's heart through him, particularly in 1:16-23, 2:18-22, 3:14-21, and 4:22-24 about knowing God and his love through his Spirit (consider pausing to read these verses). After we finished, Marie looked at me and said, "I'm ready."

We wasted no time scheduling a visit with our friend to be baptized with the Holy Spirit. When we arrived, we discussed relevant scriptures and what to expect. We talked, prayed, acknowledged any known sins, gave thanks, waited, and had hands laid on us. That evening, neither of us received the Spirit in any discernible way. In retrospect, I was distracted by not knowing what to expect and mainly by the thought that Marie might receive the Spirit, but I wouldn't. Or, far worse, we would both receive the Spirit and God would later tell us that we were to end our relationship.

Potentially losing Marie was a risk I could not avoid. Asking God to make his home in me meant surrendering everything to him. It would tear my heart if I had to let Marie go. At the same time, I often felt something was not quite right in our relationship. Something was still missing. My intuition would soon be proven true.

Our friend suggested that we come back individually to remove the potential for distraction and to recognize that we were not married and were seeking deeper relationships with God above all else. He also told us about a man he had ministered to who had not experienced Spirit baptism during his first attempt. This seeker resolutely told my friend,

"I'm coming back again, and the next time, I am not leaving until I receive the Holy Spirit."

I said, "Yes, that's me! I'm coming back, and I'm not leaving until I receive."

We scheduled time for the evening of January 22, 1993. Like our first attempt, my mind got in the way. After at least an hour of talking, praying, waiting, and giving thanks, I was tired of trying in my own effort.

Seated, with my eyes closed and arms half-raised in a receiving posture, I felt a slight pressure on my hands that seemed like God was holding and gently squeezing them to reassure me. I thought for a second that this might be the feeling of the blood draining from my hands, but I had never before nor ever again felt that same sensation, and I believe it was God's gentle touch to reassure and relax me. In a moment, I began to speak, and words poured forth in a language I did not know and had never heard before.

As I spoke, I knew that I was in the personal presence of God. I was catching up with my Father after many lost years, like visiting with an old friend you truly loved and missed. In this language I didn't understand, I knew I was telling him what was on my heart and how incredibly glad I was to be with him. In my ears were the crystal-clear words of the Spirit through me in the most beautiful and life-giving conversation I could ever have imagined. My sight (my tangible experiential knowing) had just taken a quantum leap. Before this moment, God could have been thousands of miles away, but now we were face-to-face in his throne room.

I planned to sing him a song when we met from Felix Mendelssohn's oratorio, *Elijah*. The lyrics come from Scripture, 1 Kings 18:36-37:

Draw near, all ye people, come to me!

Lord God of Abraham, Isaac, and Israel;

This day, let it be known that Thou art God,

and I am Thy Servant!

Lord God of Abraham!

O shew to all this people that I have done these things

according to Thy word!

O hear me, Lord, and answer me!

O hear me, Lord, and answer me!

Lord God of Abraham, Isaac and Israel;

O hear me and answer me;

and shew this people that Thou art Lord God;

And let their hearts again be turned![74]

After some time of talking with God in the Spirit, I remembered that I wanted to sing this song. I stood up, and as I began to sing, out of my mouth came Mendelssohn's melody but in the most beautiful Spirit-given words from a language that I did not know.

Some people long for an audience with popes, presidents, or kings, but on this occasion, I was singing in the presence of the King of Kings. Through the song, I cried tears of gratitude, and as I caught up with my Father on years of lost time, I sometimes laughed at the fact that I was so set free and that this experience of God was so real.

My conversation in the Spirit continued for about forty-five minutes, and during this time, I could speak in no other language than the

---

74 Felix Mendelssohn, "Draw Near All Ye People," *Elijah*, Op. 70, excerpted from "Elijah in Mendelssohn's Libretto," ELIJAH – Or The Jewish Artist in The Western World. *University of Notre Dame: https://sites.nd.edu/smnd-melloninterdiscplinaryproject2/the-spectacle-of-elijah/mendelssohns-elijah/* (March 4, 2024).

one the Spirit was providing. I tried to talk in English, but everything came out in this Spirit-given language.

During this conversation, I became keenly aware of why I was here, why I was born, and my life's purpose. I knew by the Spirit in me that I was made to be in a relationship with my most loving, most intimately giving, and most personal heavenly Father, now my Abba. I was made for him, to live in his presence, to be in dialogue, in collaboration with the God who made heaven and earth. He was now closer to me than any other person, "in me," as Jesus had said in John chapters 14 and 17. I had come home to the place I was always intended to live, in his presence, and in less than an hour, my life was changed forever.

When the Holy Spirit came into me, and I became one with him, I also knew by the Spirit that I would now be able to be a husband and a father. My success was no longer dependent on my broken self. My inability was now joined with his ability, and I had all the help I would ever need. The "power" that Jesus spoke of in Acts 1:8 was none other than the personal presence of God and his overwhelming love in me and through me. It was clear to me that there was no more excellent thing on this earth, no accomplishments, no accolades, no riches, no legacy, that compares with the incomparable experience of knowing him intimately through his indwelling Spirit. And on this day, it began for me.

When I could finally speak in English again, I asked my friend, "Does anyone know about this?" He replied that many did, and many did not. I also recounted to him that when I was younger and throughout my life, I had a sense that I would do something monumental that would be a defining moment in my life and that I would know when it happened that I had arrived. I once thought I might achieve fame as an opera singer, but after these forty-five minutes with God, I knew I had arrived. There would be no more quest for the monumental. I had encountered my destiny, being one with God.

At home that evening, I called Marie and shared with her what had happened. She was deeply encouraged. The following evening, she went to our friend's house for prayer/ministry and was also baptized in the Holy Spirit. While specific details of her experience vary from mine, she too spoke with God in a spiritual language for the first time.

Some Reflections

Looking back on these initial experiences, I realize that some things stand out. My relationship with God involved many stages. As a child growing up in the Roman Catholic faith, I believed in God and Jesus and participated in the sacraments. As a later teen, I appreciated the Christian community in a Congregational church and reflected on God's love, most impactfully during our youth retreats. As a young adult I lived apart from God, not at all desiring to follow him or do his will.

At the age of twenty-five, my life came crashing down. Just before my twenty-sixth birthday, I received Jesus' miraculous gift of forgiveness, had my eyes opened to who he truly was, and wanted to know him more deeply. Seven months later, God baptized me in his Holy Spirit, and my life began anew, now indwelt by the King of Kings in a union that would define the rest of my days on earth. Almost a year after that, I was baptized (fully immersed) in water as a public sign of my new covenant with God.

When I compare the critical points of my conversion to biblical examples, I see many similarities that others might also point to. Like Paul (in Acts 9), my eyes were opened to see Jesus for who he truly was. As Peter instructed the crowd, before being baptized in the Holy Spirit, I repented of my sins (Acts 2:38). Like the Samaritans (Acts 8), my Spirit baptism came well after my belief and profession of faith, and through the ministry of someone not present at the first event. Like Cornelius' household in Acts 10, my water baptism by immersion came after my baptism with the Holy Spirit. As in the Acts 2 event, I set aside time to pray and await the gift of the Holy Spirit (on those two evenings, after months of preparation). And like the Acts 2, 10, and 19 accounts, my Spirit reception came with speech in a language unknown to me.

Of all of the experiences on my journey to and with Christ, Spirit baptism was the single most radical and life-changing. Knowing I was forgiven was freeing, but experiencing God within was like going from death to life, from the old man apart from God to a new creation in Christ. I had a new vision, a new understanding, a new heart of love for God, and an experiential understanding of the immediate presence of God.

This radically altered perspective is something I reflect regularly on and have sought to understand more fully in light of Scripture. The next chapter will explore the meaning of Spirit baptism. I hope that God can use this in some way to help others put meaning to their past and possibly future experiences.

For Consideration

Perhaps you have encountered the Spirit in a way that causes you to know conclusively that he has been poured out upon you and has come to make his home in you. If that is the case, praise God!

If not, after considering the witnesses we have heard from, what will you do? Have you considered how the traditions observed in your church home(s) have influenced how you think about your relationship with God? How does the Spirit baptism of Acts figure in your worldview and your faith walk today? Putting on a risk management hat, what do you have to lose and what do you have to gain by embracing God through Spirit baptism? Do you need more understanding?

Let's move on to meaning.

8

Meaning Matters

How We View Spirit Baptism

The meaning that we ascribe to the events of Christian initiation is not unimportant. It can impact how we live and our expectations of how we will experience God. Thankfully, we have the Bible and the Holy Spirit as our guiding lights and tradition and experience as reference points. However, when many peoples, cultures (including church cultures), and experiences are involved, that inevitably leads to many views.

If we see Spirit baptism as an optional "add-on" to our faith walk, or even as nothing at all, we may be less inclined to seek it out.[75] If we see it as essential to life in Christ, possibly even bringing life in Christ, it may propel us to pursue it as if our lives depended on it. If we see Spirit baptism as primarily a receipt of power (Acts 1:8) that can benefit us in the battle against evil, helping us accomplish God's plans, we might miss the relational aspects. We may not perceive God as the source of love

---

75 Steven Studebaker summarizes that "The primary work of the Holy Spirit according to classical pentecostal theology is an add-on to Christ's saving work and thereby rendered a soteriological supplement." He challenges this perspective, noting that "The centrality of the Spirit of Pentecost in the narrative of redemption indicates that Pentecost is no an adjunct to Christ or a subsidiary experience to the salvation provided by Christ on the cross. On the contrary, the outpouring of the Holy Spirit on the Day of Pentecost is the critical nexus not only in the New Testament but for the entire history of redemption.... The substance of redemption is the opportunity to participate in Christ's fulfillment of the Spirit-breathed life." Steven M. Studebaker, "A Pentecostal Third Article Theology," *Pneuma* 45 (2023), 432, 434, 442.

and one who desires intimacy with us. If we see the promises of Acts 1:8 as the power of love actualized in our lives through the deepest possible union and closest possible proximity to him, it will likely engender a completely different mindset. We might then understand his view of us not only as soldiers in his army but also as his beloved.

Understanding the spiritual is not always straightforward. It can be helpful to have earthly examples to give us insight into spiritual realities. In the following few sections, I present some analogies to consider when thinking about Spirit baptism. These are not the only ways to understand, but I believe they can have meaningful implications for our walk with Christ and can help reconcile various doctrines, traditions, and experiences in light of Scripture.

Birth Analogy

Mary conceived Jesus by the Holy Spirit (Matthew 1:18, Luke 1:35). In due time, he was born and held in his mother's arms. Again, Jesus tells us that it is by the Spirit that *we* are spiritually born.

> "Truly, truly, I say to you, unless one is born again he cannot see the kingdom of God."... "unless one is born of water and the Spirit, he cannot enter the kingdom of God. That which is born of the flesh is flesh, and that which is born of the Spirit is spirit. Do not marvel that I said to you, 'You must be born again.' (John 3:3, 5-7)

Is it possible that there is a spiritual conception and a gestation period before spiritual birth? From a human perspective, the process that leads to birth begins with conception. We are not yet fully formed, but in an instant, we go from being no one to being someone with immense potential.

The child develops and grows in the womb environment and, in time, can feel, hear, move her body, and suck her thumb, all in the comfort and safety of her temporary home. She cannot yet visually see her parents or clearly hear their voices. She is fully enveloped, fully alive—a daughter.

In time, the child will emerge from the womb to experience the love and presence of her parents in a fantastically new way. She will feel, hear, see, and taste like never before, and what was a muffled, quiet, and dark womb will be replaced with heightened sensations and vivid experiences in a newly unveiled reality. And this child that was no less a daughter in the womb is now able to know her parents in a completely new dimension.

The change is remarkable. The child can now make noises that all can hear. She can call (at first, cry) for help and receive comfort. She can feel the touch of her parents' arms holding her closely and receive peace from the soothing song sung over her. The voices she may have heard as muffled in the womb are now clear and direct. In time, her hearing will lead to understanding, and eventually she will use those same words to communicate back to her parents and others. As she grows, she will more and more be able to know the heart of her parents and share her heart in ways that were previously impossible.

How does this relate to our journey to and with Christ? One might consider our initial decision to follow him, to accept him as Savior, to receive his forgiveness, to be our spiritual conception, a beginning of life, but also a *preparation* for birth. In the womb, we receive comfort, provision, and even love from our Father. Our hearts beat with a desire to know him, and we may sense that he is near, but we have not yet entered the deepest possible relationship. We may not yet have experienced the ongoing face-to-face-like closeness with our heavenly Parent, the warmth of his presence, the peace-giving touch of his hands, the clarity of his voice, and the sound of his singing. We also struggle to articulate our deepest heart thoughts to him. There may be joy and tears, and the weight of unforgiven sin lifted, but we still don't have unfettered access and intimacy with him. We need something more.

We may wonder if that more is something that comes afterward when we pass out of this life to be with him in heaven. We wonder because we don't understand that we haven't yet exited the womb to begin an entirely new dimension of life here on earth with our Creator. When we exit the womb, we are more able to experience him because we can hear his voice more clearly, experience his presence more fully, and recognize our oneness with the Prince of Peace. It is no longer simply (as if it were simple) a thankfulness and a removed weight of sin, but a much deeper knowing that begins when we exit the spiritual womb.

In this analogy, birth, leaving the womb, equates to being baptized in the Holy Spirit, when the life-giving Spirit is poured out upon us and within us.[76] Just as the cry of the newborn is a sign of life and health, so too, there is often a sign of spiritual language, our cry when we emerge from the spiritual womb.[77]

That is not to say that there is always a spiritual womb experience. Similar to the Orthodox all-in-one initiation into the church, some

---

76 Cheryl Peterson notes "The God who is for us also brings regeneration and rebirth, through the indwelling of the Spirit." Cheryl M. Peterson, *The Holy Spirit in the Christian Life: The Spirit's Work For, In, and Through Us*, (Grand Rapids: Baker Academic, 2024), 57.

77 Laurito describes the expression of spiritual language in Acts 2 as bringing "awareness of the Spirit's arrival" and "a visible testimony to his work of Spirit baptism.... not simply one of many signs ... but *the* sign to the gathered crowd that something supernatural had occurred." *Speaking in Tongues*, 6.

have an almost instantaneous conception/womb/birth, where the Spirit is poured out in one continuous event. But for many, the womb experience is a natural stage in our journey. Some of us have never considered that there might be more than we already have this side of heaven. But God's plan includes intimacy, peace, and joy in his presence in the here and now. The cry of "Abba" (Dad!) that the Spirit causes us to speak represents that changed relationship.

> And because you are sons, God has sent the Spirit of his Son into our hearts, crying, "Abba! Father!" (Galatians 4:6)

> For you did not receive the spirit of slavery to fall back into fear, but you have received the Spirit of adoption as sons, by whom we cry, "Abba! Father!" The Spirit himself bears witness with our spirit that we are children of God. (Romans 8:15-16)

As I described in chapter 7, I lived in that womb-like existence for seven months after my eyes were opened to Christ's forgiveness for my sin. I didn't know it was a womb until I experienced this new world of wonder in him. I would likely not have experienced this new life had someone not shared with me that there was more (Romans 10:14) and if I did not persist in belief (Luke 11:9, 13) that this "more" was for me. When I emerged Spirit baptized, neither the world nor God would ever look the same again. The vivid, unveiled presence of God was now a reality to me.

Through Spirit baptism, we are baptized into him, and he fills us with his presence. Through the power of his love in us, a love that overflows as rivers of living water (John 7:38), we become witnesses

(Acts 1:8) and vessels of his glory on the earth (2 Corinthians 4:6-7). We know that we are his and he is in us (John 14:17, 20; 1 John 4:13) as he speaks to and through us by his indwelling Spirit, bearing witness to our sonship and daughterhood. We are not only sons and daughters of God but also the Bride of Christ. Since we are his bride, it is fitting to look at a second analogy.

Marriage Analogy

> From the beginning of creation, 'God made them male and female.' 'Therefore a man shall leave his father and mother and hold fast to his wife, and the two shall become one flesh.' So they are no longer two but one flesh. (Mark 10:6-8)
>
> He who is joined to the Lord becomes one spirit with him.... Or do you not know that your body is a temple of the Holy Spirit within you, whom you have from God? (1 Corinthians 6:17, 19)

There have been many traditions regarding marriage. In our current day, marriages typically involve some form of engagement (betrothal), followed by a wedding, and if all proceeds accordingly, consummation. In ancient Jewish culture, fathers would typically arrange a marriage for their children, and the groom's father would pay a bride price [*mohar*] to the bride's father. Ceremonially, there was a betrothal [*erusin* or *kiddushin*], which was considered a legal marriage without consummation, while the woman stayed at her father's house awaiting the wedding. The wedding [*nissuin*] followed the betrothal when the groom brought his betrothed in procession to his home, and they consummated the marriage.[78] The steps in a marriage process provide another lens through which we can view our new covenant entry into life in Christ.

Using our more modern marriage example, whether arranged or by chance, we have a first encounter with a prospective spouse. Similarly, there is the first time we encounter the reality of God. Over time, two people may decide to get married. Similarly, we may decide we want to enter into a relationship with God, to give ourselves to him. The man and woman become betrothed or engaged, and through words, celebration, or an engagement ring, they communicate their intent to others.

In this analogy, betrothal is similar to our professing faith in Christ. We state our desire to follow him only and let him be our Lord, renouncing our past sins and any claim the world has on our hearts. However, this decision for Christ does not necessarily equate to a consummation. The time of betrothal is joyful as we wait in anticipation of what is to come.

Marriage was intended for man and woman to bear fruit and multiply (Genesis 1:28), and as such, it is not to remain in the betrothal phase. In time, there will be a marriage ceremony before witnesses. Similarly, for the Christian, there will typically be a baptism in water that is an outward sign observable by the community of the affirmation of the entry into covenant with God, signifying death to the old man and aligning with the resurrection of Christ (Romans 6:4).

Indeed, the anticipation, the getting acquainted, and the preparation and ceremony are rewarding and exciting, but there is an experiential

---

78 See Hayyim Schauss, "Ancient Jewish Marriage." *My Jewish Learning: https://www.myjewishlearning.com/article/ancient-jewish-marriage/* (February 28, 2024); Jamie Lash adds that like the ancient bride price, Christ was our bride price, his life given to redeem us for himself. *The Ancient Jewish Wedding...and the Return of Messiah for His Bride*, (Ft. Lauderdale, FL: Jewish Jewels, 2012), 7, accessed at *Jewish Jewels: https://www.jewishjewels.org/wp-content/uploads/2018/01/Ancient_Jewish_Wedding.pdf* (March 4, 2024). Also note, the betrothal tradition in the ancient Jewish tradition made it possible for Mary to be married and yet the virgin mother of God.

joining, the physical union of the beloved and lover, that brings an entirely different level of connection, oneness, and joy. So it is with our joining to Christ. We are not only to profess our allegiance in words and ceremony but also to make ourselves available and ask him to live within us through his Spirit (Luke 11:9-13).

I am suggesting that just as the bride and groom consummate their covenant by the two becoming one flesh, in Christ, we consummate our commitment by being baptized in the Holy Spirit, becoming one with God through the Spirit (1 Corinthians 6:17) in a personal Pentecost.[79]

For the virgin bride, there is typically a sign that follows the initial physical union. Similarly, there is usually a sign for the newly indwelt Christian. That sign on the day of Pentecost (Acts 2), in the household of Cornelius (Acts 10), and with the Ephesians (Acts 19) was the gift of inspired speech in words unknown to the speakers. In our day, that same sign often accompanies this event. In time, just as our physical union in marriage produces fruit, our spiritual union with God is to bear fruit and reproduce new life in others.

Considering that many of us are neither married nor have ever had children, let's look at a third analogy: the lottery winner. Although it is not a relational example, it still has merit.

---

79 Dunn notes that the oneness of 1 Corinthians 6:17 parallels Genesis 2:24, the two becoming one flesh and that "the one Spirit which unites believers is precisely the reality of their union with Christ." James D. G. Dunn, *Jesus and the Spirit: A Study of the Religious and Charismatic Experience of Jesus and the First Christians as Reflected in the New Testament*, (Grand Rapids, MI: William B. Eerdmans Publishing Company, 1975), 323. Hodson, in his analysis of Hebrews 6:4 notes that "one descriptor of the New Covenant life is 'sharing in the Holy Spirit'.... In Hebrews, the implication that lies behind this 'sharing in the Spirit (6:4) is not one of the Christian receiving 'power to witness' (Acts 1:8) but of entering into a 'partnership for life' with the Holy Spirit." Alan K. Hodson "Hebrews," in *A Biblical Theology of the Holy Spirit*, ed. Trevor J. Burke and Keith Warrington, (Eugene, OR: Cascade Books, 2014), 235.

Lottery Analogy

Most of us would be ecstatic to win $100 million in a lottery. Our material needs will be provided until we leave this earthly life, and we can leave a legacy of material riches for our children and loved ones. But before we receive the payout, some specific things must happen. We first must buy the ticket. The ticket purchase represents our decision to follow Christ. We must then present our ticket to the lottery administrators to validate its authenticity. Similarly, we validate our desire to be with Christ through authentic repentance before God, preparing our hearts to receive him as Lord.

Next, the lottery administrators make a public announcement, perhaps including a photo opportunity with us holding a larger-than-life check, to record this momentous occasion (and advertise for future lotteries). We are joyful to be the recognized winner, akin to the joy we experience knowing we are forgiven, and the public ceremony or announcement, like our water baptism, outwardly tells others of the change in our lives. We are the validated winner and will soon receive the payout.

The photos, fame, and confirmation by the lottery officials all come with emotion and excitement, but what we're most focused on is getting the money deposited into our bank account. Without the money, we have no purchasing power. But when the cash arrives, our lives change dramatically. We then have the authority and the ability to buy and give as we see fit in accordance with our newfound wealth.

Receiving the cash in this analogy is akin to Spirit baptism. It is what makes all (or substantially all) of the difference. We may have presented ourselves publicly to profess our faith and allegiance to God, but we are yet incomplete until he makes us his home in the fullness of his presence, love, and power. When we receive the promise of the new covenant, his Spirit within us, we are privileged to live fully as sons and daughters with unhindered access to the King of Kings. We have the riches of life in his presence that begins now, the eternal life that Jesus spoke of, intimately knowing God the Father and Jesus our Messiah (John 17:3). The fullness of this knowing does not come all at once. But the downpayment, the Spirit in us, lets us know of the wealth we have access to and allows us to taste the reality of our growth potential in investing in an ongoing, deepening relationship with him.

These three analogies, birth, marriage, and lottery, all point to an event constrained to a moment in time, which I believe, given the scriptural context, is most appropriate for our particular discussion on Spirit baptism. More recently, theologians have proposed another description, one of the intensifications of the Spirit.

Metaphor of Intensification

The metaphor of intensification is meant to describe various interactions with and fillings by the Holy Spirit in one's life. This view acknowledges that the Spirit of God is in all creation and is the source of life for every living creature and, therefore, every person. The implication is that in any subsequent filling (as some might say, at conversion, Spirit baptism, or other fillings as described in the Scripture), the "Spirit's presence becomes more intense."[80]

Intensification can be a helpful metaphor, particularly if we can

---

80 See Andrew K. Gabriel, "The Intensity of the Spirit in a Spirit-Filled World: Spirit Baptism, Subsequence, and the Spirit of Creation," *Pneuma* 34 (2012), 369-70, 377.

grasp all of the expected intensifications that can occur and can suitably pursue them. It also raises our awareness of God's involvement in many aspects of life, including those beyond our specifically spiritual pursuits. However, to understand initiation into the new covenant life, it is helpful to more narrowly define Spirit baptism in light of the events in Acts chapters 2, 8, 10, and 19. The Bible speaks of spiritual birth and being indwelt as fundamental changes in our relationship with God through his Spirit. If we say we all have the Spirit because we are alive physically, we risk obscuring the monumental change that the poured-out indwelling Spirit of God brings.

The Spirit brings life (John 6:63; Romans 8:2, 10-11, 16), a fully restored relationship with God as Father, Son, and Savior. The entry into life in the Spirit, our spiritual birth (John 3:3-6), is what Spirit baptism accomplishes. The ongoing life in the Spirit includes a continuation of filling after Spirit baptism (Acts 4:31; Ephesians 5:18). Similarly, in a marriage relationship or deep friendship, love continues to be shared and expressed in various ways over time, nourishing the relationship. And in relationship with God, his presence through the indwelling Spirit continues to transform us into Christ's image (an expression of God's love) as he renews our minds and enables us to walk in his ways more and more, in increasing glory (2 Corinthians 3:17-18).

Seeing Spirit baptism as a fundamental change in the relationship of man to God, a union or birth, breaking forth into an entirely different mode of being (we are new creations in Christ Jesus – 2 Corinthians 5:17), highlights the importance and centrality of this step in our conversion process and puts it front and center in the life of those who desire to be disciples of Christ. It cannot then be ignored, sidelined, or reasoned away. We must deal with the distinct Spirit baptism event—failure to do so risks being a detriment to the bride of Christ and all who desire to be clothed with his love and power.

If we miss this entry point, discussing what happens when we are inside the house, adopted as sons and daughters, becomes more of an academic exercise. Let's first ensure that we are fully birthed, then move to the ongoing process of growth and maturation. We must be born again of the Spirit, united to God. Without this transformative union, we remain subject to our sinful nature (Ephesians 2:1-3; Colossians 2:13) and cannot possibly bear the fullness of his love, power, and fruit in this life. We may be forgiven and accepted, but we will likely not be radically transformed from within by the Spirit. And that may well be why Jesus instructed his disciples to remain in Jerusalem to receive the Spirit (Luke 24:49; Acts 1:4-5; also John 7:39). Do you think it is possible that after Jesus' atoning death on the cross and his resurrection, Spirit baptism was the watershed event in the lives of his disciples? If so, does this change what it means to be a disciple?

Believer or Disciple?

Although the terms believer and disciple are often used interchangeably, a distinction is needed for this discussion. One may believe that God exists and that Jesus is the Savior who came to free us from the bondage of sin through his atonement, forgiveness, and the new life that he offers in close relationship with God. To believe this but not take hold of it and make it our own, to not enter into an interactive relationship with this God we believe in, does *not* make us a disciple.

Disciples in biblical times sat at the feet of their teacher, desired to know and emulate their teacher, and received direct instruction from their teacher. Discipleship takes proactive engagement, *not* simply a passive or once-and-done approach, but a heart that pursues and comes to intimately know their teacher's mind while spending as much time as possible in the teacher's presence.

We are to sit under the teaching of the Holy Spirit (John 14:26), receiving through the Spirit all that our Father desires to share with us (John 16:13-15). Partaking of the one who dwells in us (John 14:17, 20) is the only way for true discipleship to occur. It is not simply a belief but a direct experience of the Giver of Life.

The Spirit speaks and teaches, and we must be able to hear him, ask him questions, and receive responses. The need for this interactive relationship with God through the Holy Spirit elevates the importance of understanding what it means to receive the Spirit, putting Spirit baptism at the forefront of the issues related to our walk with Christ. We must not simply believe but walk with our Teacher and become his disciples, sitting at his feet, reading about and interacting with him, allowing him to transform us by his Spirit from the inside out.

Subsequent, Separate, or Same?

In our three analogies, birth, the consummation of a marriage, and receiving our lottery winnings are all steps in a larger process, not simply stand-alone events. By likening them to Spirit baptism, I am also affirming the possibility that the Spirit baptism reflected in Acts represents a pattern for the initial indwelling of the Spirit for all Christians as part of a larger process. In saying this, I understand that I am putting myself in conflict with many current doctrines that say the indwelling of the Spirit comes at the first step of our initiation, at the moment of conversion (repentance or profession of faith in Christ), or for some, perhaps through the sacrament or rite of baptism. I wonder, though, is there any possibility that this viewpoint is incorrect and the Spirit is not received until later, after our initial turn to God?

From a risk management perspective, I would rather err on the side of pursuing too much of the Holy Spirit, even if it means assuming that I do not yet have the Spirit at all, or at least, in the same way, those in Acts 2, 8, 10, and 19 did, rather than potentially missing a crucial component of my walk in Christ.

Believing that there is more opens me to the possibility of seeking more. And if we do not yet have that "more," there is no shame or inferiority, just as there is no inferiority in being married without yet having consummated, being in the womb not yet born, or being a lottery winner soon to receive payment. These are all interim states, signs of, and steps toward good things to come. There is no room for superiority for anyone who may have already experienced what some are poised to experience. Instead, there is expectant hope and joyful anticipation.

But what of the arguments that we receive the Spirit the moment we believe or are baptized or profess our faith in Christ? Many cite the writings of Paul as clearly stating this as fact, noting that we cannot belong to Christ without having the Holy Spirit (Romans 8:9), we were sealed with the Holy Spirit when we believed (Ephesians 1:13), and we all drink of one Spirit (1 Corinthians 12:13). Are there potentially alternate understandings of these statements? Is it possible that believing precedes being sealed, drinking of the Spirit, and belonging completely to Christ?

Most Pentecostals and charismatics believe that Spirit baptism (or infilling) is something separate that typically follows one's conversion experience or initial commitment to Christ. At the initial Spirit baptism event in Acts 2, the 120 disciples were all believers in Christ and followed his instruction to wait for the Holy Spirit in Jerusalem (Acts 1:5, 8). On the day of Pentecost, they received the Spirit.

Philip ministered to the Samaritans, and Luke tells us that the Samaritans, including Simon, believed and were baptized but had not yet received the Holy Spirit. The Samaritans later received the Spirit only after Peter and John ministered to them (Acts 8:14-17).

As recorded in Acts 19, Paul confirms that the Ephesians did not know of or receive the Holy Spirit "when they believed" (19:2). Some debate what they had believed, whether John's foretelling of the coming Messiah or Jesus' fulfillment. Regardless of our position on what they believed, we see that two things followed. They were first baptized in the name of Jesus (19:5), then Paul laid hands on them, and the Holy Spirit came on them, bringing forth Spirit-inspired speech (19:6).

If Paul had not followed their baptism with a laying on of hands, the Ephesians likely would not have received the Holy Spirit then. Given his ministry to the Ephesians, it seems highly probable that Paul is speaking of Spirit baptism when he tells them that they "were sealed with the promised Holy Spirit" (Ephesians 1:13). It is also conceivable that some of those receiving Paul's letter to the Ephesians were among those Paul laid hands on in Ephesus in Acts 19, those who knew experientially what it meant to receive the Spirit.

To these instances where receiving the Spirit appears to be a subsequent event, we might add Saul of Tarsus' (Paul's) experience, which we touched on in chapter 5. Paul had a direct encounter with Jesus (his voice) amid a great light on the way to Damascus and affirmed him as Lord (Acts 9:3-5; 22:6-8; 26:12-15). Three days later, Ananias laid hands on Saul to be filled with the Holy Spirit (Acts 9:17) and receive his sight.

In the reception of the Spirit by Cornelius and his household, we know Cornelius is a God-fearer (Acts 10:2), a non-Jew who worships the god of Israel, and he knows of the ministry of Jesus (10:37-38). In this case, the Spirit falls on them while Peter is talking, with no clear evidence of a preceding or accompanying conversion or profession of faith, and they are afterward baptized in water (Acts 10:47-48). So, here, there is still the possibility that Cornelius' household received the Spirit following faith in Christ. At the very least, it was concurrent with faith in Christ (not necessarily verbally confessed) and accompanied by an outward sign (Acts 10:46).

Some may agree these passages do represent biblical evidence of receiving the Spirit after conversion or faith in Christ, but may also say that these events are unique because they are associated with the ministry of the apostles or they are related to the birth of the church where God was giving unique signs that are not to be taken as a pattern for today. Many people also speak of Acts as a historical narrative and not necessarily instructive or prescriptive for today. They may also point to other evidence of those professing faith in Christ in Acts, where there is no discussion of Spirit baptism or any signs accompanying. A quick web search on "conversions in Acts" will give you lists or charts detailing their components. Some show no record of believing, water baptism, reception of the Spirit, or any outward signs. But what do we make of this variation in narratives? We might conclude that Luke chose not to provide full details of each event or that the events differed widely.

Is it possible that Luke did not find it necessary to record all details in every circumstance because his initial audience had already known and experienced receiving the Holy Spirit as a distinct component of their initiation? Said another way, as discussed in more detail in chapter 9, is it possible that those receiving his Acts record had all already received the Spirit with the same outward sign that the 120 disciples (Acts 2), the Samaritans (Acts 8), the household of Cornelius (Acts 10), and the disciples of John in Ephesus (Acts 19) received? If there is even a small chance that these two possibilities are true, is that enough to warrant further consideration of our doctrines? (*What does your heart say?*)

I am not proposing that we cannot receive the Spirit concurrent with a profession of faith or even without an outward profession, which appears to be the case in Acts 10, where the Spirit is poured out while Peter is still preaching. But I am saying that there is a strong possibility, based on the scriptural evidence alone, that the Spirit is not always received at the moment of the profession of faith, or even the sprinkling or immersion of baptism or even the anointing of confirmation, as some streams would say.

Further, if I believe that God is already in me and I have no need for a subsequent Spirit baptism, I run the risk of trying to live out the Christian life without the power and presence of the Holy Spirit within me. I may well have faith and God with me, but I will likely find it challenging to walk in the love and power seen in the early church.

In John 7:38, Jesus tells us, "Whoever believes in me, as the Scripture has said, 'Out of his heart will flow rivers of living water.'" John goes on to say that Jesus was referring here to the Spirit. Is it possible that these rivers of living water and our drinking of the Spirit (1 Corinthians 12:13) only occur as a result of baptism with the Holy Spirit? And is it conceivable, given the scriptural evidence alone, that Spirit baptism is the initial indwelling of the Holy Spirit and can come at a separate time from our initial profession of faith? I see both of these beliefs as possible.

For Consideration

If the disciples and God-fearers in Jesus' time needed to be baptized with the Holy Spirit, why would we not? Is it not possible (even slightly possible) that Spirit baptism was on the mind of the apostles in Jerusalem when they sent Peter and John to Samaria in Acts 8, on Paul's mind when he questioned and ministered to the Ephesians in Acts 19, why Ananias ministered to Saul in Acts 9, and possibly even why Priscilla and Aquila ministered to Apollos in Acts 18? And more than that, was it not what Jesus had in mind when he told the disciples to wait in Jerusalem, as recorded in Acts 1:5 and 1:8?

Do you know through experience and without doubt that Jesus lives in you (John 14:20)? Does your spirit cry "Abba" (Romans 8:15)? Do you regularly hear his voice and follow him (John 10:27)? Or is your knowledge of God confined to what you read in the Scriptures and what others may tell or teach?

If you long for a deeper relationship or more direct experience of God, I urge you to press into this question of Spirit baptism. The next chapter will look at some common questions and considerations related to Spirit baptism, including some that might hold us back from asking, seeking, and knocking.

9

Some Common Questions and Considerations

Is the Spirit Baptism of Acts for Today?

Some argue that Spirit baptism in the book of Acts was only given as a sign to let early disciples know that God was fulfilling his promises to pour out his Spirit, but after those initial events, the tangible expressions were no longer needed. Some posit that once the Bible was completed, we need only Scripture to know that Christ is in those who believe (Romans 8:9-10; Galatians 2:20; Colossians 1:27), that the Holy Spirit is given to those who believe (Romans 8:9-11; 1 Corinthians 2:12; 3:16; 6:17, 19; Galatians 4:6, among others), and that we don't need any other experiential witness to these truths. We simply need to believe and trust God's word that he has done this work.

Let me pose something for your consideration. Imagine you are a pregnant woman (or the husband of a pregnant woman) who has gone to the hospital for the delivery. As you await the newborn's arrival, the doctor enters and examines your situation, declaring, "Your little girl has been born!" You wonder for a moment and seem puzzled because you didn't feel anything, and you cannot see or hold the newborn. The doctor reassures you, "Trust me, your baby has arrived, and she is beautiful and healthy." You then press further, "But I don't recall giving birth, and I want to hold her." The doctor responds, "Trust me, it really happened," and leaves the room. The nurse then comes in and says, "Time to feed your little girl," but you cannot see or hold anything, and there is no sensation of a nursing newborn.

Just as a baby's arrival comes with sights, sounds, and sensations, so does our spiritual birth. We should expect contact, signs and sensations of life, with peace, gratitude, and joy. Do you/did you expect to tangibly experience his presence at your spiritual birth, at the entering of his Spirit into your body? Paul seems to express this when he speaks of the Spirit bearing witness that we are children of God, evoking our cry of "Abba!" (Romans 8:15-16) and that God's love is poured into our hearts through the Holy Spirit (Romans 5:5).

If God has indeed poured out his love, a greater love than any man or woman can muster or imagine, should we not know this experientially? Otherwise, rather than crying "Abba!" we might wonder, "Abba?"

If the Spirit bears witness, and his love has been poured out, should not that love be more significant than our earthly experiences? John tells us that it is "By this *we know* that we abide in him and he in us, because he has given us of his Spirit" (1 John 4:13). He doesn't say, "By this, we know that we abide in him and he in us, because Scripture says it is so." There must be a tangible way of knowing that he has given us his Spirit. I believe there is a high probability that this is the intent of Spirit baptism, not only in the days of the early church but also for us today, that we might know beyond a doubt that the God of heaven and earth has come to make his home in us. And if for some there is no tangible effect initially, potentially due to a spiritual, intellectual, or emotional block within us, it will follow not long afterward.

The tangible expression of the Spirit's entry at the home of Cornelius left no doubt that they had received the Spirit (Acts 11:15-17). Is that not both a loving (on God's part) and practical help for anyone seeking to help another receive the Spirit?

Cessationism/Continuationism

There remain various camps across the body of Christ relative to Spirit baptism and supernatural spiritual gifts. Cessationists believe that supernatural gifts of the Spirit (such as found in 1 Corinthians 12:4-11, 28-30) are no longer offered to the body of Christ.

Continuationists embrace the Pentecostal-charismatic experience of Spirit baptism (or initial Spirit infilling) and related supernatural gifts to varying degrees. A continuationist will say that supernatural gifts are available today but may say that some are in operation while others have ceased. A significant portion of the body of Christ includes those who do not discount supernatural gifts, but are wary of some of the practices they observe.[81]

Referencing our principle of biblical grounding (see the Prelude), looking at the choice between cessationism and continuationism becomes relatively straightforward. Choosing cessationism limits how God can work in the body today and denies gifts once present in the body of Christ. Returning to a risk management perspective, if there was only a 1 percent chance that cessationism is a faulty view, would you not take those odds and seek after spiritual gifts as Paul urges in 1 Corinthians 14:1?

---

81 *Are Miraculous Gifts for Today?* ed. Gundry and Grudem, 12-13.

If you argue from Scripture that Spirit baptism and associated spiritual gifts have ended, what do you do with the hundreds of millions of Pentecostal-charismatic witnesses and others worldwide today who have experienced some or many of the gifts of the Spirit described in the Bible? If you argue that they are false or wrong, then these manifestations are either carnal or demonic. A wise risk manager would ask if there is even a tiny chance that these current-day manifestations are genuine works of the Holy Spirit.

We are called to continue the work of Christ in the world and advance the Kingdom of God. Is it not more likely that we will be doing the miraculous? If we are fighting against the miraculous, is it possible we are actually aiding the enemy? If God's people are being strengthened, built up in love, and walking in the miraculous power of the Spirit, then the Kingdom of God is advancing (Matthew 12:28), and the enemy's hold is failing. Oh, let it be so!

True Fruit?

It may be evident to some that not all manifestations of the Spirit observed in Pentecostal-charismatic circles are valid experiences of the Holy Spirit. Given some descriptions of what occurred at the Azusa Street Mission, there appears to have been an intermixing of the work of the Spirit, human emotion, openness to other spiritual influences, and some learning curve regarding how to shepherd and share spiritual gifts.[82]

---

82 Robeck notes "At the Azusa Street Mission, people spoke in tongues, prophesied, preached divine healing, went into trances, saw visions, and engaged in other phenomena such as jumping, rolling, laughing, shouting, barking, and falling under the power of the Holy Spirit, that were highly unusual within the established religious community of Los Angeles." *Azusa St Mission*, 12.

This intermixing is fathomable and likely, as the people at the beginning of the 20th-century outpouring were all new participants, and it often takes time to mature in wisdom and understanding as the Scripture and Spirit inform our practices. Further, if the apostle Paul had to correct the Corinthians regarding the orderly shepherding of spiritual gifts (1 Corinthians 12-14), it is highly possible that at Azusa and elsewhere, including in our churches today, he would have at least a few loving words of correction for us.

Further, you don't have to search too far to find scandal and aberrant behavior in the Spirit-filled community. Some of the highly visible ministry scandals of the 1980s and '90s, continuing into the 21st century, have involved leaders of charismatic or Pentecostal backgrounds. Unfortunately, the behavior of the few often taints the picture of the whole. To this day, some observers and critics have rightly and wrongly labeled some of what they see as unbiblical. It is not my desire to call out every practice or doctrine that might be considered unbiblical nor to rehash positions. Some activities and views in Pentecostal-charismatic Christianity have no biblical equivalent or precedence, and some may represent emotionalism, learned behavior, and human wisdom apart from the Spirit of God.[83]

The Bible is our plumb line, and we must continually exercise discernment to foster maturity in our practices that stand up to the Spirit of Christ's scrutiny. We must operate in decency and order (1 Corinthians 14:33, 40). We are to be known by our love for one another (John 13:35). We are to be known as being indwelt by Christ and doing what he and his disciples did. Unfortunately, we are not always successful in that endeavor.

---

83 See Michael L. Brown, *Playing With Holy Fire: A Wake-up Call to the Pentecostal-Charismatic Church*, (Lake Mary, FL: Charisma House, 2018), for a survey of issues needing restoration in the renewal movement.

What Do We Do with John 20?

Recalling the principles of relational focus and biblical grounding can help evaluate what to do with John's discussion of Jesus imparting the Holy Spirit in John 20. Only Luke, in the book of Acts, provides detailed accounts of Spirit baptism. Only John provides insight into what happened when Jesus breathed on his disciples after his resurrection but before Pentecost:

> On the evening of that day, the first day of the week, the doors being locked where the disciples were for fear of the Jews, Jesus came and stood among them and said to them, "Peace be with you." When he had said this, he showed them his hands and his side. Then the disciples were glad when they saw the Lord. Jesus said to them again, "Peace be with you. As the Father has sent me, even so I am sending you." And when he had said this, *he breathed on them and said to them, "Receive the Holy Spirit.* If you forgive the sins of any, they are forgiven them; if you withhold forgiveness from any, it is withheld." (John 20:19-23, emphasis added)

How do we reconcile John 20 with the reception of the Spirit in the Acts 2 Pentecost account? Did the disciples first receive the Spirit with Jesus, as it seems in John 20, and again on Pentecost? Based on the Greek, some point to Jesus' command to "receive" as being a present-tense action and say there is no question that the disciples received the Spirit then.[84] But is there even a small possibility that this was not the moment of Spirit reception but instead that Jesus was preparing

---

84   Laurito posits that "this supernatural breathing was not merely a symbolic act. Rather, it was an actual impartation of the divine Spirit of God." *Speaking in Tongues*, 8.

them for what was to come?[85] Or might it be, as some scholars propose, that John and Luke had different theological purposes for what they shared? Perhaps John (or even Jesus) desired to evoke other instances of God breathing life in the Hebrew Bible, such as with Adam in the Garden and the valley of dry bones in Ezekiel.

> Then the Lord God formed the man of dust from the ground and breathed into his nostrils the breath of life, and the man became a living creature. (Genesis 2:7)
>
> Then he said to me, "Prophesy to the breath; prophesy, son of man, and say to the breath, Thus says the Lord God: Come from the four winds, O breath, and breathe on these slain, that they may live." So I prophesied as he commanded me, and the breath came into them, and they lived and stood on their feet, an exceedingly great army. (Ezekiel 37:9-10)

Again, could Jesus' breath have been preparatory, symbolizing God's initial breath into that which was lifeless so we could afterward become vessels of the Spirit? Whatever John's purpose for recording this event, Luke explicitly describes the events in Acts 2 and 10 as being baptized with the Holy Spirit, receiving the Holy Spirit. Is it possible we have two events of "receiving," first receiving some, then more of the Holy Spirit, or as we noted the charismatic Catholic might say, what was received in baptism and confirmation that lay dormant was now activated?[86]

---

85 Macchia takes a view that "It may be that the Johannine breathing forth of the Spirit is symbolic of what will happen at Pentecost. (Jesus engaging in prophetic drama of what will occur when the Spirit is received)." © Frank D. Macchia, *The Spirit-Baptized Church: A Dogmatic Inquiry*, (London: T&T Clark, an imprint of Bloomsbury Publishing Plc., 2021), 34.

86 ICCRS, *Baptism in the Holy Spirit*, 101.

Further, if the breath in John 20 is an initial reception and a model for how we receive the Spirit in the modern day, what is the parallel event for new Christians today? As some might say, receiving the Holy Spirit in John 20 could be an initial reception of the Spirit at conversion without the fullness, and receiving in Acts could be the fullness of the Spirit.

Does it matter if we believe we receive the Spirit the moment we believe in Christ, or later at Spirit baptism, or if we say we get some but not all initially, and the fullness or activation is what follows? If our position does *not* stop us from pursuing Spirit baptism as described in Acts, then perhaps it matters less. In practice, though, given human nature, the greater the perceived treasure, the more effort and persistence we will apply to obtain it. And if this treasure of Spirit baptism is a gateway to the most profound possible relationship with God, then much is at stake.

The New Testament Writers' Vantage Point

When we seek to understand the Scriptures, it is invaluable to understand the viewpoints and context of the writers and the intended audience. A question we might ask relative to our Spirit baptism discussion revolves around the personal experience of the writers of the New Testament. Did they each experience Spirit baptism similar to what we find in Luke's accounts (Acts 2, 8, 10, 19)? Although I am not a historian or theologian, my study has led me to several possibilities for your consideration.

Spirit Baptism: The 120 individuals at Jerusalem in Acts 2 included the twelve apostles (with Matthias as Judas' replacement), Mary, the mother of Jesus, and the brothers of Jesus (Acts 1:13-15). Luke records that Peter and the eleven stood up when Peter addressed the crowd, so we know that Matthew, John, and Peter were all present. The writer of James is identified as the brother of Jesus (Matthew 13:55), who was also the leader of the Jerusalem church (Acts 15:13-20), so he almost certainly was among Jesus' brothers who were part of the 120. Jude identifies himself as the brother of James, and some believe that James is also the brother of Jesus.[87] So Jude then is possibly one of Jesus' brothers (see also Mark 6:3), who were part of the 120. We know also that Jude urges the readers to build themselves up, praying in the Holy Spirit (Jude vv. 20-21). Prayer in the Spirit here is likely referring to prayer in a spiritual language, as Paul describes in 1 Corinthians 14,[88] making it almost certain that Jude was knowledgeable of Spirit baptism and its accompanying gifts.

We know from Acts 9 that Paul was ministered to by Ananias, who laid hands on him to receive the Holy Spirit. We also know that later, Paul ministers the same to others and cites himself as speaking in a spiritual language more than all (1 Corinthians 14:18). So, Paul's experience, regardless of timing, seems similar to the other Acts accounts of Spirit baptism. That leaves us with Luke and Mark since the authorship of the letter to the Hebrews is uncertain.

It is improbable that Luke, the author of Luke and Acts, was present as part of the 120 in Jerusalem at Pentecost, as Paul describes him as a non-Jew (Colossians 4:11). We do know that Luke was a close friend of Paul and traveled with him (Acts 16:6-11; 20:5; 27; Philippians 1:24;

---

87 See Brian Chilton, "Who Wrote the Book of Jude?" September 24, 2017. *CrossExamined.org: https://crossexamined.org/wrote-book-jude/* (February 28, 2024).

88 Laurito, *Speaking in Tongues*, 48; Fee, *God's Empowering Presence*, 229.

Colossians 4:14; 2 Timothy 4:11), and we know that Paul was concerned with the full reception of the Spirit by believers (Acts 19:2). Given their companionship, it is unlikely that Luke would have avoided or been overlooked by Paul's ministry of Spirit baptism (Acts 19). Further, it would be a stretch to think that he could function in such a crucial role in the early church, with sensitivity to keeping a record of Pentecost and Spirit baptisms, living among the apostles, and *not* having personally experienced this outpouring of the Spirit.

Mark also is not among the twelve apostles. Still, we know he accompanied Paul in ministry, and Paul would have certainly addressed any gaps in Mark's initiation, as he did with the Ephesians as recorded in Acts 19. Given these cursory observations, it is highly likely that *all* of the writers of the New Testament had experienced Spirit baptism as described in Acts.

Outward Signs: Following this observation, another question arises. Is it reasonable to assume that the authors of the New Testament and the apostles expected an outward expression to validate or prove Spirit baptism? If so, would they not have sought to minister the baptism of the Holy Spirit to new converts? As with many of these questions, there may be no conclusive answer. However, we might ask, "If it happened to them, why would they not expect it to happen to others?" And if it is not for others, is there any prescriptive scriptural evidence that supports that view? It seems entirely possible that these early events set a pattern for the future.

Further, without the outward sign of Spirit reception, how would Peter otherwise have known that the Spirit had fallen on Cornelius' household (Acts 11:15; 15:8)? And if they did not expect an observable Spirit baptism, why did the apostles in Jerusalem send Peter and John to Samaria to pray that the Samaritan's who had received God's word would also receive the Holy Spirit (Acts 8)? And why would Paul lay hands on the Ephesians (Acts 19) if they had received the Spirit upon profession of faith and water baptism? Again, the record seems to show that in the early church, the experience of Spirit baptism with some evidential sign was a fact not under debate.

Spiritual Language: From the testimony of Acts 8, 10, and 19, there at least exists the possibility—however small—that speech in a spiritual language commonly accompanied Spirit baptism. Moreover, it is possible, though not proven, that this was considered normative. If it were normative, giving full details of every conversion account would not be necessary. As we mentioned in chapter 8, in the book of Acts, we see varying levels of detail regarding belief, water baptism, and Spirit baptism. If Luke was writing to Christians who held a common understanding of the steps of initiation, what was not written could easily have been understood to have occurred and would not need to be explained *ad infinitum*.

Philip's Ministry

Some might ask, "Why did Philip not minister Spirit baptism to the Samaritans in Acts 8, and why did Peter and John have to come to complete that work after Philip preached the Gospel?" Is it possible that Philip was more gifted as an evangelist and preacher, and others were more equipped to facilitate Spirit baptism? Perhaps the Holy Spirit instructed Philip to move on and allow Peter and John to finish the work he had begun, a sharing of joy and responsibility. Key to this story is not so much who is ministering but that the Samaritans receive the

Spirit just as the Jews at Pentecost and the Gentiles at Cornelius' house. That Jews, Gentiles, and the despised Samaritans whose bloodlines were mixed received the Holy Spirit indicates that the gift of the Holy Spirit is for everyone. Philip's lack of ministering Spirit baptism does not argue against Philp having been baptized with the Spirit or that he believed it was unimportant.

Taking this a step further, others in Luke's Acts record (Silas, Barnabas, Stephen, Simeon, Lucius, Manaen, Priscilla, Aquila, etc.) spent time with Paul and would likely not have been deficient in their initiation into the new covenant. It follows that as they ministered, it would be reasonable to expect them to pray for or lay hands on others to receive the Spirit. It would be shocking if they did not.

Isn't It My Belief That Matters?

"If you confess with your mouth that Jesus is Lord and believe in your heart that God raised him from the dead, you will be saved. For with the heart one believes and is justified, and with the mouth one confesses and is saved.... "Everyone who calls on the name of the Lord will be saved." (Romans 10:9-10, 13)

The Scripture above is an anchor for many when they share the good news with others. I confess with my mouth and believe in my heart, and I am then saved, which is how most people read this. From the discussion in chapter 4 about salvation as a moment in time versus a process and relationship, it seems that it may be possible to see these verses a bit differently. We hear from Peter in Acts 11, after seeing that the household of Cornelius had received the Holy Spirit, just as the

120 did on the day of Pentecost (v. 15), that God gave the "same gift to them as he gave to us *when we believed in the Lord Jesus Christ*" (v. 17, emphasis added) and that "God has granted *repentance that leads to life*" (v. 18, emphasis added).

Peter speaks of belief, repentance, *and* receipt of the Spirit in the context of "life." In the Acts 10 narrative, we see not repentance or a moment of belief but rather the outpouring of the Holy Spirit. If eternal life is knowing God and Christ (John 17:3), and this knowing is walked out in relationship with God through the indwelling Spirit, then this progression of belief should lead to Spirit baptism.

As noted in chapter 8, based on the record of Acts, it is not an ironclad assumption that the Spirit is received at the moment of belief or profession of faith, but it seems that these "lead to" (Acts 11:18) life. Our engagement with God enters a new dimension through becoming one with him (1 Corinthians 6:17; John 17:21, 23) in the reception of his Spirit to our bodies, the temple of his Holy Spirit (1 Corinthians 6:19).

The 120 believed Jesus when he told them to wait for the promised Holy Spirit in Jerusalem. They did what he said and were baptized with the Holy Spirit (Acts 1-2). The weight of Scripture points to God's desire that believers seek and experience Spirit baptism. Jesus wants us to receive his Spirit (John 7:39).

> And I tell you, ask, and it will be given to you; seek, and you will find; knock, and it will be opened to you. For everyone who asks receives, and the one who seeks finds, and to the one who knocks it will be opened. What father among you, if his son asks for a fish, will instead of a fish give him a serpent; or if he asks for an egg, will give him a scorpion? If you then, who are evil, know how to give good gifts to your children, how

> much more will the heavenly Father give the Holy Spirit to those who ask him!" (Luke 11:9-13)

In the above passage, the Greek verb tense of Jesus's words indicates a command to the hearers to ask and keep on asking, seek and keep on seeking, knock and keep on knocking.[89] Luke pairs this admonition with another parable of persistence in Luke 11:5-8. By persisting, we demonstrate trust in Jesus' words.

If Romans 10:13 existed in isolation, then its statement about everyone who calls on the name of the Lord being saved would support those who deny Spirit baptism. But he has instructed us to call on his name, to call on him, *and* ask for his Holy Spirit.

Baptized into Christ

Some say the Holy Spirit first baptizes us into Jesus (1 Corinthians 12:13, 27; Galatians 3:27), and then Jesus baptizes us in the Holy Spirit (Luke 3:16, among others). But I then ask, if Jesus has become the life-giving Spirit and Jesus and the Spirit are one, as are Jesus and the Father, how can we be baptized into Jesus but not be baptized into the Holy Spirit?

> Thus it is written, "The first man Adam became a living being"; the last Adam became a life-giving spirit. (1 Corinthians 15:45)

> Do you not know that all of us who have been baptized into Christ Jesus were baptized into his death?... Now if we have died with Christ, we believe

---

89 These verbs are Present-Active-Imperative tense. "αἰτέω." *Bill Mounce: https://www.billmounce.com/greek-dictionary/aiteo* (February 28, 2024).

> that we will also live with him.... So you also must consider yourselves dead to sin and alive to God in Christ Jesus. (Romans 6:3, 8, 11)

> As many of you as were baptized into Christ have put on Christ. There is neither Jew nor Greek, there is neither slave nor free, there is no male and female, for you are all one in Christ Jesus. (Galatians 3:27-28)

> He who is joined to the Lord becomes one spirit with him. (1 Corinthians 6:17)

As Paul says above in 1 Corinthians, if we are joined to the Lord, we become one spirit with him. How might we be one spirit apart from the Spirit in us? Paul and Jesus agree that it is the Spirit who gives life (John 6:63; 2 Corinthians 3:6). Again, Jesus tells us that we must partake of him to have eternal life (John 6:53-54), and we know that eternal life is knowing Jesus and the Father (John 17:3). So, the life flowing from Christ is a life of the Spirit in us, nourishing us relationally, creating intimacy with God as we partake of his presence in us.

Paul speaks often of being "in Christ" (Romans 12:5; 2 Corinthians 5:17; 12:2, among others), and again, John shares with us Jesus' words foretelling this reality:

> That they may all be one, just as you, Father, are in me, and I in you, that they also may be in us, so that the world may believe that you have sent me. The glory that you have given me I have given to them, that they may be one even as we are one, I in them and you in me, that they may become perfectly one, so that the world may know that you sent me and loved them even as you loved me. (John 17:21-23)

As we have noted previously, Jesus says that it is the Spirit that will be in us (John 14:17), Jesus himself will be in us (John 14:20), and he and the Father will make their home with us (John 14:23). The intertwining, indwelling oneness that Jesus spoke of in John 17:21-23 is only accomplished by the Spirit in us.

To have Christ in us and to be in Christ, we must have the Spirit in us.[90] We cannot separate the two, and this reaffirms the importance of ensuring we have not missed any steps related to the entry point of the Spirit into our bodies. What are we to do, then? Let us walk in Christ, Christ in us, baptized in the Spirit, indwelt by the Spirit of the Father and Son, with God's love permeating every cell of our being, in a symphony of praise that brings Glory to our Father!

Belonging to Christ

> You, however, are not in the flesh but in the Spirit, if in fact the Spirit of God dwells in you. *Anyone who does not have the Spirit of Christ does not belong to him.* But if Christ is in you, although the body is dead because of sin, the Spirit is life because of righteousness. If the Spirit of him who raised Jesus from the dead dwells in you, he who raised Christ Jesus from the dead will also give life to your mortal bodies through his Spirit who dwells in you. (Romans 8:9-11, emphasis added)

In the passage above, Paul contrasts two types of people—those with Christ and those without. Given his experience of the Spirit and

---

90 Dunn concurs that "One cannot experience Christ without experiencing Spirit, which also means that one cannot experience Spirit except as Christ." *Jesus and the Spirit*, 323. I would add that one may also experience the Spirit as Father/Abba, as he is both the Spirit of God and of Christ, as discussed in chapter 4.

evidence of his ministry of Spirit baptism (Acts 19), it seems reasonable to think that he would not consider leaving someone who wanted to follow Christ in an interim state without Spirit baptism. So, when he is speaking about those who are in Christ or who have the Spirit, it follows that those are among the Spirit baptized.

Today, due to the wide variances in doctrine and (mis)understanding about Spirit baptism, many have not experienced the Spirit baptism of Acts. Under Paul's ministry, if this was the case, there should be no significant delay until he ministers to them to receive the Spirit. Can we profess to be Christians but still be soulish, led by our "old man"? Without fully surrendering to the Spirit, we will likely walk habitually in the flesh. Even our religiosity can be flesh-led if it is not the result of the Spirit in us.

To be his and belong to Christ, we must be one with him through the Spirit. Our human effort and willpower can bring a measure of kindness and devotion, but only the Spirit can bring true surrender and transformation. God acknowledges and receives what we give as an offering to him, like Cornelius' almsgiving (Acts 10:1-2), but there is so much more that he wants to provide us with. Cornelius received that "more" when Peter came and spoke to him and his family (Acts 10:34-47). How much more Cornelius must have been able to give of himself to God and others when he received the indwelling power and love of the Spirit!

Paul shares his perspective on his past in Philippians 3:5-11, that he was a Hebrew of Hebrews and blameless under the law (vv. 5-6). Yet, he confesses that "whatever gain I had, I counted as loss for the sake of Christ" (v. 7). He speaks of the superiority of knowing Christ and being found in him (vv. 8-9). To be in him, he in us, is the work and witness of the Holy Spirit in us. We can only wholly belong to Christ by the Spirit in us. Yet even after he has entered, we must continue to surrender and allow him to heal and strengthen us and nurture our relationship with him so we can walk based on our union with God rather than live from our old minds (Romans 12:2).

Is Our Confession of Christ Proof or Fruit?

> By this we know that we abide in him and he in us, because he has given us of his Spirit. And we have seen and testify that the Father has sent his Son to be the Savior of the world. Whoever confesses that Jesus is the Son of God, God abides in him, and he in God. (1 John 4:13-15)

> I want you to understand that no one speaking in the Spirit of God ever says "Jesus is accursed!" and no one can say "Jesus is Lord" except in the Holy Spirit. (1 Corinthians 12:3)

Can we say from 1 John 4 above that if I have confessed Jesus as Lord, which many do who practice the Christian faith, I must have the Holy Spirit living in me? Where does this view logically leave me relative to Spirit baptism? If he is already in me, with proof that I confessed Jesus as Lord or the Son of God, I will not need to receive him again. And if Spirit baptism is supposed to represent receiving the Holy Spirit, then I will be more likely to think that is not a good doctrinal position and not pursue it. Furthermore, if a confession is proof, then what do we do with demons who both believe that God is one (James 2:19) and say that Jesus is the Son of God (Luke 8:28, 30)? Is this evidence of the Holy Spirit in them? Is it possible that our confession discussed here is not necessarily proof of the Spirit within?

Those that have the Spirit will confess him as Lord. Lordship connotes giving him rule and reign in every aspect of our lives. Can we truly and fully do this apart from the Spirit within us? Let's consider again the Samaritans ministered to by Philip. They believed and were baptized (Acts 8:12-13) and likely could have articulated a confession at that point that Jesus was the Son of God and was Lord. But they had not yet received the Holy Spirit (Acts 8:16).

Before receiving the Spirit, they could know intellectually because they heard Phillip's words and believed (trusted) his testimony. The Spirit with them—but not yet in them—opened their minds to understand and believe. After Peter and John laid their hands on the Samaritans to impart the Holy Spirit (Acts 8:17), the Samaritans could say from experiential, first-hand knowledge that Jesus was both Lord and the Son of God and that he had taken up residence in them. Similarly, our "Abba, Father" cry is by the Spirit in us (Romans 8:15).

Let's look at a similar statement:

> Whoever keeps his commandments abides in God, and God in him. And by this we know that he abides in us, by the Spirit whom he has given us. (1 John 3:24)

This verse seems to say that if I keep his commandments, I am abiding in God. But both 1 John 3:24 and 1 John 4:13-15 are paired with similar statements of knowing *by the Holy Spirit* that he lives in us. So, we could understand that the Holy Spirit in us confirms our mutual abiding, not solely our statements of belief or even our keeping the commandments. We are not called to keep the letter of the commandments without his Spirit in us. We walk in the new covenant with hearts of flesh that are alive and responsive to God, keeping his commandments as a fruit of the Spirit of God in us (Ezekiel 36:25-27; Galatians 5:22-24).

So, seeing our confession and obedience as fruit, we can say that the Spirit first imparts God's presence (first with us, and then in us through Spirit baptism). As a result of his presence in us, we can then truly confess him as Lord and walk in his ways.

How Much Time Do I Have?

What do we do with those who have made a profession of faith but have not sought God to pour out his Spirit upon them, to baptize them with the Holy Spirit? Is there a distinction between those who have heard and ignored versus those who never heard, and what if there was not sufficient time to address this in the life of an individual because they were on their deathbed? What if they never lived a moment in the Spirit but repented and turned toward God at the last moment, like the thief on the cross next to Jesus (Luke 23:39-43)? My conclusion is simply because God is love, I will trust that he is merciful and just.

I believe that if I had left this earth seven months before I was baptized with the Holy Spirit, I would have been with God. I had repented, received his forgiveness, and saw Christ as my Savior. Like the birth analogy from chapter 8, I was still in a womb state, did not see, hear, or experience him in a way that I would later, but I was no less a son. My heart was turned toward him, and I was pursuing him. I wanted to walk in his ways and to know him. I would not have said I wanted to live without him, but I was still walking in some of the same sinful ways, with my flesh still playing a large part in my walk, and I sometimes looked for ways to interpret the Bible to suit my desire or even ignored it in some cases. I did not have a closeness to God or sense his presence within me, but I knew he loved me. I did not know his voice but saw at least some of his signs.

I am not the first to say this, but I believe many who look down on others may be very surprised who they will meet in God's presence on the other side of this earth-bound life. God looks upon the heart and actions (1 Samuel 16:7; Jeremiah 17:10), not the label or brand.

Each person's relationship with God is unique, and only God knows the heart (1 Kings 8:39; Proverbs 21:2; Luke 16:15; John 2:25). So we should seek to understand one another and find room to learn from one another, to challenge and to encourage one another, standing together in awe of God. And let God be the judge of man's heart (Romans 2:6-11; James 4:12; 5:9).

I do not believe that avoiding divisiveness means we should not teach or discuss Spirit baptism with others, but rather that we should teach, discuss, and even challenge prayerfully and as the Spirit leads. I believe this sentiment was also the heart of the apostles in Acts 8, 10, and 19, to serve and see God's purposes fulfilled through the outpoured Spirit.

Power, Love, or Both?

But you will receive power when the Holy Spirit has come upon you, and you will be my witnesses in Jerusalem and in all Judea and Samaria, and to the end of the earth." (Acts 1:8)

Beloved, let us love one another, for love is from God, and whoever loves has been born of God and knows God. Anyone who does not love does not

> know God, because God is love. In this the love of God was made manifest among us, that God sent his only Son into the world, so that we might live through him. (1 John 4:7-9)

I mentioned this concept briefly at the beginning of chapter 8, but I believe it bears additional discussion. It is common within Pentecostalism to see Spirit baptism as empowerment for witnessing. In the verses quoted above, Jesus tells his disciples to wait in Jerusalem to receive power, and John tells us that God is love. But what does it mean to have power, and are these two related? We might think of having the "Most Powerful One," God himself, living in us. If God is in us, *anything* he can do apart from us, the miracles that Jesus performed when he walked the earth, healing, deliverance, and provision, he could potentially do through us. These works also exhibit power granted in a relationship, the delegation of authority. As a kingdom of priests (Exodus 19:6; Revelation 1:6; 5:10), we exercise his authority by serving with his love, bringing all we do as a sacrifice before him, interceding on behalf of others, even overcoming sickness and evil (Luke 9:1-2; Acts 3:1-8; 5:12-16; 1 Corinthians 12:9-10).

At their core, the powerful things God does through us result from our God-breathed trust in him. Through trust, we can forgive the unforgivable, love the unlovable, and bring light and life to those in need, truly loving our neighbor. Our trust is a response to the God who has shed his love abroad in our hearts through the Holy Spirit (Romans 5:5), causing his fruit to be borne in and through us (Galatians 5:22). The power of our witness is the love of God poured out in Christ and lived through his sons and daughters. As we exercise this power of his love, we become more and more like him.

Gifts of the Spirit

My purpose is not to provide details on all the spiritual or supernatural giftings that may come in Christ or accompany Spirit baptism. I have focused on spiritual language (expanded in part 3) because that gift is foundational for all in a relationship with Christ through the Spirit, just as foundational as the reception of our earthly language from those who raised us. For other spiritual gifts (Romans 12:6-8; 1 Corinthians 12:4-11, 28; Ephesians 4:11-12; 1 Peter 4:10-11), you can find many excellent resources in book form or on the internet that describe them and how they might be used.

Many church doctrinal statements state that we each receive at least one gift for the benefit of others, and then they may list a host of natural and supernatural giftings that one might identify as theirs. Using this approach seems to potentially limit God, particularly when we do not see the gift as the Holy Spirit, God himself in us, capable of working through us in any manner, from the mundane to the miraculous. Paul tells us: "To each is given the manifestation of the Spirit for the common good" (1 Corinthians 12:7), which gives wide latitude for the Spirit to work.

So, as Paul says, let us eagerly pursue spiritual gifts (1 Corinthians 14:1), empowerments of the Spirit within us. Let us broaden our impact and dependence on God to allow him to do what he desires through each of us. That is not to say that everyone will operate in every gift or calling, as the body has many parts (1 Corinthians 12:12-27), but we should not be limited to the thought that we have one, or maybe two gifts to share and expect to operate only in those lanes. We should always seek, trust, listen, and collaborate with God, giving him the latitude to work through us however he chooses, in any gift he wants to give in a moment or over time. He gives us gifts at his good pleasure, and they sometimes may surprise us.

Head versus Heart

Some raise the issue that Pentecostals and charismatics are often more driven by experience and emotion (more heart-focused) and less grounded or focused on the exposition of the Word of God (less head-focused). But is this still true today? As the Pentecostal-charismatic movement has matured, so have its members and influence. Craig Keener provides a more than cursory summary of the breadth of impact that scholars with a Pentecostal, charismatic, or continuationist background have within the fields of biblical and theological scholarship across a broad cross-section of educational institutions and disciplines.[91]

There are also more than a few scholarly organizations worldwide that focus on Pentecostal and charismatic theology. One such organization in the United States is the Society for Pentecostal Studies (SPS), whose purpose is to foster discussion across academic disciplines, encourage, recognize, and publicize work of Pentecostal and charismatic scholars and scholars of Pentecostalism, for the benefit of the body of Christ and those in front line ministry.[92] Many of these organizations collaborate across denominations and within the academic and pastoral communities.[93] Each has a role in influencing the church's culture locally and globally.

---

91 Keener, *Spirit Hermeneutics*, 296-303.
92 See *Society for Pentecostal Studies: https://sps-usa.org/about.html.*
93 For a listing of some key academic and ecclesiastical organizations, see *Pentecostalism and Christian Unity: Ecumenical Documents and Critical Assessments*, ed. Wolfgang Vondey (Eugene, OR: Pickwick Publications, 2010), 30.

PART THREE

PRACTICAL
CONSIDERATIONS

10

Individual Renewal

God Our Deliverer

Before discussing receiving the Holy Spirit in this chapter, the first three sections (including this one) will explore some foundational elements of entering into a relationship with God. Each of us has a different starting point for our journey in Christ. For some, these thoughts may be rudimentary, and for others, helpful.

God is in the rescue and transformation business. Whether we like to acknowledge it or not, just as the Jews were in slavery in Egypt and needed God's strong hand to deliver them, there are many forms of slavery in our world today, from the darkest forms of human trafficking to the insidious slavery of worshipping false gods. God desires to deliver us from anything that keeps us from him.

We are groomed by the messages, expectations, and appetites of the world around us that show no regard for our well-being but would instead use us for what it can get from us, unmoved by our suffering and pain. But God knows where we are, and he wages a campaign to extract us from our captor(s), bring us to safety, and give us new life, removing and healing the scars of our brokenness in the process. Such is the good news, and it impacts not only a city or a culture but also the individuals within who are unaware of his presence. The new life he is offering is one of connectedness to him, where we find hope, refuge, and restoration. And what we experience of his hand in our lives often depends on our expectations and motivation. Let's turn next to our motivation for our relationship with God.

What Type of Friend Do You Want?

A friend loves at all times, and a brother is born for adversity. (Proverbs 17:17)

A man of many companions may come to ruin, but there is a friend who sticks closer than a brother. (Proverbs 18:24)

Faithful are the wounds of a friend; profuse are the kisses of an enemy. (Proverbs 27:6)

Greater love has no one than this, that someone lay down his life for his friends. (John 15:13)

The Greek Philosopher Aristotle, in his *Nicomachean Ethics*, describes three types of friendships that can arise in our interpersonal relationships. A friend shared these with me, and I found them helpful in examining my motivation for relationships with others and God. Aristotle describes the first type as a friendship of utility, which is based on what others do for us. Friendships of utility are typical in a work environment, project, or event, where we come together to accomplish a goal. Once we meet the goal, our need for the other diminishes.

Aristotle's second type is a friendship of pleasure, which is based on mutually enjoying activities or pursuits. The relationship may end if one or both no longer find pleasure or joy in the common pursuit. In utility- and pleasure-based relationships, the desire for deeper mutual knowing is not a high priority or is not present at all.

Aristotle calls the third type the perfect friendship, a friendship between two people who are "good," virtuous, and desire the good of the other. This perfect friendship describes how we, as Christians, ought to care for and love one another. [94] It also describes how God loves us (for our good), and we are to respond to him and those around us in the love he has given us (1 John 4:7-12). He alone is truly good (Mark 10:18) and transforms us to be like him (2 Cor 3:17-18).

Which of these three types of friendship best describes how you relate to God and how you perceive him? How would you assess your ability (goodness and virtue) to be a "perfect" friend to others?

If you desire a deeper relationship with God through the Holy Spirit, I encourage you to examine your motivation. Do you want to be closer to him because of what he can give you, how he will make you feel, or because you desire to love him and see his will done on earth? Or is it some mixture of the three? If your motivation is other than love, ask and trust him to transform that desire into a perfect friendship by the Spirit.

Some Context for Spirit Baptism

"For God so loved the world, that he gave his only Son, that whoever believes in him should not perish but have eternal life. For God did not

---

94 Aristotle, *Nicomachean Ethics*, trans. D.P. Chase, [Book VIII, Chapters IV and V] *Gutenberg.org: https://www.gutenberg.org/files/8438/8438-h/8438-h.htm#chap08* (February 28, 2024). See also, Scotty Hendricks, "3 kinds of friendship, according to Aristotle," September 30, 2017. *BigThink: https://bigthink.com/personal-growth/do-you-have-true-friendships-why-aristotle-thinks-you-dont/* (February 28, 2024).

> send his Son into the world to condemn the world, but in order that the
> world might be saved through him. (John 3:16-17)

> For *those whom he foreknew he also predestined to be conformed to the*
> *image of his Son*, in order that he might be the firstborn among many
> brothers. And those whom he predestined he also *called*, and those whom
> he called he also *justified*, and those whom he justified he also *glorified*.
> (Romans 8:29-30, emphasis added)

When we consider the good news, the gospel, we are faced first with understanding God's desire to bring us to him. His will is that no one should perish and that all should come to repentance and return to him (2 Peter 3:9). Paul tells us above in Romans 8:30 that God's call goes out (we are *called*). Those who respond are restored to a right relationship with him through Christ's atonement, forgiveness, and our union with the Holy Spirit (we are *justified*). As we walk with him and are transformed by his indwelling Spirit, he reveals himself in and through us: that is, we are *glorified*, or rather, he is glorified in us.

The gospel is great news to those who struggle with sin, suffer shame, experience condemnation, and lack love. Let's look a little closer at the process.

A firm foundation and a clear plan are needed to build a house. The most solid foundation is what Christ himself set. A foundation that does not have receipt of the Spirit as a fundamental entry point into a life in Christ is at a high risk of being devoid of the gospel's full power. Attempting to build on anything else is like building on sand.

Using another word picture, it is like wearing athletic shoes that are four sizes too small and trying to run a marathon. But we can run unhindered when given a shoe with a perfect fit and the perfect combination of support and flexibility. It is this way with the gospel. If we don't get the right one, the full-sized gospel intended for us, we are hindered in our ability to run the race of life in Christ.

And there are not supposed to be many different gospels. Instead, there is one true gospel that is complete, perfect, and available to everyone. How we make our way to God may be unique, but the destination that he has provided for us, the goal of our race (at least for now before his return) is the same: intimacy with God our Father and Christ (John 17:3) through his indwelling Spirit, in the here and now, the hope of glory (Colossians 1:27), God revealing himself in and through us.

We might start this journey with curiosity or trauma, and somewhere along the way, we are introduced to the thought that there is a God who created all things. We may come to this viewpoint on our own, through seeing the heavens at night and the billions upon billions of stars in the sky, the beauty of a majestic mountain, or the vastness and the power of the oceans or mighty rivers. We may feel his presence or hear him speak. We may see him in the life of a parent, a brother or sister, or a friend or acquaintance. Or someone may have spoken to us and introduced us to God's heart in Scripture.

However it happens, our awareness is aroused. We may wrestle with whom to attribute these observations, but at some point, we arrive at the place of belief that there is a real God who made everything. We might seek to gather information, to know more about him, and at some point, we may seek to meet him, to know him, and to develop a relationship with him. Our relationship can take many forms, even before learning about the works of Christ. We might even worship him, give of our resources, and pray to him as Cornelius did in Acts 10.

At some point, we become aware of the barrier that remains between us, the sin-death that keeps us from intimacy with him. That awareness may come through reading the Bible, hearing the words of or experiencing the care of a friend or stranger, or even an encounter with God or a convicting dream or vision that speaks to our ailing spirit. Whatever the means, the Spirit draws us to actively repent of our sins and accept the forgiveness Jesus offers through his atoning sacrifice. Jesus wipes away our sins, removing the burden he never intended us to bear. We experience a newfound freedom, a lightness, even a supernatural elation that we no longer have to carry that weight. His forgiveness is a gift of his love for us and brings about a measure of change. However, we may recognize that we continue to battle against our sinful nature, and even though we have forgiveness, sin still rules our bodies. We long to be set free, victorious over sin—like Christ.

We may serve and give of ourselves, but there is a limit. Sometimes, we may see God work through us, our actions, choices, and words. But thoughts may still linger. Is there more? Why am I not changing? How do I grow, how do I bear fruit, and why do I not do the things I see others doing in the Bible or my community or church in the name of Christ? Why am I not at peace? Am I truly saved? Or, perhaps I have a measure of peace and thankfulness, and someone suggests that there is more. I must contemplate and adjust my views, possibly even take a risk.

I asked some of these same questions even after Christ took away the weight of my past sins. Although I had confessed my sins, and he had forgiven me, as I noted, I was still led mainly by my earthly desires. Then, someone told me about something that was entirely new to me—Spirit baptism. This last gateway was one that I had not yet walked through, and I believed that there was something more on the other side. I was excited to draw closer.

Many have never come to this point. But if we hear, we have a choice – will we surrender ourselves entirely to this God of Love? As we persist in our belief, will we take action and knock, seek, and ask? Jesus clearly states that God's desire, his will, is to give us his Spirit (Luke 11:13).

For some, receiving the Spirit through Spirit baptism will come easily. For others, it will take time and intent. In either case, God will *not* withhold his Spirit. After we receive his Spirit comes the process of transformation, renewing our minds, receiving healing for the trauma of the past, uncovering any areas of unrepentance, and empowering us to repent. We receive his ongoing forgiveness and are cleansed from our unrighteousness (1 John 1:9). We spend time in his presence, seeking his face, becoming more attentive to his written and spoken words, and often the still small voice within. We learn of his ways and develop spiritual strength by practicing obedience to what he calls us to do. Again, the Spirit changes us from within, imparting God's glory to us (2 Corinthians 3:17-18), causing us to look, speak, and act more and more like our Father.

As it is with earthly relationships, so it is with the heavenly. Challenges come, failures come, persecutions come, victories come, and in all these things, we come to know God better. During the storms of life, he speaks to us, "Peace, be still" (Mark 4:39), and we learn to trust him, irrespective of our life circumstances. We bear a sweet fragrance of his presence among others. Some are drawn to this fragrance. Others, unfortunately, find it repelling (2 Corinthians 2:14-16). But God works the redemption and salvation of others through the witness of our lives, causing the light of his glory to shine collectively brighter.

Is the fire yet burning brightly within you, and do you have a ready supply of the oil of his Spirit? If so, then let's burn brightly together. If not, then "Ask, and it will be given to you; seek, and you will find; knock, and it will be opened to you" (Matthew 7:7). And if you don't ask, don't complain that you do not have, but keep asking, be persistent, don't give up or give in. And certainly, don't listen to the voice that tells you the fullness of Spirit in this gospel is not for you.

Some Potential Personal Barriers to Spirit Baptism

We have already discussed doctrine's role in what we believe and in shaping our practices. There is a potential that what we have heard, learned, or experienced may cause us to avoid the subject of Spirit baptism. Our doctrines, intended to draw us closer to God, can sadly do the opposite.[95] Demystifying Spirit baptism is a primary aim of this book, and if it is hitting its mark, it may be challenging some of your beliefs. Ask God to speak to you, lead you through the Scriptures, give you insight, and show you the path forward.

As you might suspect, doctrine is not the only barrier to openness to Spirit baptism. Another critical influence can be the relationship we have or had with our parents, primary caregivers, or any person of authority in our lives.

If we were blessed with people around us who could love with a healthy, communicative love, modeling God's grace and mercy, then it

---

95 "There is generally a direct correlation between what is preached and what is experienced. Sound preaching and teaching open people to being touched by God and equip them to properly interpret what they experience." ICCRS, *Baptism in the Holy Spirit*, 84. Suenens notes that "There is evidence that in many of the early Christian communities, persons not only asked for and received the Spirit during the celebration of initiation, but they expected that the Spirit would demonstrate his power by the transformation he would effect in their lives." Suenens, *Theological and Pastoral Orientations on the Catholic Charismatic Renewal*, 15-16.

may be easier for us to embrace the indwelling love of our heavenly Father. If we experienced abusive, overly critical, restrictive, or neglectful parenting or oversight, we may have an aversion to allowing God to come closer to us. Any emotional injury and trauma can have this same effect. Inviting him in, his Spirit into us, to become one with us, is a life-altering event. If we can't conceive of this as a good thing or it raises fear, we will likely avoid it altogether. We may keep God at arm's length, creating a "safe space" where he is not allowed in.

If you struggle with this, consider seeking the help of a minister, counselor, or friend who can walk you through the steps of forgiveness (both giving and receiving) and prayer for healing.[96] It is also a good practice to confess any known sin, as this puts us in a posture of humility and vulnerability, which opens us up to receiving.

We also may not know how to invite the Holy Spirit in. Looking at Scripture, we see some precursors that include united prayer (Acts 2), hearing preaching/teaching (Acts 10), prayer, and the laying on of hands (Acts 8, 9, 19). Some may receive the Spirit while alone, others with someone ministering to them, and others may receive as part of a group of people praying. Experiences can range from the dramatic to the calm, and no two are the same. Some have even received the Spirit amidst an alcohol or drug-induced stupor or while in imminent danger of death. While this is not the norm and certainly not recommended, God is not put off by our situations or inadequacies because receiving his Spirit is not dependent on our ability. If our heart desires, God will meet us where we are.

---

96 "Many individuals have been wounded by family dysfunction and other effects of the culture of death; thus inner healing is often needed before people can open themselves fully to the grace of the Holy Spirit." ICCRS, *Baptism in the Holy Spirit*, 84.

The next section will provide some practical suggestions for receiving the Spirit, and there are also many other helpful resources on this subject available from seasoned ministers and ministries. [97]

How Do I Become Spirit-Baptized?

If you have read this far and have not previously experienced Spirit baptism in your walk with God (you have no tangible recollection or experience of the Spirit in you), and you desire to, here are some practical steps you might consider. I do not mean to discount the providential way God may pour out his Spirit upon a person without their focused pursuit.[98] These suggestions are intended for those who may desire to ask, seek, and knock for that to occur.

1. If you have unconfessed sin, acknowledge it before God and ask his forgiveness.

2. Similarly, if you have known unreconciled offenses with others (you or they have an offense), seek God about what to do and when. He may call you to go to others before seeking Spirit baptism but also may want to equip you with his Spirit before such encounters.

3. In preparation, you might read Bible passages about the Spirit being poured out to stir your faith and expectation. (See chapter 5 for New Testament and Hebrew Bible references.)

---

97 Among others, see Clark and Healy, *Spiritual Gifts Handbook*, 129-131; Jack Hayford, *Beauty of Spiritual Language*, 258-265 regarding Spirit baptism and 299-309 regarding spiritual language; Dennis and Rita Bennett, *The Holy Spirit & You: A Guide to the Spirit-Filled Life*, (Alachua, FL: Bridge-Logos, 2010), 31-75; Don Basham, *A Handbook on Holy Spirit Baptism*, (New Kensington, PA: Whitaker House, 1969), 134-143; ICCRS, *Baptism in the Holy Spirit*, 91-94.

98 Clark and Healy share some examples in *Spiritual Gifts Handbook*, 131-134.

4. Reaffirm your belief in God's love for you and his desire for a relationship with you (see chapter 3), particularly the promise of the new covenant (chapter 4).

5. You might talk with others who have experienced Spirit baptism and ask them about their experiences or read testimonies online.

6. Tell God your thoughts, apprehensions, hopes, and desires, and ask him to fill you with his Holy Spirit.

7. Express your thanks through prayer, reading or singing psalms of praise and thanksgiving, or even singing uplifting hymns and worship songs. Thanksgiving expresses trust and allows us to loosen our grip on control.

8. An aspect of receiving the Holy Spirit can include expectant waiting, similar to the disciples in Jerusalem leading up to Pentecost in Acts. They devoted themselves to prayer in one accord (Acts 1:14). They agreed on God's purpose for their gathering, united in trusting him and waiting as he directed.

9. Expect God to give you a spiritual language. As mentioned, I waited, prayed, and gave thanks for over two hours over two successive nights. My error was that I thought I just needed to sit still, and the Spirit would take control. When I finally started speaking, I realized it would have been a shorter labor if I had cooperated and begun to speak anything that came to mind or came out. Receiving a spiritual language is covered in more depth later in this chapter.

10. Are you fearful about surrendering? Ask God to help you surrender.

11. Do you not know what to expect, and is your adrenaline

causing fight or flight emotions? Consider this example my friend shared before my Spirit baptism: What if I told you I would give you a million dollars, which I had next to me, no strings attached, and you had to do nothing for it except put out your hand to receive? How would you feel? Would you be excited with anticipation? Would you be thankful before or only after you received the money? Don't worry, be thankful, even before receiving! He is a good God!

God will pour out his Spirit upon you just as he did in the book of Acts. I have no doubt that he will do this in and for you. Join me in faith, believe, and persist, and God will prove himself faithful. And you will have a testimony that the God who poured out his Spirit two thousand years ago is still doing the same today. Because he is, and he will do it in you. As Jesus spoke by the Spirit in him, "These things I have spoken to you, that my joy may be in you, and that your joy may be full" (John 15:11). That joy is both in anticipation of his life in us and a fruit of that experienced reality. So rejoice, clap for joy (read Psalm 47!), and even dance before God in his presence (2 Samuel 6:14) in anticipation of his filling you.

If all this sounds daunting, you may want to find someone locally to lead you through receiving the Holy Spirit. There are plenty who can help.[99] There are no degrees or ordination required. It is the Holy Spirit who does the work.

---

99 Some possible local resources include your Spirit-baptized friends, the charismatic population within your own church or any local Pentecostal or charismatic congregation or fellowship group.

The Gift of Language

Have you considered that every parent, at least under normal circumstances, gives the gift of language to their child? As we noted in chapter 8, parents speak and often sing to their infant in words the child cannot comprehend. Many parents can attest to a baby being calmed and soothed by a lullaby, bringing peace to the uncertainty and discomfort of their new world. Although the baby may not understand the words, he or she responds to the tone of voice and the love expressed.

For a time, the child cannot understand what is being said and can only reply with nonsensical words. Children may express their thoughts, but the average person cannot comprehend them. In time, the words bring new and fascinating insight into the child's mind, heart, and personality and begin a new phase of sharing that will grow over a lifetime.

The gift of language is extraordinary but not so surprising when we consider that we are made in the image of God, and from the beginning, he has revealed himself with speech. Genesis tells us that he created the heavens, earth, and everything in them through his words. He conversed with man and woman in the Garden of Eden, with Abraham and Moses, and with many others. He spoke to his people through Moses, the prophets, and later through Jesus. Through Spirit baptism, the Spirit continues to speak through us, inspiring our speech in known and unknown languages to build up the individual and the body of Christ in the love of God.

Expect that he will enable you to speak to him and that he will communicate with you through the language that he gives you. You are his child. What parent would withhold the gift of his voice from them?

What lover would silence his beloved? And it may very well be that through partaking of his words of life by the Spirit, we who thirst for the living God (Psalm 42:1-2) are satisfied and found drinking from the fountain of life (John 4:14; 7:37).

How Does One Receive a Spiritual Language?

Have you ever had an experience where a thought from God came to your mind to share with someone else? Or some words of wisdom came out of your mouth that were clearly not yours, and you said, "That was definitely not from me; it had to be from God?" Speaking in a spiritual language is similar; it is a gift from God, except that all you are saying is not from you, and you can keep speaking, hearing the Spirit's words through your voice for as long as you would like.

As noted earlier, it is common to speak in a spiritual language as part of Spirit baptism, but if you know you have received the Holy Spirit yet have not spoken in a spiritual language, you can ask God for that gift, too. Thank him for his provision. Regardless of the timing, when you begin to receive a spiritual language, it may pour forth or come with a thought of a syllable or word. In simple faith, speak that word and allow the Spirit to fill your mouth with more. By this, I mean that you will not need to hear the words internally before you continue to speak, but you will speak them as naturally as you speak in your native language without having first to think about every word you will say.

Some might begin praying in their native language and transition into a spiritual language. As I mentioned earlier, when I was being prayed for to be baptized in the Spirit, I thought that the Spirit would take control of my vocal apparatus, make me talk, and make my mouth and tongue form words. I did not realize until afterward that at any moment in my waiting, as I yielded, I could have begun voluntarily speaking syllables that came to me, cooperating with the Spirit rather than waiting to be uncontrollably spoken through. Once I yielded and began to make a sound with my voice, the words flowed freely in a language I could not understand. I was still in control of whether I spoke (I could have stopped at any moment), but in no way did I want to.

Also, as I shared in chapter 7, while this is not always the case, I could not speak English during this first conversation with God in the Spirit. Anything I tried to say came out in a spiritual language. In retrospect, it may be that God knew that I might doubt my experience, so he gave me indisputable evidence that this was not me speaking, akin to making Zechariah mute (Luke 1:20) or Saul blind (Acts 9:8). For my analytical mind, it left no room for doubt.

So, after a first syllable or word comes, continue to speak, believing that God will continue to give you words by his Spirit, and of all things, don't overthink or try to analyze what is going on. Just talk. Talk, and then talk some more. Don't worry about how you sound. As you speak, tell him how you feel about him. Feel free to intersperse words in your natural and spiritual languages. Enjoy and thank him! Just as each physical birth is unique, each is a praiseworthy event.[100]

A One-Syllable Prayer

Some of us often judge our experiences as inferior to what we've heard about or observed, and at times, we don't understand what we're

---

100 Sees testimonies of receiving a spiritual language in Sam Storms, *The Language of Heaven: Crucial Questions About Speaking in Tongues*, (Lake Mary, FL: Charisma House, 2019) 229-238.

experiencing. Not long after Marie and I experienced Spirit baptism, another young woman came to receive the Holy Spirit. She experienced being baptized in the Holy Spirit, but rather than a flow of words in a spiritual language, for the first several days, her prayer in the Spirit consisted of a single syllable.[101] She was initially discouraged, thinking she was somehow defective, but with some consolation and encouragement, she continued to pray that same syllable day after day in faith. By the end of the week, what began as a single syllable spoken in faith blossomed into a much more complex language, bringing an increased assurance of God's work within her and joy and thankfulness in his presence. By trusting the Holy Spirit and persevering through her discouragement, she fully received the spiritual language God wanted to give her.

After being prayed for to be baptized with the Holy Spirit, another sister in Christ had only a few initial words and found it difficult to pray in the Spirit freely. A week later, while standing in breaking waves at the beach, she was overcome by the vastness of God's love and began to speak fluently in her spiritual language. The gift of the beauty and power of the waves spoke to her and freed her to surrender more fully to God. From then on, she was unhindered in her prayer in a spiritual language.

Don't worry or try to evaluate simple beginnings. Thank God and let him bring the increase. As we persevere and wait, we glorify God in our trust.

---

101 The Bennetts mention a similar occurrence in *Holy Spirit & You*, 69.

Will I Understand What I'm Saying?

When conversing with God in a spiritual language, it is entirely normal not to understand any of what you are saying. That does not mean you will never know. At times, you might have a sense of the subject matter and God's or your own sentiment and emotion, but not specific words. You might also find that occasionally, God gives you an interpretation or understanding of what is being said. This understanding can occur in the same way as God's gift of interpretation in public settings, which is discussed in the next chapter.

I have found that over time, I have become more in touch with God's heart, and when I'm actively engaged in the prayer (not distracted), I more often sense what I'm praying about or, at times, what God is saying to me. You have nothing to lose by asking God to give you an interpretation or understanding, and don't be surprised if he does or disappointed if he doesn't.

While praying in the Spirit, God often speaks to me internally in my native language, giving me not interpretations but sometimes thoughts (ideas, understanding, and direction) to guide my actions. I typically keep something nearby to capture these thoughts so I don't forget what I've heard (I use a notes app or text myself.) Many of the topics and thoughts in this book were generated by listening to God's guidance amid prayer. Collaboration with God through the Spirit is a joy, not a burden. That is how we are to be walking in our everyday lives, letting him speak in prayer, journaling, through the Scriptures, other people, signs of various kinds, and the still small voice within. Through this communication, we learn to know his will, and he confirms his care for us as our Good Shepherd.

What Happens as I Pray in the Spirit?

God is the Shepherd over the smallest to the most significant details of life and is interested in helping us if we are willing to make ourselves available to him. Praying in a spiritual language is an active sign of our willingness to surrender and let him care for us. When we pray in this way, we yield our speaking faculties and allow the Holy Spirit to speak *anything* on our behalf. Our prayers might include praise, petition, sharing one's heart and thoughts, intercession, and anything else you might speak in your native tongue. They may even include speaking things we would typically not ask for in our native tongue, such as asking God to refine or strengthen us or a loved one through a challenging trial.[102] Through our prayer in the Spirit, we might also speak forth God's words to us, which we will discuss more in the next chapter, and we may be speaking things that are simply beyond human comprehension, spirit to Spirit—expressing the inexpressible.

As we pray in the Spirit, we express the perfect words at the perfect time in full accordance with God's will (Romans 8:26-27). Our flesh is completely put to the side. In surrendering to the Spirit, we nurture our ability to surrender our entire lives to him. James 3:2-10 speaks of the power of the tongue, like a rudder for a large ship or a spark that can set a forest ablaze. As we yield our tongues to these words given by God, he transforms us into those who speak blessing and not cursing. As we yield to the Spirit's words through us, we become more sensitive

---

102 Menzies shares that "It is a risky thing to encounter God. Speaking in tongues symbolizes this risk, for it requires that we surrender control of that most significant and defining organ of our body, our tongue (James 3:1-12; Proverbs 18:21)." Robert P. Menzies, *Speaking in Tongues: Jesus and the Apostolic Church as Models for the Church Today*, (Cleveland, TN: CPT Press, 2016), 6.

to yielding when we are talking in our native language and when we are contemplating an action or response to others or God.[103]

We become the brush in the hand of the Master Painter, the clay in the Potter's hands, allowing him to create what he wills with our lives, shaping us into the image of Christ through the Spirit in us (2 Corinthians 3:17-18).

How Do I Pray After Spirit Baptism?

If you surveyed Christians who have been baptized in the Holy Spirit and speak in a spiritual language, you would find a wide range of responses about their ongoing practices. Some might tell you that they spoke only once. Others might say they rarely speak in a spiritual language, perhaps only when they are particularly weighed down with an issue of life and have no other way of expressing their hearts. Others might say they pray in the Spirit for a few minutes during their daily prayer time. Still others might say they spend considerable time praying in a spiritual language each day.

Because the conversation is spirit to Spirit, unless you are speaking with another person, you can talk with God in your spiritual language at any time, as quietly or audibly as your situation allows. While your mind may be engaged in listening for God's heart and thoughts as you pray, it is also possible to pray and intercede in the Spirit while doing many tasks, such as driving or even reading the Bible. (If you are driving, though, and God overwhelms you with his words or love, you should pull over and give him your full attention.)

---

103 Clark and Healy note "Many people find that tongues becomes a doorway to other gifts of the Holy Spirit because it gives us practice in yielding to the Spirit without being completely passive." *Spiritual Gifts Handbook*, 187.

The apostle Paul, arguably the most influential of the apostles and a man who walked in the Spirit of Christ in power and love, tells us that he prayed in the Spirit more than all of the Corinthians – perhaps even more than all of them put together (1 Corinthians 14:18). In my first days after being Spirit baptized, I wanted to spend more and more time with God in the Spirit—one hour led to two, and even three or more at times. My honeymoon with the Holy Spirit was glorious. However, as life became more complex I did not keep up that initial pace or fervor.

The demands of life, raising children, work, church, and home, brought a different balance than in my days as a single man and in our newlywed year living in an apartment with no children. (Paul speaks about some of this shift in balance in 1 Corinthians 7:33-34.) There may have also been some performance mentality in my efforts to pray early on, thinking that more was always better. Speaking with God in a spiritual language is now part of my ongoing conversation with him intermittently throughout the day, in my comings and goings, and in set-apart individual and corporate prayer time, which varies in length.

You might ask, how long should I pray in the Spirit as part of my set-apart time with God? I would say as long as the Spirit guides you. If you're just starting out, any amount of time is better than none, and your appetite and desire will typically grow as you develop more intimacy and interactivity with God. I have found that if I don't set a limit on the amount of time I'm praying in the Spirit, eventually, I will sense the Spirit's leading to conclude. I might shift from praying in a spiritual language to singing in a spiritual language, praying and singing in English, and ultimately moving on to the day's activities.

Paul's words in 1 Corinthians 14:15 can be applied to your personal prayer time (in addition to the context of mutual edification in a public setting), so praying and singing in your native tongue interspersed with praying and singing in the Spirit are things you might expect the Spirit to put on your heart. Your prayer and praise are a collaboration with and inspired by the Spirit. Let him lead you in it.

If you have spoken in a spiritual language at one time, but it is not a regular and ingrained part of your life, I encourage you to consider following Paul as he yielded his life to God in this way. We are a people called to pray unceasingly (1 Thessalonians 5:17), pray at all times and on every occasion in the Spirit (Ephesians 6:18), coming boldly to the King of Kings on the throne of Grace (Ephesians 3:12; Hebrews 4:16). To that end, spend daily quality and quantity time in Spirit-enabled conversation with your Savior. It can strengthen us in unique ways we often do not understand.

An Intercessory Anecdote

> Likewise the Spirit helps us in our weakness. For we do not know what to pray for as we ought, but the Spirit himself intercedes for us with groanings too deep for words. (Romans 8:26)

During the spring and summer of 2009, our family was in transition between homes and spent five months living with Marie's parents in northwest Virginia. One afternoon, as I was driving home from work praying in a spiritual language, I knew I was interceding for many challenges that were present at the time. During this prayer, for what seemed to be about five minutes, I heard in my head a verbatim translation of the

Spirit's words. I was overcome with tears of thankfulness and amazed at how perfectly he interceded through me. I could *not* have prayed such a prayer in my own ability and language. While I had trusted God's prayer through me to be effective before this time, when I heard how magnificently the Holy Spirit spoke exactly what was needed, I was convinced beyond any doubt of the power of intercessory prayer in the Spirit. This experience encouraged me to pray in my spiritual language all the more and is a constant reminder of the joy of collaborating with the Spirit.

You may have issues and people you regularly bring to God in intercession. If you do not already, consider yielding some of that time to let the Spirit intercede through you in words you don't understand as well as those you do.[104]

Rose-Colored Glasses

When I was first Spirit baptized, I wore rose-colored glasses and honestly thought that with the Spirit of God in me, my entire life would go perfectly, with every small thing put in the right order. So much so that I thought my eyesight, which wasn't horrible, would be healed and that I would no longer need glasses. I thought parenting would be a breeze and our children would flourish simply because God was in and with us. I was in an extended honeymoon phase with God, delighting in my newfound relationship with him, praying a lot, and experiencing his peace and presence. During this time, Marie and I were also part of a

---

104 See also Clark and Healy, *Spiritual Gifts Handbook*, 179-181; Laurito, *Speaking in Tongues*, 49-50; Storms, *Language of Heaven*, 94, 142, 149-156; and Fee, *Paul, the Spirit, and the People of God*, 147-149, for discussion on prayer in a spiritual language for intercession and spiritual warfare.

home-church community where we all sought to live out the love and fellowship with God and each other like that experienced in the first century. It seemed like a taste of heaven on earth.

What was not at the forefront of my mind was that in this life, we would have troubles and trials (John 16:33) that would test our faith. And I didn't consider that every person I talked to about my newfound relationship with God would *not* be glad to hear my story. Looking back, I am sure that I was a bit overzealous and possibly even over-disclosing of what was happening in my life with many I encountered. Had I had more sensitivity, love, and maturity, I would have listened more and been better able to hear the Spirit's leading for when and what to share. But even with this, every day was a joy and seemed to include some newfound wonder of God. Worship and study in our home church was something I looked forward to because God always spoke to us with words, prayer, and songs in perfect timing for the life issues we were dealing with and with wisdom, understanding, and gifts that reflected his Spirit at work. But in time, the words of James would come into view as we experienced trials I would have never imagined.

> Count it all joy, my brothers, when you meet trials of various kinds, for you know that the testing of your faith produces steadfastness. And let steadfastness have its full effect, that you may be perfect and complete, lacking in nothing. (James 1:2-4)

Through life's trials, God's presence, care, and provision have become a source of refuge, and he has proven himself as the Prince of Peace, the One who calms the storm. May the words of our brother Peter resound in our ears:

> Beloved, do not be surprised at the fiery trial when it comes upon you to test you, as though something strange were happening to you. But rejoice insofar as you share Christ's sufferings, that you may also rejoice and be glad when his glory is revealed. If you are insulted for the name of Christ, you are blessed, because the Spirit of glory and of God rests upon you. (1 Peter 4:12-14)

Can I Help Others to Receive?

As I noted earlier, no ordination, licensure, or training is required to pray for others to receive the Holy Spirit. If you've never done it before, it can be helpful to team up with someone experienced in this ministry to prepare you to help others through the process, but this is not absolutely necessary. If you find yourself ministering to another, ask Jesus what to do and what to say. Ask, pray, and trust that he will lead you. As noted earlier, many resources on this topic are available online and in book form to help guide you.

An Easy Wager ...

As I wrote this section, the U.S. Powerball jackpot prize was at $1.9 billion U.S. dollars (a lump sum payout of $929 million), with a drawing set for that evening. A single lottery ticket was just two dollars. If you win, you will have more money than most people could ever spend in a lifetime—such a small risk for such a potentially large return. It's no wonder the frenzy of lottery ticket buyers grows as the jackpot increases. However, the odds of winning this prize are approximately 1 in 292 million (0.0000003 percent), far less likely than the chances of being struck by lightning, which is under one in a million,[105] but who's counting?

Now, my confession. While writing and reading about the lottery, I found that I could buy Powerball tickets online. This easy access is just one of the problems with the internet. As I considered purchasing a ticket, I also considered my principles and biblical and moral outlook. I rationalized that I would be fine winning just a one-million-dollar prize (the odds are still extraordinarily unfavorable) because that would allow us to do things in the current season of life that God wants us to do, including blessing others. But did I really need the lottery? What about Proverbs 10:2: "Treasures gained by wickedness do not profit, but righteousness delivers from death," and Proverbs 12:11, "Whoever works his land will have plenty of bread, but he who follows worthless pursuits lacks sense," or Proverbs 13:11, "Wealth gained hastily will dwindle, but whoever gathers little by little will increase it"?

After talking it over with Marie, I decided to essentially "donate" $6 to the lottery fund. I had no expectation of winning, but some questions swirled in my head. Was this potentially an open door for the enemy to attack me, not trusting God for my family's provision and future? Would buying the tickets derail my writing and ability to listen and hear God's voice? These were just my thoughts about buying the tickets, not even winning one of several possible prizes.

The results are in. I didn't win. This book was written, and no curse was put on my family. But I learned something valuable. My biggest fear was not being a fool and losing the $6, but what would happen if I won a prize? What would this do to my life, my wife and children, friends,

105 "Lightning Strike Victim Data," Natural Disasters and Severe Weather. *Centers for Disease Control and Prevention: https://www.cdc.gov/disasters/lightning/victimdata.html* (February 28, 2024).

and family? Would it put a wall between me and God? This experiment reinforced for me that nothing is worth the possibility of losing my relationship with God.

Do you fear what Spirit baptism might do to your current life, beliefs, and relationships? What might you possibly lose? As I shared earlier, I faced this fear in January of 1993 when I surrendered to God the possibility that I might have to let Marie go. To me, at the time, the risk of loss that I took was huge, but it was infinitesimally small compared to the gain in my relationship with God. And in his incredible generosity and love, he added to that by giving me Marie as my incredible wife and partner in life's pursuits.

... Without Cost

As we touched on earlier, during the Feast of Tabernacles (*Sukkot*), Jesus, speaking of the Spirit, told the crowds, "If anyone thirsts, let him come to me and drink. Whoever believes in me, as the Scripture has said, 'Out of his heart will flow rivers of living water'" (John 7:37-39). He was alluding to the words of the prophet Isaiah, spoken hundreds of years before:

> "*Come, everyone who thirsts, come to the waters; and he who has no money, come, buy and eat! Come, buy wine and milk without money and without price.* Why do you spend your money for that which is not bread, and your labor for that which does not satisfy? Listen diligently to me, and eat what is good, and delight yourselves in rich food. Incline your ear, and *come to me; hear, that your soul may live*; and I will make with you an everlasting covenant, my steadfast, sure love for David. (Isaiah 55:1-3, emphasis added)

The water, wine, and milk are without price, yet free to us for the taking. He is offering himself, through his Spirit, the source of eternal life. The price has already been paid. There is an ongoing, endless supply of living water, a God who is never exhausted or too tired to speak with us, help us, and pour out his love into us. We only have to give our time and the little faith we have to believe he will do what he has spoken. How extravagant a prize for such a meager cost. No lottery can even come close to the riches available in him—he beckons us to come into his rest (Matthew 11:28).

I say this offer is free, but it may have a cost. God might ask you to give up your earthly love for a heavenly one. Not unlike Pascal's wager, you would be surrendering your very self to God. Everything you have and are responsible for—your time, finances, possessions, and relationships—would be subject to God's guidance and direction as you respond to the love he pours into your life. What you receive in return is immeasurable peace, joy, provision, comfort, guidance, wisdom, and direct access to the King of Kings, to the mercy seat in the heavenlies, to the temple of the Holy Spirit, which you now become, a temple not made with human hands. You begin eternal life in the here and now (Ephesians 2:6).

If you have only partially heard him in the past, you will more clearly hear him afterward. If you are living for yourself with some small offering to God, you will increasingly want to give all of yourself to him. If you are not able to understand the Scriptures, the Holy Spirit will teach you and provide insight and hunger for his Word as you read and listen (John 14:26).

I wonder why there is not more of a frenzy around this Spirit baptism wager than there is about Powerball? Thankfully, God seeks us out and provides us with evidence of the reality of the availability of his Spirit. Just as we can observe the beauty of creation and, in a moment, connect that to the Creator, we can also have "the eyes of our hearts enlightened" (Ephesians 1:18) to know the hope he has called us to, our inheritance of the riches through Christ. This hope was the gift of Pentecost, God's Spirit in us, which continues in our current day.

If you are still searching for peace, an understanding of why you were born, your purpose, and knowing when you've arrived, look no further. Jesus wants to baptize you with his Holy Spirit and change you forever. He will join himself to you, in you, and you will know that he is in you (John 14:20).

I believe God taking up residence in man through Spirit baptism is the greatest miracle of all of the works of God in the Bible.[106] This promised union with God is what Moses' deliverance through the Red Sea was pointing to. This defeat of the enemy is what David's victory over Goliath of Gath foreshadowed. This overcoming of death is what Jesus began when he went to the cross and was resurrected by the power of the Holy Spirit to walk once again with his disciples. He is the God who overcomes, searches out and saves, and gives life from death. The life he desires to give is the life of his Spirit in us.

I will ask once again, have you experienced the unmistakable joining of God with your spirit? Do you know experientially that he is in you? What are you waiting for? Is there anything you may be holding back on in your relationship with God because you fear what might happen if it is true or comes to pass? Do you think that complete surrender to

---

106 Yong also shares this sentiment, noting that "The most miraculous signs and wonders are not merely astounding healings or even the resurrection from the dead, but the vivifying of peoples and communities touched by the Spirit as the flame of love." *Spirit of Love*, 111.

anyone or anything is a fearsome prospect? Do you fear giving every part of yourself to God and no longer being the master of certain areas of your life? If any of these are true, ask God what's happening and why you feel this way and listen for his answer.

11

Thoughts on Spiritual Language

A Restoration of What Once Was

Now *the whole earth had one language and the same words.* And as people migrated from the east, they found a plain in the land of Shinar and settled there. And they said to one another, "Come, let us make bricks, and burn them thoroughly." And they had brick for stone, and bitumen for mortar. Then they said, "Come, let us build ourselves a city and a tower with its top in the heavens, and let us make a name for ourselves, *lest we be dispersed over the face of the whole earth.*" And the Lord came down to see the city and the tower, which the children of man had built. And the Lord said, *"Behold, they are one people, and they have all one language, and this is only the beginning of what they will do. And nothing that they propose to do will now be impossible for them. Come, let us go down and there confuse their language, so that they may not understand one another's speech."* So the Lord *dispersed them from there over the face of all the earth*, and they left off building the city. Therefore its name was called Babel, because there the Lord confused the language of all the earth. And from there the Lord dispersed them over the face of all the earth. (Genesis 11:1-9, emphasis added)

In the passage above, God confused the languages because of the imminent risk that man would walk in his own ways in all things, using his collective intellectual and physical gifting apart from a relationship with God to navigate life and not carry out God's plan to the detriment of creation and all mankind. The dispersion of the people echoes God's sending Adam and Eve out of the Garden, where he originally intended to nurture this first couple in a relationship with himself. Adam and Eve went their own way and rebelled by not heeding God's word, and God cast them out of the Garden (dispersed them) so they would not eat from the Tree of Life and remain in that fallen condition forever (Genesis 3:22-23). In both cases, God acted in the best interest of his children, for humanity, in less-than-ideal circumstances. In both cases, God worked to further his goal of filling the earth with his glory.[107]

Something miraculous changed in the time between Genesis and Acts 2. Through Christ, God not only opened the way back to himself (Matthew 27:51; Hebrews 10:19-22), but he also purified his new dwelling place on earth, his bride, the body of Christ (1 Corinthians 12:13, 27; Hebrews 9:14). His desire to have a people rightly related to him was accomplished by putting his transforming and life-giving Spirit in them, becoming one with them (John 17:21-23; 1 Corinthians 6:17). The risk of living on forever in that marred garden-state of sin is now mitigated, and man can partake of the Bread of Life himself (John 6:35), the source of eternal life, through the Spirit. Instead of

---

107 Macchia notes that "God confused the tongues and dispersed the peoples at Babel in order to lead them to Pentecost and, through Pentecost, to the liberating story of Jesus. For God determined the time and places of all peoples so that they might reach for and find God (Acts 17:24-27)." Frank Macchia, "Babel and the Tongues of Pentecost: Reversal or Fulfillment," in *Speaking in Tongues: Multi-Disciplinary Perspectives*, ed. Mark J. Cartledge (Eugene, OR: Wipf and Stock Publishers, 2012), 46.

language uniting man apart from God, the language of the Spirit unites man to God.[108]

> "For at that time I will change the speech of the peoples to a *pure speech,* that all of them may call upon the name of the Lord and serve him with one accord." (Zephaniah 3:9, emphasis added)
>
> May the God of endurance and encouragement grant you to live in such harmony with one another, in accord with Christ Jesus, that together you may *with one voice* glorify the God and Father of our Lord Jesus Christ. (Romans 15:5-6, emphasis added)
>
> For through him we both have *access in one Spirit* to the Father. So then you are no longer strangers and aliens, but *you are fellow citizens with the saints and members of the household of God,* built on the foundation of the apostles and prophets, Christ Jesus himself being the cornerstone, in whom the whole structure, being joined together, grows into a holy temple in the Lord. *In him you also are being built together into a dwelling place for God by the Spirit.* (Ephesians 2:18-22, emphasis added. See also 1 Peter 2:5)

Through this new language, we can draw near to God, spirit to Spirit, strengthened with power in the inner man (Ephesians 3:16; Jude v. 20), as witnesses of him doing "far more abundantly than all that we ask or think, according to the power at work within us" (Ephesians

---

108 Laurito mentions tongues as a "unifying agent within the early church," uniting Jew and Gentile and reversing Babel with spiritual language, "reunifying the languages of humanity." *Speaking in Tongues,* 22, 81-82. Macchia notes that tongues shared among Jews and Gentiles becomes "a sign of a reconciled community." "Babel and the Tongues of Pentecost," 47.

3:20). By his indwelling Spirit, he gives us the mind of Christ so that we can love with his love and walk in his ways, not to collaborate with man in his ways of death, but to collaborate with God whose ways are only good (Mark 10:18). We become the Temple of the Living God, not the work of man's hands and intellect. Man and woman, Jew and Gentile, are redeemed and transformed to bring his glory and personal presence on the earth collectively.

What Is a Spiritual Language?

> For one who speaks in a tongue speaks not to men but to God; for no one understands him, but he utters mysteries in the Spirit.... The one who speaks in a tongue builds up himself, but the one who prophesies builds up the church. (1 Corinthians 14:2,4)

> But you, beloved, building yourselves up in your most holy faith and praying in the Holy Spirit, keep yourselves in the love of God, waiting for the mercy of our Lord Jesus Christ that leads to eternal life. (Jude vv. 20-21)

> For by one Spirit are we all baptized into one body, whether we be Jews or Gentiles, whether we be bond or free; and have been all made to drink into one Spirit. (1 Corinthians 12:13)

As discussed in earlier chapters, conversation is a primary way to build relationships. As an earthly parent gives a language, so does our heavenly Father. Just as we can use our earthly language to communicate exclusively with those we love, our Father provides a way to communicate exclusively with him. The language he gives connects us spirit to Spirit. Rather than relying on our comparatively small (when compared with God's) intellect to process words, the Spirit enables us to speak hidden things that are only between us and God, bypassing our intellect. Paul calls these mysteries (Greek *mysterion* in 1 Corinthians 14:2), and they include not only communication to God but also from God, as it also builds us up (1 Corinthians 14:4) and enables us to experience the love of God (Jude vv. 20-21).[109] The English word used most often in the Bible for this speech is "tongues" (meaning "languages") or "unknown tongues."

In Acts 2, we hear of this communication being languages unknown to the speaker (verses 4-11). Paul tells us that the Spirit-given words in Corinth were "speech that is not intelligible" (1 Corinthians 14:9) and that "no one understands." Given these descriptions, it is possible that the languages in Corinth are not earthly languages but spiritual or even angelic (1 Corinthians 13:1) or simply earthly languages that a typical Corinthian may not be familiar with. I have been referring to "tongues" as "spiritual language," that is, a language 1) given by the Holy Spirit, 2) unknown to the speaker, and 3) may be either an earthly or heavenly language/dialect.[110] And when speaking, this is not a wild and uncontrollable frenzy, like some frothy form of ecstasy. It is speech, two-way communication, a conversation with

---

109 Yong builds on Jude's sentiment, noting that "Prayer in the Spirit is in the end the only possible means of experiencing the rapturous love of God and, in turn, of "articulating" the incomprehensible and ecstatic character of His love." *Spirit of Love*, 53.

110 I am not including in the term "spiritual language" the somewhat rare phenomenon sometimes experienced after traumatic events where a person is instantaneously fluent (both speaking and understanding) an earthly language previously unknown to them. While that may (or may not) be a miraculous gift from God, that is not our focus. The Bennetts recount some instances of a similar miraculous occurrence in *Holy Spirit & You*, 95-96. See also Doctrinal Commission, "Glossolalia, Xenolalia and Xenoglossia," July 28, 2021. *CHARIS: https://www.charis.international/en/glossolalia-xenolalia-and-xenoglossia/* (February 29, 2024), and Clark and Healy, *Spiritual Gifts Handbook*, 182.

God.[111] As Paul wrote, this speech is always controlled by the speaker, who can decide when to speak (1 Corinthians 14:27-28, 31-33).

The Languages of Acts 2

Some argue that tongues today cannot be the same as what was experienced in Acts because the Acts events, particularly Acts 2, involved known human languages. They do not typically dispute that the speakers did not previously know these languages.

> Now there were dwelling in Jerusalem Jews, devout men from every nation under heaven. And at this sound the multitude came together, and they were bewildered, because each one was hearing them speak in his own language. And they were amazed and astonished, saying, "Are not all these who are speaking Galileans? And how is it that we hear, each of us in his own native language? Parthians and Medes and Elamites and residents of Mesopotamia, Judea and Cappadocia, Pontus and Asia, Phrygia and Pamphylia, Egypt and the parts of Libya belonging to Cyrene, and visitors from Rome, both Jews and proselytes, Cretans and Arabians—we hear them telling in our own tongues the mighty works of God." (Acts 2:5-11)

The crowd testifies of what they hear, but it is not conclusive that this results from the disciples speaking in earthly languages, a miracle

---

111 Laurito notes that "Glossolalic prayer is a beautiful union of human and divine prayer as Spirit-filled individuals allow the Spirit to pray through them.... Pentecostals view prayer as more than merely a monologue to God – it is an opportunity to experience a divine dialogue through the Spirit." *Speaking in Tongues*, 50-51. Mark Cartledge notes that "glossolalia is a prayer language that is used when words of one's normal language prove inadequate. It transcends language and yet embodies language. It is a language of the Spirit rather than the mind; it is of the heart rather than of the head. It functions as both a sign, as evidence of the presence of God in a special way, through baptism of the Spirit, and as a gift of prayer and prophecy (when interpreted) in private or corporate settings," in Mark J. Cartledge, *Charismatic Glossolalia: An empirical—theological study*, (New York: Routledge, 2002), 135.

of hearing, or some combination of both. It is plausible, for instance, that as the languages from the regions in verses 9-11 above were distributed across the 120 who were speaking, people in the crowd could have directly heard at least some of what some of them were saying. But is it also plausible that the speakers were all speaking in some form of heavenly language, and God was giving the listeners an interpretation in their own tongue? Some think not. Whatever the answer is to these questions is less important to me than someone trying to use Acts 2 to say that modern spiritual language cannot be what was experienced in Acts because the modern versions are not known earthly languages, and, therefore, today's version is likely a counterfeit.

The words I speak when praying in the Spirit are not from any language I know, but they sometimes sound as if they have Semitic origins. Absent someone hearing me pray in a spiritual language who can recognize that language, I have no conclusive way of knowing if it is one of over seven thousand earthly languages.[112] I also am unaware of a tool that can accurately identify all known world languages based on an audio sample, so it would be challenging to prove that a spiritual language was or was not an earthly tongue, particularly if it were not a common language. Whether the language I speak is earthly or heavenly is of no consequence to me as I know it is a language given to me by the Holy Spirit. When speaking or praying in this spiritual language, I directly communicate with God and tangibly sense his presence and love.

---

112 "How many languages are there in the world?" *Ethnologue: https://www.ethnologue.com/insights/how-many-languages/* (February 29, 2024).

Might Everyone Speak?

The two explicit references to Spirit baptism (Acts 2 and 10) included speech in a spiritual language, and one additional similar event (Acts 19) contains the same. So, are we then to assume that anyone baptized with the Holy Spirit will speak in a spiritual language? If you have some time and love to read, volumes have been written from many perspectives on this topic. Rather than revisiting them, I propose a view here based on the testimony of Scripture, the experience of others, and my own experience. Let us first look at Paul's words to the Corinthians as he lists some of the spiritual gifts:

> Are all apostles? Are all prophets? Are all teachers? Do all work miracles? Do all possess gifts of healing? Do all speak with tongues? Do all interpret? But earnestly desire the higher gifts. (1 Corinthians 12:29-31)

The question posed by Paul above has been a perennial favorite for those affirming that it is not a universal expectation that all Christians will or could speak in a spiritual language. Given our risk management perspective, is there any possibility that this view is incorrect? Some believe that there are explanations that could dispel that view. Some understand the context of 1 Corinthians 12 as the community, the assembly, and gifts shared publicly. If this is the context, and not referring to a personal prayer in a spiritual language, then it would make perfect sense that not everyone would have the gift of bringing a public word in a Spirit-given language or an interpretation to share for the building up of others (1 Corinthians 14:3-4, 12, 17, 19). Based on Paul's guidelines to Corinth (1 Corinthians 14:26-33), God distributes those gifts as he sees fit. Only a few would share those particular gifts in a public setting. Looking again at 1 Corinthians 12, Paul says:

> Now there are varieties of gifts, but the same Spirit; and there are varieties of service, but the same Lord; and there are varieties of activities, but it is the same God who empowers them all in everyone. To each is given the manifestation of the Spirit *for the common good.* (1 Corinthians 12:4-7, emphasis added)

This "common good" served by sharing spiritual gifts aligns with Paul's theme of love in 1 Corinthians 13 and 14. He further says:

> For one who speaks in a tongue speaks not to men but to God; for no one understands him, but he utters mysteries in the Spirit. On the other hand, the one who prophesies speaks to people for their upbuilding and encouragement and consolation. The one who speaks in a tongue builds up himself, but the one who prophesies builds up the church. (1 Corinthians 14:2-4)

Paul continues:

> If any speak in a tongue, let there be only two or at most three, and each in turn, and let someone interpret. (1 Corinthians 14:27)

The words in a spiritual language build up the individual speaking, and an interpretation, similar to prophecy, edifies the hearers. Regarding whether all can speak, Paul expresses his heart:

> Now I want you all to speak in tongues, but even more to prophesy.... If, therefore, the whole church comes together and all speak in tongues, and outsiders or unbelievers enter, will they not say that you are out of your minds? (1 Cor 14:5, 23)

Paul's desire that they all speak in tongues concerns their personal edification (1 Corinthians 14:2, 4; Ephesians 6:10, 18). But in the context of a gathering, Paul wants them to bring gifts for each other. (See also Matthew 23:11; Acts 20:35; 1 Peter 4:10.) In the case that there were unbelievers present, their greatest need is not an indiscernible spiritual manifestation but to encounter the love of God. God's love considers where the unbeliever is and looks to shepherd him into God's presence. So, while supernatural manifestations can be beneficial, they must be administered in love. Therefore, it would be unloving to withhold a word in a spiritual language that the Holy Spirit wanted you to share in a public setting (to be covered more in the next chapter).

In the public setting, as we are proposing for the context of Paul's question in 1 Corinthians 12, "Do all speak in tongues," the most edifying approach for others relative to this Spirit-inspired speech would be to have an accompanying interpretation (1 Corinthians 14:13-16). Paul also closes this section, noting that we should "not forbid speaking in tongues" (1 Corinthians 14:39), endorsing the continued exercise of this gift. So, Paul seems to leave the door open so that, at least in Corinth, all might speak in a spiritual language, and he expresses his desire that all speak habitually. We also need to note that Paul's desire, as captured in 1 Corinthians, is part of the revealed Word of God for all those who believe, not solely the Corinthians of the first century.

Must Everyone Speak?

From the scriptural record in Acts 2, 10, and 19, it appears that all of those who were baptized with the Holy Spirit on those occasions spoke in a Spirit-given language.[113] If the gift were only for some, one might ask, why did at least a few not talk in a Spirit-given language? Again, some might say these events were different; they were at the church's birth, and God used them as a sign, not a normative experience.

In my home church experience over fifteen years, all but one person who came to receive ministry to be Spirit baptized received the Spirit and spoke in a spiritual language. All members regularly prayed in a spiritual language as part of their relationship with God. One person attended our home church for several years without speaking in a spiritual language but eventually asked to be baptized in the Holy Spirit. She ultimately received a spiritual language. Although my sample is small, it is remarkable that all members spoke, particularly if the gift is only for some. Again, as with the Scriptures on Spirit baptism, our small sample does not mean it must be normative.

For some time, I believed that one must speak in a spiritual language to evidence Spirit baptism until I heard the testimony of a prominent minister. He described three stages in his Christian life. As a young child, he professed faith in Christ but, through his teen years, exhibited no evidence of change, power, victory, or revelation. In his later teens, he earnestly sought a deeper relationship with God and was filled with

---

113 This Spirit-inspired speech fulfilled Jesus' prophetic words that "those who believe ... will speak in new tongues" (Mark 16:17). Some question the authenticity of Mark 16:9-20. From a risk management perspective, there is no benefit to disregarding verse 17. Further, Luke's record provides ample evidence of Spirit-given languages accompanying those who believe.

the Holy Spirit, though he had not been taught about Spirit baptism. He described an immediate change, a powerful inner transformation, revelation and understanding of God, power and boldness to preach and pray for healing, and an outward zeal for God. Still, he did not speak in a spiritual language. Not that he couldn't have. He was taught it was not of God and, therefore, did not pursue it.

It was not until three years later, months after he understood that speaking in a spiritual language was a valid gift of the Spirit, that he began to speak. To him, receiving this gift was like being Spirit baptized anew. From then on, prayer in a spiritual language was a regular part of his life, and his closeness with God and his ministry continued to grow and prosper.

Many can testify of receiving the Spirit without a spiritual language. Still, I believe this is not meant to be the norm, and it may be due to a lack of supportive teaching or ministry or some other barrier that needs to be addressed before surrendering to God in this way. As I suggested in chapter 10, if you've unmistakably received the Spirit but have never prayed in a spiritual language, ask God to give you that ability, and if necessary, find someone to help you get started. Giving the gift of spiritual language is not difficult for God. As it is in most, if not all, aspects of our relationship with God, the difficulty resides with *our* unwillingness or lack of capacity to receive.

If you've heard a voice telling you, "Prayer in a spiritual language is not for you, so stop trying," I would consider the possibility that those words were not from the Spirit of God. In contrast, the Word commands us to pursue spiritual gifts earnestly (1 Corinthians 14:1).

A few years ago, a friend introduced us to an older woman who had been walking closely with God for years. She had many experiences of

God's presence and would regularly hear him speaking to her, but she had never prayed in a spiritual language and wanted that as part of her life. She asked us to come to her home and pray for her, which we did one Pentecost Sunday. After walking through some key Bible verses, Marie, our friends, and I prayed with her, and in a short time, she was catching up with her Father in this newfound gift. Age is never a barrier!

What To Do While Waiting

People who have not spoken in a spiritual language should not feel in any way condemned or less than. As some have said, it is a gift we get to experience, but we do not have to experience it. I would wonder, though, why anyone would not want this gift. If receiving a spiritual language takes longer than you would like (it was years for the woman I mentioned in the prior section), be patient, trust God, and continue to communicate and be with him in all the ways you have until now. If you are not in a regular practice of conversation with God, set aside some daily time to talk. Talk with him throughout the day and as you come and go. Read Scripture and participate in a community with other disciples who can share in your walk with Christ and help you grow and mature. God feeds, speaks, teaches, and challenges us through his written Word and our brothers and sisters in Christ.

In the past, I looked at the Bible as words on a page. Over time, I realized that these words bear the power and love of God. As it says in Hebrews 4:12, "The word of God is living and active, sharper than any two-edged sword, piercing to the division of soul and of spirit, of joints and marrow, and discerning the thoughts and intentions of the heart." Coupled with his presence within us, they come even more alive as the Holy Spirit teaches us. Ask him what you should read and expect him to highlight words you need for the day or issue or to receive his encouragement and love. Ask him questions and listen for his response. He still speaks, both outside of and through the Scriptures, imparting life through his words.

Songs in a Spiritual Language

In 1 Corinthians 14:13-15 (mentioned in the prior chapter), Paul talks of speaking and singing in a spiritual language and having an interpretation, which the mind can process. In our private time with God, both are applicable and possible in various combinations. A song sung in a spiritual language can be in a familiar tune (this was my first experience singing in the Spirit, the Elijah aria I mentioned in chapter 7). It may also be a new Spirit-given tune. God might also give a new song (words and tune) in our native and spiritual languages. I believe both can be considered spiritual songs, as Paul mentions in Ephesians 5:19 and Colossians 3:16, encouraging his readers to sing psalms, hymns, and spiritual songs to one another.

Paul's instruction to sing Spirit-given songs aligns perfectly with God's heart in the Hebrew Bible. The Spirit tells us through Zephaniah that God himself rejoices and sings over us:

> The Lord your God is in your midst, a mighty one who will save; he will rejoice over you with gladness; he will quiet you by his love; he will exult over you with loud singing. (Zephaniah 3:17)

Can you imagine God rejoicing and singing over you, his voice working within you with the same power that created the universe, called Lazarus out of the tomb, and resurrected Christ? Can you imagine his joy and peace overflowing from your heart? Our experience of God's voice is integral to Spirit baptism and our relationship with God. He puts his Spirit in us, and we collaborate with the Spirit, joined with our spirit, to speak and sing in words given by the Spirit. What a marvelous gift!

For Prayer, Praise, and Thanksgiving Only?

Some say that speaking or singing in a spiritual language is for praise/prayer and thanksgiving only,[114] citing 1 Corinthians 14:15-17:

> What am I to do? I will *pray* with my spirit, but I will pray with my mind also; I will sing *praise* with my spirit, but I will sing with my mind also. Otherwise, if you *give thanks* with your spirit, how can anyone in the position of an outsider say "Amen" to your thanksgiving when he does not know what you are saying? For you may be giving thanks well enough, but the other person is not being built up. (emphasis added)

Prayer includes intercession (Romans 8:26), as we discussed earlier. However, prayer is more than petition and praise. It is also a two-way conversation.

We mentioned Zephaniah's words that God rejoices and sings over us (Zephaniah 3:17). In the context of his discussion on spiritual language, Paul recounts to the Corinthians that "By people of strange tongues and by the lips of foreigners *will I speak to this people*, and even

---

114 See Laurito, *Speaking in Tongues*, 39, 41-42, and Fee, *God's Empowering Presence*, 218.

then they will not listen to me, says the Lord" (1 Corinthians 14:21, quoting Isaiah 28:11, emphasis added). While an aspect of that passage speaks to the witness of the nations to the children of Israel, some also associate this verse with God speaking to us through spiritual language and interpretation.[115] Consider also that when speaking in a spiritual language, our mind may be unfruitful (1 Corinthians 14:14), but what is the effect on my spirit? Just as the infant hears her parents' voices (as mentioned in chapter 10), we are receiving from God.

Tongues, interpretation, and prophecy are all forms of speaking Spirit-given words. We are built up by the private use of spiritual language (1 Corinthians 14:4; Jude v. 20) and the public gifts of prophecy and tongues with interpretation (1 Corinthians 14:3-5, 24-26, 31). If both build us up, then is it not probable that what is being spoken and heard includes God's heart for us, not only ours for him? Might some of the mysteries spoken (1 Corinthians 14:2) be for our benefit too?

Hearing the Voice of God

In a sermon I heard several years ago, the pastor asked, "How many of you have heard God's voice?" Most people will immediately think about whether they have heard God's audible voice or his still, small voice within. But have you considered that when we hear or speak in a spiritual language, we hear the words of the Spirit, perfect words of God, spoken through our voices? And if the Spirit is the Spirit of Christ, Christ in us, we are hearing the voice of his Spirit, tangible daily evidence of Jesus' resurrection and his indwelling presence.

---

115 See Bennett, *Holy Spirit & You*, 86-87. Storms also holds open the possibility of tongues as a message for one or more believers. *Language of Heaven*, 94-96, 131.

Having the living Christ as Spirit, speaking through us and to us at will at any time of day or night, is an unfathomable gift to us as disciples. Perhaps this, at least in part, is what is meant by having unhindered access to the throne of grace (Hebrews 4:16) and approaching God boldly (Ephesians 3:12). In both passages, as well as the Hebrews passage cited below, the root word *parrésia* is used, meaning "freedom of speech" and "confidence." We can draw near to our King, as Esther did to Ahasuerus, without fear of death (Esther 4:11-5:3), because we have been cleansed. Just as Ahasuerus extended his golden scepter to Esther, sparing her life and listening to her plea (Esther 5:2), God has extended his wondrous Spirit of Life to us so we can speak freely with him.

> Therefore, brothers, since *we have confidence to enter the holy places by the blood of Jesus, by the new and living way that he opened for us through the curtain, that is, through his flesh*, and since we have a great priest over the house of God, *let us draw near with a true heart in full assurance of faith*, with our hearts sprinkled clean from an evil conscience and our bodies washed with pure water. (Hebrews 10:19-22, emphasis added).

The Wandering Mind

A common experience among newly Spirit-baptized and seasoned Christians is a wandering mind when praying in a spiritual language. You may be enraptured in God's presence one minute and two minutes later, thinking about walking the dog or baking a pie. Before you know it, you might even stop praying and go off to do those very things. You might also feel bored, concluding that praying in the Spirit is not worth the effort or is ineffective, or you might think you are a "noisy gong or clanging cymbal" (1 Corinthians 13:1).

Let me encourage you. First, you are not alone. Second, you can overcome this tendency. One thing you might find helpful is to consider that Jesus is in you, and you are conversing with him. If your mind is wandering to miscellaneous thoughts or topics that do not require prayer, pause and ask God to help quiet your mind and help you connect with him on a heart level. It may take a while, but in time, you will be fully connected in conversation with God, and you will frequently experience appropriate emotion (peace, assurance, fortification, comfort) and a sense of his presence. If your thoughts contain issues you are concerned about or know need intervention or prayer, he is likely raising those.

Remember to listen as you pray. God may share thoughts, interpretations, encouragement, and direction during these times of communion.

Personal or Impersonal?

I believe there is a risk that if we see speaking in a spiritual language as a source of power only, or a tool for warfare, intercession, or praise, and not a relationship-building conversation, we may miss out on a core component of its purpose. We are not merely soldiers wielding weapons in battle. We are God's beloved, called to intimacy with the One who made heaven and earth, called to bear his love, the most powerful force for good ever conceived. Our prayers and speech with God should mirror that reality.

In human relationships, our conversations with a beloved involve words spoken, tone, and body language. Words can convey multiple meanings, depending on their context. Tone and body language help the hearer to know the mood and emotion of the speaker, providing context to the words spoken and communicating the speaker's heart. We process all of these through our ears, eyes, and mind, as well as our bodies, and experience them as information and emotions.

If speaking in a spiritual language involves two-way conversation, the Spirit can also give us inflection, tone, and emotion that express our heart to God and his heart toward us.[116] I'm suggesting that we should expect and be open to experiencing the emotion and "body language" accompanying the Spirit within. Most often, prayer in the Spirit will bear the characteristics of a conversation. At times, though, it may be more exuberant and exclamatory, even shouts of praise and joy in the Spirit that recognize the majesty and greatness of our Father, who is both intimately knowable and King of Kings. It may also bear a sense of the powerful intercession we may be engaged in.

If you find prayer in a spiritual language impersonal, ask God to help you surrender your faculties to connect with the heart of the Spirit, the heart of the Father and Son, more deeply.

---

116 Beautiful representations of this genuine human expression in conversation with the Divine occur in the movie *Ushpizin*, a Hebrew film centered around a Sukkot (Feast of Tabernacles) celebration, where Mali (Michal Batsheva Rand) and Moshe (Shuli Rand) converse with God. *Ushpizin*, directed by Gidi Dar, (2004 Gilgamesh Productions; Los Angeles: New Line Home Entertainment, Inc., 2006), DVD.

12

Engaging the Spirit in Christian Gatherings

The Importance of Community

> And he gave the apostles, the prophets, the evangelists, the shepherds and teachers, to *equip the saints* for the work of ministry, for *building up the body* of Christ, until we all attain to the unity of the faith and of the knowledge of the Son of God, to mature manhood, to the measure of the stature of the fullness of Christ, so that we may no longer be children, tossed to and fro by the waves and carried about by every wind of doctrine, by human cunning, by craftiness in deceitful schemes. Rather, speaking the truth in love, we are to grow up in every way into him who is the head, into Christ, from whom *the whole body, joined and held together by every joint with which it is equipped, when each part is working properly, makes the body grow so that it builds itself up in love.* (Ephesians 4:11-16, emphasis added)

Paul's words to the Ephesians in the above passage highlight the need to be in community. By participating with others in the body of Christ and by functioning in God's design, we help each other grow in love. God does not leave us alone to figure out how we must live but calls us to come together with gifted others and share what he has put in each of us so we can progress toward Christlikeness. As noted in chapter 4, in many cultures worldwide, participation in the community is the core of life, and identity is found in relationships with others. In the modern Western world, we tend to be more cerebral and individualistic, but the ancient world's culture emphasized community.

There is a dimension of the experience of God in a community that we cannot experience in isolation. Consider the difference between a choir and a soloist. The soloist may have a beautiful voice and meaningful expression, but alone, she or he cannot produce the sheer power, harmony, and unity experienced in a choir of skilled singers. While experiencing God's presence alone is wonderful, being immersed in a community mutually seeking God, walking in the Spirit, and exercising God's gifts to build one another up brings an entirely different dimension to our relationship with God.

In any community, people will be at various stages of spiritual and relational maturity. With mature leadership and the Spirit at work, the community fosters growth in love for God and one another, healing of the heart, discernment, development of giftings and callings, deepening relationships, empowerment to walk in faith, and a challenge to follow Christ. We strengthen one another in worship and prayer. God works through others to counsel and guide (Proverbs 11:14; 15:22; 24:6). These all happen in the context of the Christian community as we engage with one another, bringing the presence, gifts, and fruit of God in us through the Holy Spirit.

I have experienced spiritual community in various forms: small and large congregations, home/house church, small groups, men's groups, church choir, drama troupes, mission and ministry teams, conferences,

Bible studies, and many one-on-one relationships arising from those contexts. I've also been through seasons where there was less connectedness individually and communally for various reasons (busyness of life, misplaced priorities, transitions, etc.).

In my current season, I have come to treasure this interconnectedness as a staple for healthy living. Disconnectedness has a tangible impact when I neglect relationships with those around me, and I find myself longing to return to those wells of life. The effect is similar to going through a dry season in prayer life. The relationships God gives us in the body of Christ are meant to nurture and encourage; without them operating in the proper order, we tend to wither. Let's turn next to the community at Corinth.

Reflections on Corinth and Spirit-Filled Gatherings

Many of the epistles were written to address specific issues happening at a particular location. The First Letter to the Corinthians is the primary source of information addressing issues related to the exercise of vocal spiritual gifts. Paul knew of Corinth's circumstances and gave them guidelines for operating in spiritual gifts that suited their situation. His instructions, particularly those in 1 Corinthians 14, may not have addressed different occasions or environments.[117] Scripture provides guidance that we must use to adapt to different situations—small gatherings, large gatherings, and gatherings where unbelievers are present or not.

For example, if there is no chance that an unbeliever or uninitiated person would be present (1 Corinthians 14:23-25), other instruction

---

117 Storms makes a similar observation. *Language of Heaven*, 104.

might be appropriate. In our home church gatherings, on most occasions, all attendees were Spirit baptized, all speaking in spiritual languages as part of their regular prayer life. At times, particularly if we were interceding in prayer, all might pray together in their spiritual languages without interpretation. We also would occasionally be led to sing together a spontaneous song in the Spirit to harmonies that the Spirit provided. This mutual experience of God and the heavenly harmonies that poured forth were always uplifting and unifying. It deepened our appreciation for the mutual indwelling Spirit that sang through us this heaven-sent song. There was typically no interpretation, but our experience of the heart of God and the peace in his presence spoke for themselves.

This collaboration with the Spirit in song is not mentioned explicitly in 1 Corinthians, but it certainly could fall under Paul's instruction for spiritual songs in Ephesians 5:19 and Colossians 3:16. Corporate song in a spiritual language was present at Azusa Street[118] and is a recurring feature in the Catholic charismatic expression[119] and many others in our current day and throughout time.[120]

While Paul's concern was loving others, there are some loving practices we might consider that are not included in Paul's letter. For example, in our home church, whenever we had a visitor unfamiliar with spiritual gifts or how we would worship, we would spend a few minutes explaining what they might see or experience, as well as the significance and biblical grounding. Our worship times might include prophetic words, prayer in a spiritual language with interpretation,

---

118 Robeck, *Azusa St Mission*, 149-153.

119 See Doctrinal Commission, "Can several people pray or sing in tongues at once?" July 28, 2021. *CHARIS: https://www.charis.international/en/can-several-people-pray-or-sing-in-tongues-at-once/* (2/29/2024).

120 See Clark and Healy, *Spiritual Gifts Handbook*, 178; Cartledge, *Speaking in Tongues*, 232; Storms, *Language of Heaven*, 102-104; Bennett, *Holy Spirit & You*, 90.

songs in the Spirit, and the like, and this short tutorial was helpful to orient the newcomers as well as set their expectations to experience God's presence.

Where love is preeminent, sensitivity to those in attendance will also be present. We should desire to include and not repel or confuse participants. And where Scripture may not have addressed our specific situation, we may need the Spirit's guidance, directly or through mature elders and leaders, to exercise wisdom in how we relate to God in our gatherings.

Does the public experience of the Spirit that you see in the Pentecostal-charismatic renewal draw you closer, leave you curious, or repel you? Have you considered whether there is anything in your current gatherings that might confuse a visitor, and how do you address this?

Public Words in a Spiritual Language

In chapter 11, we discussed the differences between public and private use of spiritual language. This section examines how we navigate sharing this gift publicly. While we can speak in a spiritual language at will in our private conversation with God, there are some differences to consider when gathered with others in God's presence. Paul gives the following instruction to the Corinthians:

> For one who speaks in a tongue speaks not to men but to God; for no one understands him, but he utters mysteries in the Spirit.... If any speak in a tongue, let there be only two or at most three, and each in turn, and let someone interpret. But if there is no one to interpret, let each of them keep silent in church and speak to himself and to God. (1 Corinthians 14:2, 27-28)

Because we are called to seek the good of others, not our own glory or what we can receive, we should first be sensitive to the question: "Am I supposed to speak a word at all? Is God giving me something to share publicly?" In some settings, a moderator may guide you on whether to share or not. In other settings, there may be no moderator. In either case, the presence of a thought or idea does not mean you should share it. Ask God first, then proceed within the designated order of the gathering.

If you believe God is giving you a word or song in a spiritual language as a gift to those gathered, and you don't have a complete sense of what the word may be saying, ask him (and any moderator, if one is present) if you may share. If the answer is yes, and such sharing is acceptable in your gathering, then at an appropriate time, act in faith and speak the word in the Spirit, trusting that he will provide the words both in the Spirit and an interpretation (either from you or another.) Our obedience in faith allows the Spirit to work in and through us and generally makes hearing an interpretation of what was said all the easier. You may have only the first few words in your mind as you begin to share, and the rest of the word in the Spirit (or interpretation) comes forth without premeditation. You might also hear an interpretation or sense of what is being said internally as you speak in a spiritual language and can share what you've heard afterward.

If this is a meeting where others are sharing, leave sufficient time between you and the prior person to allow yourself and others time to absorb, consider, and potentially respond to what was shared. If someone is speaking, wait and consider what they have said before approaching a moderator with what you feel led to share. What the speaker is sharing may well be for you, too, as much as what you have to share may be for others. If there is no designated time in the public setting for people to share what God is giving them, certainly don't interrupt a speaker and blurt out in a disruptive manner. If possible, ask a leader for permission to share or write down what you are hearing and share it later. As Paul tells us: "The spirits of prophets are subject to prophets. For God is not a God of confusion but of peace." (1 Corinthians 14:32-33).

Public Gift of Spiritual Songs

God gives songs (Psalm 40:3). He also delights to collaborate with us in singing, even using our voices as the instrument of his song sung to us and through us. Some might call a spontaneous song in our native language a prophetic song or even a psalm. If we publicly share a song in a spiritual language, it would commonly be expected to have an interpretation, either sung or spoken, just as Paul instructs for the spoken word in a spiritual language. Any such interpretation may also be a sense of or paraphrase of what was spoken in the Spirit, or perhaps an image or impression, all supernatural gifts of God through the interpreter. And just as words spoken, this song can express our heart toward God, or his toward us.

I also believe that there are times when the Spirit of God might prompt an individual to sing a song in the Spirit where there is not an immediate interpretation, as a form of ministry to the soul of another, allowing God to emote meaning Spirit to spirit.[121] In our private prayer, an uninterpreted song we sing in the Spirit may quiet our soul or encourage us. In a secular setting, even a wordless symphony can move

---

121 The Bennetts share an occasion of an uninterpreted message in a spiritual language being a catalyst for salvation. *Holy Spirit & You*, 88.

one to tears or joy, elevating and praising God with sublime melodies. The parent's song over an inconsolable infant can bring peace and rest. Similarly, the Holy Spirit can use inspired violin or cello music as a catalyst for inner and physical healing, exhibiting the power to transform.

If these wordless expressions of music on instruments can touch the heart profoundly, how much then might Spirit-given melodies carried by the human voice do the same, particularly if they are humbly shared in love and deference to the Holy Spirit, and those responsible for governing? In such an experience, God may speak to the hearer, or the hearer can at least express what they experienced during the song, in keeping with Paul's desire for there to be an interpretation and edification.

Some might argue against this uninterpreted spiritual language in public, mainly because of Paul's words to Corinth (1 Corinthians 14:6-17). I believe, though, that because Corinth was in such disarray and was visited by uninformed outsiders (1 Corinthians 14:23), Paul's instruction to them may have needed to be more restrictive. I don't believe sharing a public uninterpreted song in a spiritual language would be a regular practice, but this might be done in certain times of ministry as the Spirit leads. The posture afterward should still be one of listening and receptivity to any interpretation or sense of what God was doing in the moment, even by the one singing or anyone hearing the song.

Spiritual Language and Interpretation versus Prophecy

Now I want you all to speak in tongues, but even more to prophesy. The one who prophesies is greater than the one who speaks in tongues, *unless someone interprets*, so that the church may be built up. (1 Corinthians 14:5, emphasis added)

Some believe an interpretation cannot be the same as prophecy,[122] and others believe it can serve the same function. An interpretation is a gift of the Spirit given in the native language of the speaker, first given in part (even as little as a first word) or whole in the speaker's mind, then spoken. So, too, is prophecy.

As noted earlier, some say that public words in a spiritual language and their interpretation must be only words *to* God. It seems within reason that just as one could speak prophetic words *from* God in their native language, we can also speak words from God in an unknown language.[123] It follows that if there is an interpretation of the words in a spiritual language *from* God, the interpreted words can be another form of delivering a prophetic word.[124]

One might also ask, why should the public word be in a spiritual language if there needs to be an interpretation that God also gives? Why not go straight to the known language? Here's how I process this. First and foremost, both are gifts from God (1 Corinthians 12:10). Why would we need to question his wisdom in giving these gifts? We should trust that he has a reason for sharing with us in that way and receive it with joy. Second, the use of a spiritual language is a supernatural sign of God's presence for all hearing. Third, the process is both relational and faith-building. We must be relationally engaged and present to him, aware and listening for his prompting. And faith is required to believe that God will provide an interpretation (or else why speak in the first place). Listening and speaking what we hear cultivates listening and

---

122 See Laurito, *Speaking in Tongues*, 41-42.
123 There are numerous accounts of words shared in a spiritual language that were messages from God for an individual(s) translated by someone who spoke the language or interpreted through the spiritual gift of interpretation. See Bennett, *Holy Spirit & You*, 87-89 and Hayford, *Beauty of Spiritual Language*, 90-97.
124 See Clark and Healy, *Spiritual Gifs Handbook*, 179.

obedience to his direction in all areas of our lives, not only in corporate gatherings.

When we listen, trust, and obey, collaborating with our Great Shepherd, we usually experience peace, joy, provision, and satisfaction. Prophetic words can bring the hearers to their knees, declaring, "God is really among you," as Paul says (1 Corinthians 14:25). The same can result from a word in an unknown language and interpretation or from any shared gift. It is not necessarily the specific gift but the presence of God, the One who knows our hearts, that brings us to our knees.

Insights from Quaker Meetings

There is a practice in meetings among the modern-day Quakers (The Religious Society of Friends) that is called "expectant waiting"[125] or "waiting worship." As described by a member, "We prepare ourselves and wait for the presence and guidance of the Divine to be made manifest among us."[126] In these "unprogrammed" meetings, there is a silent expectation that the Spirit may or may not prompt someone to share words of vocal ministry, which is said to be similar to how God gave prophetic words to individuals in the early church.[127] Thus, there are periods of silence with spoken ministry interspersed until there is a sense of being done, usually after an hour or so.

While I am not endorsing Quaker meetings or some of their varied beliefs and practices, I believe there is something to be observed in

---

125 "Traditional Quaker Worship," May 5, 2011. *Quaker Information Center https://quakerinfo.org/quakerism/ worship* (February 29, 2024).

126 "Why Do Quakers Worship in Silence?" October 18, 2018. *Quaker Speak: https://quakerspeak.com/video/why- do-quakers-worship-in-silence/* (February 29, 2024).

127 "Quaker Meeting for Worship Pt 2: Giving Vocal Ministry," September 25, 2014. *YouTube: https://www.youtube. com/watch?v=gws5EmDTFY0&t=10s* (February 29, 2024).

this posture that contrasts sharply with many of our Christian worship gatherings. While some services allow the Spirit to move beyond what has been preplanned, most services in both liturgical and non-liturgical settings are scripted and leave little time for listening to what the Spirit may be saying or directing in the moment. Lest we think this is just a modern phenomenon, this was the lament of some in the Azusa Mission after the first couple of years of the outpouring of the Spirit.[128] We, as humans, like to pour concrete around the movement of the Spirit in a well-meaning attempt to preserve the beauty of the experience. Sadly, this practice often stifles the spontaneity found in living and growing relationships.

God can and does speak through Scripture, liturgy, sacrament, sermon, and song. These elements can be an essential part of our gatherings, but many often find themselves in a passive-participatory audience-type role rather than being part of the drama.

An intriguing aspect of Quaker meetings is that there is an expectation that anyone present can participate and share what they are sensing or hearing. A helpful feature is that these meetings are typically small enough to make this approach manageable.[129] Let's consider how this approach might impact the larger body of Christ.

---

128 Robeck recounts that by 1909, the revival that had begun in 1906 "entered a steady decline." Frank Bartleman, who was present and recorded much of the history of the revival, "complained about what he termed 'a spirit of dictatorship' in the mission leadership. Services were 'programmed' 'from start to finish,' he growled. There was no longer any room for the Holy Spirit to break in." *Azusa St Mission*, 312.

129 Quaker meetings in Britain average approximately 20 people, with some of the largest upwards of 80 on average. "The Changing shape of Quaker meetings," March 18, 2021. *Quakers in Britain: https://quaker.org.uk/blog/the-changing-shape-of-quaker-meetings* (February 29, 2024).

A Listening Tapestry

> What then, brothers? When you come together, each one has a hymn, a lesson, a revelation, a tongue, or an interpretation. Let all things be done for building up. If any speak in a tongue, let there be only two or at most three, and each in turn, and let someone interpret. But if there is no one to interpret, let each of them keep silent in church and speak to himself and to God. Let two or three prophets speak, and let the others weigh what is said. If a revelation is made to another sitting there, let the first be silent. For you can all prophesy one by one, so that all may learn and all be encouraged, and the spirits of prophets are subject to prophets. For God is not a God of confusion but of peace. (1 Corinthians 14:26-33)

When planning time with our significant other or a friend, we create an atmosphere for two people to connect and share themselves and their hearts in space and time. In healthy relationships, this time will be filled with giving and receiving, talking and listening, creating an interweaving of lives and hearts. What if, in addition to our gatherings with planned preaching, praise, and proclamation, we held gatherings that set aside time to specifically listen to what God wanted to say or do in and through us in the moment?

In 1 Corinthians 14:26, Paul describes God working through a multiplicity (even "each one") of the people gathered together. In that context, gifts from God are shared, and there is an expectation that there will be mutual edification through what the Spirit provides.[130]

---

130 This seems to also be how William Seymour led at the Azusa Street Mission: "He invited them to a space made sacred both by the presence of God and by Seymour's commitment to take seriously whatever gifts the people brough to share. He made it clear that it was an open space." Robeck, *Azusa St Mission*, 92.

Paul was bringing order to gatherings that were in disorder, but when these gatherings were operating in love, there was order, building up, and strengthening for the body.

As God's Holy Spirit indwells us, he can speak to and through man, woman, and child for the benefit of all.[131] When we come together with the express purpose of listening for the heart of God and sharing what we hear, we engage in an in-the-moment surrender to the One who knows perfectly how to care for us.[132] And God is more than willing to fill our open hands and hearts.

> To each is given the manifestation of the Spirit *for the common good.* For to one is given through the Spirit the utterance of wisdom, and to another the utterance of knowledge according to the same Spirit, to another faith by the same Spirit, to another gifts of healing by the one Spirit, to another the working of miracles, to another prophecy, to another the ability to distinguish between spirits, to another various kinds of tongues, to another the interpretation of tongues. *All these are empowered by one and the same Spirit, who apportions to each one individually as he wills.* (1 Corinthians 12:7-11, emphasis added)

While the above gifts are not exclusive to gatherings (most could be exercised at any time in the ordinary course of relationships), when we gather, we are to share what he gives out of the overflow of our intimacy with him.

---

131 Fee observes regarding community worship: "Perhaps most noteworthy from the available evidence is the free, spontaneous nature of worship in Paul's churches, apparently orchestrated by the Spirit himself. Worship is expressed in a variety of ways with the [potential] participation of everyone (1 Cor 14:26)." *Paul, the Spirit, and the People of God,* 154.

132 Pinnock shares that "To know the Spirit we must become persons of prayer who are willing to yield in complete openness to God. Waiting in silence and patient receptivity will cultivate a heart-knowledge of our life-giver.... The picture Paul paints for us is that of a people waiting on God and listening to the Spirit." *Flame of Love,* 6, 152.

> And do not get drunk with wine, for that is debauchery, but be filled with the Spirit, addressing one another in psalms and hymns and spiritual songs, singing and making melody to the Lord with your heart, giving thanks always and for everything to God the Father in the name of our Lord Jesus Christ, (Ephesians 5:18-20)

> Let the word of Christ dwell in you richly, teaching and admonishing one another in all wisdom, singing psalms and hymns and spiritual songs, with thankfulness in your hearts to God. (Colossians 3:16)

In Paul's words, connecting in community is not solely directed to God; we are bringing "for one another" psalms, hymns, and spiritual songs. In this our love for God overflows to love for one another. When we come together, he can also guide us in ministering to one another through prayers for physical healing, confession of sins, and healing of the heart (James 5:13-16). In our gatherings, we are to "stir up one another to love and good works … encouraging one another" (Hebrews 10:24-25). And our listening to the heart of Christ through one another can continue in our fellowship over food, teaching, and prayer (Acts 2:42, 46; 1 Corinthians 11:33).

Our Sabbath with God was usually an all-day venture at our home church. We typically began in the morning with prayer, praise, and teaching/preaching that took us through the noon hour. We followed this with a brief break and then moved on to a time of waiting worship.

Our waiting worship was largely unscripted, allowing the Holy Spirit to guide and direct us, although we usually included candle lighting (reciting Isaiah 11:1-6), communion, and songs as the Spirit led.

During this entire time, we would be together in the presence of God, awaiting his guidance and sharing what he put on our hearts. As there were typically ten to twelve of us at any gathering, everyone usually had something to share. Sharing might include reading or singing a psalm, sharing a Bible passage or verse, words of encouragement, brief teaching, testimony (something God did or shared during the preceding week), prayers of thanksgiving or petition, requesting and receiving prayer, sharing a word from God (prophecy, spoken to us), words or songs in a spiritual language with interpretation, hymns, insights, visions, and at times, praying or singing together in a spiritual language. We listened and shared until our hearts were clear and there was nothing else to give—there was no scheduled or expected time to end.

Our time of listening, sharing, and worship in God's presence was often a couple of hours as he weaved his tapestry of love through us. Afterward, we would share dinner, closing the day together. This extended time may seem extreme to some. But we usually experienced this as a taste of heaven, partaking with the Eternal One in timeless communion, a "love feast" prepared by our King.

The small group setting does not have to be the only setting where we can allow God to weave this listening tapestry. The practice in larger gatherings in some churches includes a time of worship that provides for some sharing by members of what God has spoken to them or shown them in the form of testimony, prophetic word, encouragement, challenge, impression, or vision, and even occasionally, a word in a spiritual language with an interpretation. As noted earlier in this chapter, some have a moderator. In our small home church setting, we didn't need a moderator, although on rare occasions, what was shared might need to be clarified. In larger settings, having a moderator allows openness to hearing from God spontaneously and preserves order in the gathering.

Perhaps we might make time in our larger gatherings to listen in silence for his prompts and see what God does. We might also have extended time listening together in smaller group settings. What might this bring to our worship and prayer time together? Would your church family or small group consider such a practice? Consider starting small and see what God does.

PART FOUR

WHERE BLOWS THE WIND?

13

Where Is the Body Today?

The Renewal Today

Our individual and local corporate expressions within the body of Christ are parts of the larger whole, and we each have a stake in the success and health of every member. Beginning with the state of the Spirit baptism-fueled renewal in the global church, in this part of the book some thoughts are provided for your consideration and prayer.

From the numbers I shared in chapter 6, the renewal in the body is no small ripple. The outpouring of the Holy Spirit at the post-resurrection Pentecost began a tectonic shift that spread from Jerusalem to Judea, Samaria, and the ends of the earth. Jews, Gentiles, religious, irreligious, men, women, and children alike were all profoundly changed. In the 20th century, its force overwhelmed denominational walls despite the many efforts to decry and defeat it. Powerful and life-changing, it ushered in the joy of the presence of God and continues to this day.

The estimated 1.9 billion Christians that have not directly experienced this renewal (through Spirit baptism/infilling) represent a considerable opportunity for growth. Observing statistical trends, Johnson and Zurlo project that by 2050, one billion Christians will have experienced renewal (an increase of over 300 million).[133] The fastest growth is found in the Global South (Africa, Latin America, Asia, and Oceania), where most of the world's current Pentecostal-charismatic population reside (555 million as of 2020). Growth rates remain positive but slower in the Global North (including Europe and Northern America), where the remainder (89 million) live.[134]

Because Pentecostal-charismatics are a cross-organizational, cross-denominational population comprised of varied people groups in many geographic locations, there is no unified or uniting influence across the renewal that supports a shared understanding of what it means to live as Spirit-filled Christians.[135] While Spirit baptism (or Spirit infilling) is a common feature, there is also much diversity in beliefs and practices. A feature of the renewal is that it does not necessarily impose structure on those it impacts but tends to integrate with the cultures or religious structures it touches, such as seen in the charismatic renewal in mainline denominations. This flexibility often fosters openness to the gospel in varied contexts. Unfortunately, those varied contexts can also be a source of divisiveness.

While we might see some of the same spiritual signs, gifts, and fruit

---

133 Johnson and Zurlo, *Introducing Spirit-Empowered Christianity*, 11.

134 Johnson and Zurlo, *Introducing Spirit-Empowered Christianity*, 37. For related resources on the renewal and its impacts, see: the list in Johnson and Zurlo, *Introducing Spirit-Empowered Christianity*, 7-8; *Spirit-Empowered Christianity in the 21st Century*, ed. Vinson Synan; *The New International Dictionary of the Pentecostal and Charismatic Movements*, ed. Burgess and van der Mass; *Center for the Study of Global Christianity*: https://www.gordonconwell.edu/center-for-global-christianity/; Todd M. Johnson and Gina A. Zurlo, *The World Christian Encyclopedia*, 3rd ed. (Edinburgh, Scotland: Edinburgh University Press, 2019); *The Cambridge Companion to Pentecostalism*, ed. Cecil M. Robeck, Jr. and Amos Yong (Cambridge: Cambridge University Press, 2014); Hocken, *Challenges of the Pentecostal, Charismatic, and Messianic Jewish Movements*, among others.

135 Many mainline denominations impacted by the charismatic renewal have support organizations that foster education, fellowship, and growth. Some examples are: Sharing of Ministries Abroad (SOMA, Anglican), Presbyterian-Reformed Ministries International (PRMI, Presbyterian/Reformed), Aldersgate Renewal Ministries (Methodist/Wesleyan), Catholic Charismatic Renewal International Service/CHARIS and Pentecost Today USA (Roman Catholic), St. Symeon the New Theologian (Orthodox). Lutheran Renewal (Lutheran) ceased operation in 2014. Independent charismatics and Pentecostals have a variety of denominational support, apostolic networks, colleges and universities, and parachurch organizations that provide resources to foster adherent growth.

present today as in the first-century church, not all Pentecostal-charismatics are flourishing or retaining their distinctives. Pentecostals in the U.S. observe that Spirit baptism with tongues/spiritual language as evidence are, in some cases, becoming less prominent, making their congregations outwardly appear more like other non-charismatic evangelical churches. Further, not unique to the renewal, many Pentecostal-charismatics are challenged in the areas of spiritual formation, discipleship, and strong connection in Christian community.

Echoing Moses' Desire

Moses' desired that all of God's people would be prophets and that his Spirit would be upon them. At Pentecost in Acts 2, Peter explained to the onlookers that they were seeing the beginning of the fulfillment of God's desire to pour out his Spirit on all flesh (Acts 2:17). Just as the Spirit came upon Moses in his day and spoke through Peter on that day, God can speak through and guide individuals today, even fallible men and women like you and me. While what I share in this section are not the only instances you will find across the body of Christ, I was surprised and encouraged to hear the following calls.

In the same timeframe as Episcopal Priest Dennis Bennett's reception of the Holy Spirit in 1960 (the beginning of the charismatic outpouring in other Protestant denominations), Pope John XXIII preceded the Second Vatican Council (1962-1965) with a call for a "new Pentecost," which many Catholic charismatics see as answered in the Roman Catholic charismatic renewal.[136] Pope Francis, in his June

---

136 ICCRS, *Baptism in the Holy Spirit*, 65-66.

2017 address to a cross-denominational crowd at the Golden Jubilee (the fiftieth anniversary of the beginning of the Catholic charismatic renewal), called the renewal "a flood of grace of the Spirit … for the whole Church," imploring the movement to "share baptism in the Holy Spirit with everyone in the Church," and "walk together with Christians of different Churches and Ecclesial Communities in prayer and activity on behalf of those in greatest need."[137]

The pope reiterated his call in his June 2019 in an address to international leaders within the Catholic Charismatic Renewal International Service (CHARIS), again urging them to "share the baptism in the Holy Spirit with everyone in the Church," noting that "It is the grace you have received. Share it! Don't keep it to yourselves!"[138] I find it remarkable that the head of the largest Christian denomination in the world would call for all of its members to be baptized with the Holy Spirit. Regardless of the pope's record and views on other subjects, his words on Spirit baptism prophetically expressed the desire of God's heart.

National Service Center/Pentecost Today USA, comprised of charismatic lay members and clergy of the RCC, has launched a nine-year devotional prayer effort called Holy Spirit 2033, begun on Pentecost 2024. Its mission is to "bring baptism in the Holy Spirit to the whole Church," and they are imploring people to join them in "crying out for a new & ongoing Pentecost in the Renewal, in the Church, and in the world."[139] Similarly, a group of Pentecostal-charismatic leaders

---

137 "Pentecost Vigil of Prayer, Address of His Holiness Pope Francis" June 3, 2017. *Vatican: https://www.vatican.va/content/francesco/en/speeches/2017/june/documents/papa-francesco_20170603_veglia-pentecoste.html* (February 29, 2024).

138 "Address of His Holiness Pope Francis to Participants in the International Conference of Leaders of the Catholic Charismatic Renewal International Service – CHARIS" June 8, 2019. *Vatican: https://www.vatican.va/content/francesco/en/speeches/2019/june/documents/papa-francesco_20190608_charis.html* (February 29, 2024).

139 "Holy Spirit 2033." *Pentecost Today USA: https://www.pentecosttodayusa.org/hs2033/* (February 29, 2024).

have come together under the global alliance Empowered21, aiming that "every person on earth would have an authentic encounter with Jesus Christ through the power and presence of the Holy Spirit … by Pentecost 2033."[140] The sentiments of these two groups represent the heart of many praying Christians across the globe.

Signs Pointing to Future Unity?

Jesus' prayer in John 17:20-23 expresses the oneness he desires for us. Paul tells the Colossians of his desire that we be "knit together in love" (Colossians 2:2), and he reminds the Ephesians that Jew and Gentile have become "one new man" with "access in one Spirit to the Father" (Ephesians 2:15, 18). God's desire for all his followers is a unity in love and Spirit. In the book of Acts, we see an initial fruit of unity and selflessness. Those indwelt by the Spirit shared in fellowship, prayer, praise, and material goods and possessions, including proceeds from the sale of land and homes, to care for those in need (Acts 2:42-47).[141] Do we regularly see or experience this level of selflessness in our current day, and if not, do we ever wonder why?

The Pentecostal revival that began in earnest in Los Angeles in 1906 saw barriers come down between those of various classes, cultures, ethnicities, and denominations.[142] People joined together in praise and prayer, ministering to spiritual and physical needs in a multicultural setting that saw even racism evaporate, if only for a while.[143]

---

140 "We are Empowered21," *Empowered21: https://empowered21.com/about/* (February 29, 2024).

141 They were not all walking in such generosity (for example, Ananias and Sapphira in Acts 5:1-11), but it was a start.

142 Yong observes that the outpouring at Azusa "reembodied the eschatological outpouring of the Spirit on the day of Pentecost and in the life of the early church," binding "Samaritans, Ethiopians and other Gentiles together with Jews," reconciling "haves and have-nots." Amos Yong, *The Spirit Poured Out on All Flesh: Pentecostalism and the Possibility of Global Theology*, (Grand Rapids: Baker Academic, 2005), 137.

143 Robeck, *Azusa St Mission*, 88, 138.

The charismatic renewal of the 1960s saw denominational walls come down as Spirit-baptized Christians met for prayer with brothers and sisters from different streams. Peter Hocken (Catholic) and Vinson Synan (Pentecostal) concur that there was a "charismatic ecumenism," a coming together that was Spirit breathed.[144]

Some at the Golden Jubilee of the RCC charismatic renewal observed an "ecumenism of Love" that came from the presence of the Spirit within, bringing people together from across the body of Christ to celebrate.[145] Interestingly, this Spirit-ecumenism birthed in the 20th century within Protestantism first made its way to the RCC through the intermingling of Catholics with Protestants, resulting in a mutual sharing in the gift of the Spirit. Where man divides, the Spirit unites.

Since Vatican II in the 1960s, there has been a dialogue between the RCC and representatives from various Christian denominations (including Pentecostals and charismatics) and Judaism. Participants share about their beliefs and practices with a desire to foster stronger relationships and community in the larger body of Christ. They are not required to relinquish their beliefs. Instead, they look for common ground and areas of disagreement that will fuel future discussion and interaction.[146]

Dialogue is a beginning point. Finding common ground is hopeful and, at the very least, is a sign pointing in the right direction. Even more encouraging are the relationships forged through the dialogue. When identifying areas of unity, however, it seems there always remain areas of division, and there can still be underlying suspicions and viewpoints

---

144 "Fr. Peter Hocken on CCR Golden Jubilee. A Current of Grace for the Whole Church," June 17, 2017. *YouTube: https://www.youtube.com/watch?v=veAYfCa3kVk&t=1960s*, (February 26, 2024).

145 "A Current of Grace The Catholic Charismatic Renewal Golden Jubilee," November 30, 2017. *YouTube: https://www.youtube.com/watch?v=AOvg9G5Qs64&t=537s* (February 29, 2024).

146 See documentation at "Ecumenical Relations," *Dicastery for Promoting Christian Unity: http://www.christianunity.va/content/unitacristiani/en/dialoghi.html* (February 29, 2024).

that perhaps only God, through his Spirit, can resolve. Regardless of its shortcomings, this intermingling of streams points to a *desire for unity*, and many are at the table seeking the Spirit's way forward.

Dialogues alone cannot bring the true oneness Jesus spoke of in John 17:20-23. This oneness is only possible when we are vitally connected to God through his Spirit and transformed in his presence, resulting in our prejudices melting away.[147] Through intimacy with God, we see Christ in each other and recognize our mutual value. We desire to love as he has loved us. Jesus enables us to do what is impossible for man (Matthew 19:26; John 14:12).

---

147 Dunn also observes that "*fundamental to Christian community for Paul was the shared experience of Spirit/grace.* Without this, 'fellowship' (κοινωνία) lacks all substance; it remains a jargon word or ideal and never becomes an existential reality. So too unity hinges on this common experience." *Jesus and the Spirit*, 262.

14

What Hinders Us?

The War Against God's People

We are commanded to love God and one another (Mark 12:30-31), and it is through our love that we will be known as his (John 13:35). The enemy seeks to thwart the transformative power of this love by keeping us from intimacy with God. The enemy does not want God's plans or people to advance or succeed, and his tactics are not difficult to see.

Overt attacks often arise as religious persecution or the attempt to marginalize and belittle Christians and Christianity in the culture. The enemy desires to defeat our advance at every turn. If he can get us so focused on our worldly goals, priorities, and accomplishments as a means of fulfillment, he will use that. If he can get us chemically addicted to drugs or alcohol or the use and abuse of ourselves and others, he will do that. If he can make us run after false gods and the philosophies of man, he will do that. And sometimes, he keeps us so distracted with benign activities that we remain distracted from our calling, disarmed in the fight.

The enemy prowls around like a roaring lion, seeking to devour (1 Peter 5:8). And if we happen to hear the message of Christ and are drawn to a relationship with God, receiving his forgiveness, the enemy will try to stop us from receiving the Spirit. He battles against Spirit baptism as a work of Christ. He knows that if he can keep the Holy Spirit from indwelling us, we cannot be fully nourished, our fruit will not be as plentiful, we will lack true sacrificial love for God and one another, and God's presence will not be experienced to its fullest potential in and through us. We are also unable to bring others into the fullness of Spirit-filled life that we ourselves do not have.

When God makes his home in us, when we become one with him, immersed in him, baptized with the Holy Spirit, the battle changes. The enemy continues to fight, attempting to take us off track and distort what a walk with God looks like so others will be repelled and deterred from pursuing a relationship with God through the Holy Spirit. The enemy plays on our unhealed or unforgiven wounds, so our emotions rule, and our decisions and actions are flesh-led. He leverages our pride, even at times spiritual pride, letting us gain fame and influence only to cut us down when our hidden failings are exposed. He attempts to dilute the impact of the Spirit in our lives, slowly lulling us to sleep so we look more and more like the world, unaware of our slide into mediocrity. He distracts us from pursuing God with our entire heart, soul, mind, and strength, diminishing our prayer life, intending that we ultimately forsake God and return completely to the world's ways.

We are called as Christians to embrace life in the Spirit and to seek a relationship with God as our highest priority. We are not here to be entertained and led by our emotions, chasing after experiences.[148]

We are to walk in the fear (holy awe) of God. We are not just to become a "better self" but a new creation united with Christ in us. We are to

---

148 Chan laments that within Pentecostalism, "instead of serious discipleship we have virtual fan clubs revolving around the mega-church leader. Seldom is worship an encounter with the awesome God; it has become an occasion for cheap thrills and continuous festivity dubiously called 'praise and worship.'" *Pentecostal Theology*, 9.

live sacrificially, serving in the footsteps of our Savior and walking in his strength and stability. The enemy may attack, but the Holy Spirit fortifies our faith in response. We are to trust God unwaveringly, know him and his Word, walk in victory in this life, bring others with us, and bear the plans of God on the earth. Whatever the enemy's plan, God has a better and greater plan, filling us with the love, power, and wisdom to carry it out.

Through various means, the enemy has had some success in keeping the body of Christ from walking in the fullness of the Spirit and the fullness of the new covenant. He has kept many from receiving the Spirit as the first apostles and Jewish and Gentile disciples did in the early days of the church. If the fullness of our salvation is tied to the indwelling Holy Spirit, stopping God's indwelling is a key tactic in the enemy's war for our souls. And as mentioned, some of our churches' teachings and practices have blocked the Spirit's movement.

Leon Morris notes in his commentary on Romans 8:9 that "The Presence of the Spirit in believers is not an interesting extra to be seen in a few unusual people…. It is the normal and necessary feature of being a Christian at all."[149]

Do we give a verbal nod to the Holy Spirit and put his name on our works while he is nowhere near what we are doing? Do we invoke his presence or recognize the Acts 2 outpourings as meaningful events?

In some denominations, we amplify our Christmas and Easter celebrations but ignore Pentecost. In some congregations, the phrase used by Jesus and John the Baptist, that we would be "baptized with the Holy Spirit," is missing from our vocabulary and teachings. As noted earlier, even some denominations whose distinctive is Spirit baptism are now

---

149 Leon Morris, *The Pillar New Testament Commentary: The Epistle to the Romans*, (Grand Rapids, MI: William B. Eerdmans Publishing Company, 1988), 308.

more ambiguous about their doctrine.[150] Have you observed this, and why do you think this is?

God is pouring out his Spirit in current times in many corners of the world. Through the renewal that began in the 20th century, God's offensive against the works of the enemy continues today. In a battle that involves the Spirit of the Living God, complete victory as God defines it will come.

When we recognize this gift of the Spirit as Christ and the Father in us, with full access behind the veil (Hebrews 10:19) to commune with the King of Kings, we stop the enemy's lies. When we pursue the Holy Spirit with all diligence, asking, seeking, and knocking until we have received (Luke 11:9-13), we defeat the enemy's plan.

When we receive the Spirit, we enter a new phase of relationship intended to transform us into the image of Christ. If we miss the Spirit's entry, we miss drinking from the fountain of Life (John 4:13-14), partaking fully of Christ, and experiencing his rivers of living water (John 7:37-39). It is only by the Spirit that spiritual strength, maturity, and victory come.

Church Walls?

As noted, the outpouring of the Spirit beginning in the 20th century was not constrained by denominational boundaries. It was abundantly

---

150 Perry reports, regarding spiritual language as an evidence of Spirit baptism, that "Without strong theological underpinning a practice can fall into disuse, and there is already evidence of this in the contemporary Pentecostal church." *Spirit Baptism*, 29. Warrington notes that within Pentecostalism "there has been a decrease in the numbers of people who claim to have experienced the baptism in the Spirit, especially in the West, to which may be added the fact that the experience is only encouraged to a limited extent by Pentecostal leaders." Keith Warrington, "Challenges facing Pentecostals today," *Journal of the European Pentecostal Theological Association* 31:2 (2011), 202.

clear that no denomination or stream within the body of Christ had a corner on the presence of God. Through concrete actions, God drew our attention back to his words spoken through Ezekiel, that he would put his Spirit in us (Ezekiel 36:27). He rekindled the desire to fulfill Joel's prophecy recounted in Acts 2, that God would pour out his Spirit upon *all* flesh.

The Spirit of God determines where and who the church is, indifferent to the walls we build.[151] As Moses declared:

> "If your presence will not go with me, do not bring us up from here. For how shall it be known that I have found favor in your sight, I and your people? Is it not in your going with us, so that we are distinct, I and your people, from every other people on the face of the earth?" (Exodus 33:15-16)

That is not to say that there should be no visible structures and organizations, for the Spirit works through men and women to bring order to God's family. Unfortunately, we tend to reap results that don't align with God's heart when we build with human effort. We draw lines that God never intended, fostering confusion, inconsistency, and even misdirection. The following two sections explore some teachings I wonder about that may be obscuring the importance of Spirit baptism and unity within the church. I offer these as examples that have directly impacted me, but there are many others that one might also add.

---

151 Timothy Ware sees the church as the place where the Spirit is (Timothy Ware, *The Orthodox Church*, (London: Penguin Books, 1997), 242). Macchia concludes "The church is the Spirit-baptized people of God.... a communion of love that is open to the world and involved in self-giving, abundantly so, to the point of being described as overflowing love, the love revealed from the incarnation to Pentecost" (*The Spirit-Baptized Church*, 56). Hodson notes that "Hebrews 2.4 and 6.4 make it clear that the presence of the Holy Spirit with a people authenticates them as new-covenant people." Hodson "Hebrews," 236.

The Real Presence

Pretend with me for a moment that I am blind and want to know the truth about the current weather. You tell me it is raining outside. I have some options to confirm what you've said. I might ask another person to see if they agree. Of course, they might be lying or unable to know for sure. I might listen to the sound of rain on the roof, but I may not know conclusively if it is light rain. The best way to confirm the truth is to go outside and experience the weather for myself. If it is raining, I will hear it; if I step out, I will feel it. That was my approach to Spirit baptism in 1993. I wanted to experience what the Bible and my friend described, so I sought God for that experience. I came to know tangibly, experientially, and scripturally that I had received the Holy Spirit. The Spirit of God, of the Father and Son, had come to dwell in me just as he had for Jesus' disciples in the first century.

In June 2023, I spent two wonderful days at a charismatic Catholic retreat. It was a time of reconnection to my Catholic roots and my first experience attending a charismatic mass. At times during the worship, the entire room was filled with prayer and song in spiritual languages. Before each lecture, everyone would pray in spiritual languages with hands outstretched toward the speaker, interceding for him or her and thanking God for what we were about to hear. This experience made me think back to the folk masses I attended in my local parish in the 1970s and the singers who seemed full of genuine joy in worship. It made me wonder if at least some of them had that joy because they were part of the early Catholic charismatic renewal.

When it came time during mass for the Eucharist, I knew I had to refrain because I was not a practicing Catholic. I was communing with my brothers and sisters whom I knew intuitively and experientially as my family in Christ through the Spirit, yet I could not share this sacrament with them. The topic was reintroduced later at one of our breakfast table discussions when there was time for us to share our backgrounds. I gave some of my testimony, including my Spirit baptism and how God had brought me out of darkness into his glorious light. A kind couple responded, "Jeff, you seem to have most of the pie, and that is wonderful, but you are still missing one very important slice." I didn't have to ask because I knew what they would say: the Eucharist.

They wanted me to partake of the Eucharist because that is, according to Catholic teaching, where we experience the Real Presence, the bread and wine transformed into the body and blood of Christ.[152] In the Catholic tradition, the RCC is a steward of this gift because, according to its tradition, the RCC has true apostolic succession through a continual line from the original twelve apostles under the leadership of Peter and the ability to represent Christ in consecrating the elements.[153] So, if there was anywhere to step outside to see if it was raining or if there was something to the Real Presence, the Catholic mass would be a fine starting point.

As I meditated on these thoughts, the risk manager in me said: "If the Real Presence in the Eucharist was a way to experience the risen Christ, what did I have to lose in seeking that experience?" When I shared my thoughts, my Catholic friends said that to be in right order I should first go through the sacrament of confession. Of course, there

---

152 "In the most blessed sacrament of the Eucharist 'the body and blood, together with the soul and divinity, of our Lord Jesus Christ and, therefore, the whole Christ is truly, really, and substantially contained'" (CCC 1374).

153 The RCC also recognizes the validity of sacraments in the Orthodox Church. Peter Jesserer Smith, "When Orthodox Come Into Communion: No RCIA Required," April 9, 2019. *National Catholic Register: https://www. ncregister.com/features/when-orthodox-come-into-communion-no-rcia-required* (February 29, 2024).

was no such restriction to participate in the adoration of the Eucharistic host, which I did from 2-2:30 a.m. that night.

When I entered the sanctuary, the host (bread) was on the altar in a monstrance (a decorative vessel used for display). I sat and kneeled at times, gazing at the host, contemplating Christ's sacrifice for me, and wondering if he would, in some particular way, communicate with me or make his presence known during this time. As I sat, I sensed a silent emptiness—no revelation, no communication—just quietness. I began to pray quietly in my spiritual language, experiencing the same peace and presence typical when I pray. I was not done yet, though. I still wanted to walk outside to see if it was raining, and in the back of my mind, I thought about the sacrament of confession.

A few days after the retreat, I went to our local Catholic church and waited in line at a weekday pre-mass confession. When it was time to see the priest, I knelt in the confessional and told him it had been at least forty-three years since my last confession. He laughed and said it was a long time but not the longest he had experienced. His longest was a man who had waited seventy-two years. I spent a short time with the priest and shared my confession, and he gave me some prayers to recite. Afterward, I stayed for the noon mass. Whether fully sanctioned or not, I followed the couple's advice from the retreat and got in line to partake of the Eucharist. I had to know.

What I experienced was nothing remarkably different from the many times I partook of the Eucharist in the RCC as a child and teen, nor from the many times I have participated in communion or breaking of bread outside the RCC. Nothing extraordinary happened. What was different, though, was me. I went back to my seat, and some thoughts came to mind.

I stopped trying to determine what additional effect I might receive from partaking in the Eucharist. Instead, I thought of the people who come to mass and adoration in the middle of the week. They are genuinely seeking to know, experience, and be transformed by the presence of God. In many cases, their devotion is well beyond that of many others who identify as Christians.

My heart was encouraged, and I felt a deeper love for my Catholic brothers and sisters. This experience made the truth that God looks upon the heart vividly clear. It led me to ask hard questions. Am I seeking him with all my heart, soul, mind, and strength? Am I seeking him with that same or deeper fervor? And if I seek him, will he not reveal himself to me and draw me nearer in relationship with him?

If we desire to know God, he will respond to us where we are. Can we experience the presence of God in a Catholic Mass? Absolutely. Can someone receive physical healing while partaking in the bread and wine? Most definitely. Even if the bread and wine were not transformed into the body and blood of Christ as the RCC teaches, the Spirit of Christ can be present and reveal himself through the sacrament, particularly if we are seeking him, and often much less so if we are merely participating out of obligation or tradition.

In May 2024, I had the opportunity to celebrate communion at a local church formerly part of the United Methodist denomination. Although I was unfamiliar with their practices, I discovered their liturgy was very similar to its RCC counterpart. The church member guiding me through the celebration instructed that when distributing the bread and wine/juice, we would look the recipient in the eyes and declare "the body of Christ broken for you" or "the blood of Christ poured out for you."

I was responsible for breaking the bread and passing it out as attendees came forward. As I looked into their eyes, I repeated, "The body of Christ, broken for you," placing the bread into their open hands. By the time the fourth or fifth person came up, I was overcome with tears at the intensity of Christ's love for us and his desire to nourish his flock. I could also sense the appreciation of those receiving communion and their response to his presence in our midst. It was an unforgettable experience.

Whether the bread and wine are turned into the body and blood of Christ, I am still not sure, but I am immensely more appreciative of Christ's presence in the midst of the sacrament. I also desire to honor my brothers and sisters who may view the sacrament differently.[154]

I am now less concerned about what I might be missing in the Eucharist but still more concerned about whether our participation in any sacrament, ritual, practice, or tradition in any denomination or stream is possibly diverting or at least delaying us from pursuing being baptized in the Holy Spirit as a means of entering a deeper communion with God.

What if many who rely on communion in any denomination as their experience of Christ *par excellence* (as the RCC says, "the source and summit of the Christian life"[155]) are actually experiencing far less of his presence than is available through the continually indwelling Spirit received in Spirit baptism?[156] What if the primary real presence in the new covenant is the presence of the Spirit of God in us?

---

154 Randy Clark provides a helpful perspective on how we can navigate different beliefs about the sacrament in "A Special Message on Communion," *https://www.youtube.com/watch?v=E3ELssiGLuI* (June 2, 2024).

155 CCC 1324

156 From an Orthodox perspective, Ware sees unity with Christ and others as enabled by the sacraments, particularly the Eucharist (*The Orthodox Church*, 241-242). Paul writes that "For in one Spirit we were all baptized into one body—Jews or Greeks, slaves or free—and all were made to drink of one Spirit" (1 Corinthians 12:13). Dunn observes: "Paul does not say 'one baptism, therefore one body', but 'one *Spirit*, therefore one body'. The Corinthians knew they were members of the one body because the metaphors of being 'baptized in one Spirit' and of being 'drenched in one Spirit' were living realities in their common experience and memory ('all')." *Jesus and the Spirit*, 261-262.

A sacrament can be defined as an outward sign of an inward grace. Is it conceivable that prayer in a spiritual language is a biblical sign *par excellence* of the inner activity of the indwelling Spirit? And was this sign not divinely and supernaturally instituted on the day of Pentecost, as the disciples heeded Christ's command to wait in Jerusalem (Luke 24:49)?

Could it be that experiencing the Spirit and praying in the Spirit (communion with God) was a primary source of the nourishment and edification (1 Corinthians 14:4) that Jesus spoke of when mentioning the bread in chapter 6 of John's Gospel? Again, Jesus says he is the bread of life (John 6:35) and summarizes that the Spirit gives life (John 6:63; Romans 8:9-11). The Spirit is to fill us (Ephesians 5:18) and pour forth as rivers of living water (John 7:38-39).

Could the hunger for God's presence also be fueling the modern-day call for a Eucharistic revival within the RCC? According to Pew Research, today, only 30 percent of Catholics believe in the Real Presence, while others view the bread and wine as symbolic.[157] How many who have experienced Spirit baptism could say it was symbolic only?

Pentecost and the resulting life of the indwelling Spirit were the aims of Jesus' ministry. The crucifixion and resurrection were pointing to and preparing for the indwelling of the bride. What if our highest form of communion is a living, breathing relationship with the living, breathing God through the one who is the very Breath of Life, the Holy Spirit in us? To this table, partaking of the Spirit, there is no restriction,

---

157 Gregory A. Smith, "Just one-third of U.S. Catholics agree with their church that Eucharist is body, blood of Christ." August 5, 2019. *Pew Research Center: https://www.pewresearch.org/short-reads/2019/08/05/transubstantiation-eucharist-u-s-catholics/* (February 29, 2024).

no denominational boundary, only union with God and true life shared with one another.[158]

Confirmation, Chrismation, or Spirit Baptism?

As noted in chapter 6, both the Catholic and Orthodox traditions see confirmation/chrismation as bringing to bear the experience of Pentecost in the believer's lives, and several other streams see confirmation at least related to Spirit baptism events in Acts. I asked if these sacraments, rites, and ordinances actually equate to Spirit baptism, or if they merely point in its direction. Are they possibly vestigial remains of what was more fully experienced as Spirit baptism by the early Christians?

As noted in chapter 6, Charismatic Catholics perceive that through baptism in the Holy Spirit, "Pentecost is made present and alive in the Church today." Spirit baptism typically takes place apart from the sacrament of confirmation and in a completely different setting.[159] However, seemingly in competition with this, the RCC Catechism states that the effect of confirmation is "the full outpouring of the Holy Spirit as once granted to the apostles on the day of Pentecost."[160]

Which, then, is true? Is the full outpouring of Pentecost present at Spirit baptism, confirmation, or both? And if both, is a second needed because the first was somehow deficient? The explanation offered is that Spirit baptism brings alive, releases, or actualizes the grace of baptism

---

158 Kärkkäinen notes that "*koinonia/communion* denotes 'a sharing in one reality held in common.'... The church is a communion in the Spirit since it is the Spirit of Christ that unites all Christians together into one church." Veli-Matti Kärkkäinen, *An Introduction to Ecclesiology: Ecumenical, Historical & Global Perspectives*, (Downers Grove, IL: InterVarsity Press, 2002), 87.

159 ICCRS, *Baptism in the Holy Spirit*, 69, 91-92.

160 CCC 1302

and confirmation.[161] The need for actualization seems to point to confirmation alone being ineffective at bringing about the fullness of Holy Spirit reception.

If I have received the Holy Spirit through confirmation, do I only get part, just the presence which somehow comes without the power, love, and awareness of his proximity that will be imparted later? When Jesus walked into a room, could those with him experientially recognize him as present? Could they see and hear him and experience his love, wisdom, and power? Similarly, shouldn't we be able to know when the Spirit has entered us? Again, after speaking of the Spirit who will be in us (John 14:17), Jesus says that we will *know* that he is in us (John 14:20).

What of those who have never been confirmed or water-baptized but are first baptized in the Holy Spirit? Are they missing a part of the Holy Spirit? Even the position of many Pentecostals, who assert that we receive the Holy Spirit at conversion, then later receive the fullness or power to witness at Spirit baptism, seems like a potentially confusing proposition. Was the initial receipt of the Spirit somehow deficient? Does the Spirit within, if he makes his home in us at conversion, baptism, confirmation, or some other time, withhold the effect of his presence within, or somehow stay "all cramped up in a tiny space within our souls,"[162] dormant[163] until we have been baptized in the Spirit, then not a receiving of the Spirit, but an activation?

As noted earlier, at the urging of the Jerusalem apostles, Peter and John went to the converts at Samaria and placed their hands on them to

---

161 ICCRS, *Baptism in the Holy Spirit*, 75-76.
162 Boucher, *Catholic Charismatic Renewal*, 15, 61.
163 ICCRS, *Baptism in the Holy Spirit*, 101.

impart the Holy Spirit (Acts 8:17). It seems reasonable to assume then that they had not previously received the Spirit. The same occurs with Paul in Ephesus (Acts 19:6). *After* the Ephesians were baptized in the name of Jesus, Paul laid his hands on them to receive the Spirit.

I wonder if it is possible (even a tiny chance) that the Holy Spirit is most often not received at confirmation or any time prior but is received at Spirit baptism. Not having received the Spirit would bring a simple explanation to the testimony of many, myself included, that nothing happened at my confirmation or in the years that followed that bore any evidence of having experienced a personal Pentecost.[164] My confirmation in the RCC contrasts sharply with the life-transforming Spirit baptism I experienced more than a decade later, accompanied by the same biblical signs recorded in Acts.

The picture within the Orthodox church is much the same, except, as we mentioned earlier, the renewal did not have a significant impact there. Similar to the RCC, the Orthodox see themselves as the "One Holy, Catholic and Apostolic Church" and possessors of the "fullness of the faith,"[165] and Spirit baptism, in the Pentecostal-charismatic sense, is not regularly experienced as part of the Orthodox sacramental life. However, their theology elevates the importance of union with God (*theosis*), which should theoretically open the door widely to the experience of Spirit baptism. The 18th-century Russian Orthodox elder, Saint Seraphim of Savrov, taught that "the true aim of the Christian life is the acquisition of the Holy Spirit of God." If Spirit baptism is the receipt

---

164 See testimony in Boucher, *Catholic Charismatic Renewal*, 4-5. Clark and Healy note "Few of those who are confirmed today manifest anything like what Scripture and the Church hold as the intended effects of that sacrament. On the other hand, when people experience baptism in the Holy Spirit, sometimes years later, their lives do begin to manifest the normal effects of confirmation." *Spiritual Gifts Handbook*, 116.

165 Cremeens, *Marginalized Voices*, 161.

of the Spirit, then Saint Seraphim provides a strong endorsement for a greater renewal in the Orthodox church. Again, let it be so!

A leader in the Orthodox renewal described his Spirit baptism experience after years of "praying for a greater infilling of the Holy Spirit" and "seeking that heavenly language by which to praise Jesus ineffably." He shared that while in his home, "an instantaneous feeling came over me of God's presence that seemed to fill the room and it overwhelmed me to the point where I began weeping uncontrollably.... It was like a father's embrace had enveloped me in all tenderness and loving affection.... A wonderful sense of peace and calm filled me." He further reported, "It was the following Paschal week when my tongue broke loose to express the gift of speaking in that heavenly language."[166] As in the Charismatic Catholic descriptions, this encounter with the Spirit involved a tangible inner experience with external evidence. Is it possible—even likely—that the Spirit is not received in the Orthodox chrismation, but rather in Spirit baptism?

Have you experienced the sacrament or rite of confirmation (or chrismation) in any stream of Christianity? If so, were you in any way aware of the actual reception of the Holy Spirit in these events? Was there any accompanying inward or outward sign or experience you can point to that lets you know that you received the Spirit? After this time, did you experience or notice any fundamental change in your relationship with God, closeness, enablement of spiritual gifts not previously present, growing in love for God and others, more profound understanding

---

166 Eusebius Stephanou, "Rekindling the Gift of God for a More Effectual Witness," *The Logos*, 5, no. 6 (June-July 1972), 17-18 in Cremeens, *Marginalized Voices*, 77. Stephanou wrote in his last will and testament a charge to the church to focus on "The need for the extraordinary provision of the Holy Spirit Baptism that comes directly from Heaven for infusing in believers a nuptial love for the Divine Bridegroom in preparation for the Marriage Supper of the Lamb (Rev. 19:9)." Joseph Abbate, "Remembering the Life of Father Eusebius Stephanou," *The Orthodox Evangelist*, 50, no. 2 (Summer 2016), 1.

of the Scriptures, or ability to hear his voice, among other things? Have you ever considered if your experience in these events was the same or close to the Spirit baptism experienced in the Book of Acts?

I don't deny that some may have experienced a genuine Spirit baptism at confirmation or chrismation, just as some might receive the Spirit during water baptism or even with their profession of faith. Unfortunately, these life-changing events are more the exception than the rule.

15

Where Are We Headed?

Another Like Hurricane Michael?

While Hurricane Michael's worst impact was limited to a swath of the Florida Gulf Coast (see chapter 1), there is another event that will impact the life of every human being.

> As were the days of Noah, so will be *the coming of the Son of Man*. For as in those days before the flood they were eating and drinking, marrying and giving in marriage, until the day when Noah entered the ark, and they were unaware until the flood came and swept them all away, so will be the coming of the Son of Man. Then two men will be in the field; one will be taken and one left. Two women will be grinding at the mill; one will be taken and one left. Therefore, *stay awake, for you do not know on what day your Lord is coming*. But know this, that if the master of the house had known in what part of the night the thief was coming, he would have stayed awake and would not have let his house be broken into. Therefore *you also must be ready, for the Son of Man is coming at an hour you do not expect*. (Matthew 24:37-44, emphasis added)

> The *day of the Lord will come like a thief*, and then the heavens will pass away with a roar, and the heavenly bodies will be burned up and dissolved,

> and the earth and the works that are done on it will be exposed. Since all
> these things are thus to be dissolved, *what sort of people ought you to be*
> *in lives of holiness and godliness, waiting for and hastening the coming*
> *of the day of God,* because of which the heavens will be set on fire and
> dissolved, and the heavenly bodies will melt as they burn! But according
> to his promise we are waiting for new heavens and a new earth in which
> righteousness dwells. (2 Peter 3:10-13, emphasis added)

> Therefore, preparing your minds for action, and being sober-minded, set
> your hope fully on the grace that will be brought to you at the revelation
> of Jesus Christ. (1 Peter 1:13)

I shared these verses to emphasize the reality of our mutual futures, hoping that it will help us to be even more sober-minded about our lives than the owners of the Sand Palace were about their vacation home.

If some of us are right, we may be able to get by with a mediocre life in Christ and become lifelong citizens of the new heaven and earth one day (Isaiah 65:17; 2 Peter 3:10-13; Revelation 21:1), as long as we have met the minimum requirements, the minimum building code (profession of faith, baptism, sinner's prayer, or whatever our faith stream teaches).

But if we choose a path of mediocrity, how well will we bear fruit in this life or for eternity? How will we be God's ambassadors on this earth?

Being overcomers in this life (1 John 4:4; 5:4-5; Revelation 2:7, 17, 26; 3:5, 12, 21) takes a measure of persistence and fortitude that can only come from one source—not by our might, nor our power, but by the Spirit of God (Zechariah 4:6).

Do you have a faith that can stand against persecution? Are you firmly built upon the Rock and know well his stability, power, and love? Are you able to walk in excellence—living and working as unto God? Do you experience his peace and joy during life's trials? Have you sought out what it was that so impacted the apostles and the first disciples?

Consider again the parables of the kingdom of heaven and the five virgins with no oil in Matthew 25:1-13. The bridegroom responds to the five virgins: "I do not know you." And to those that prophesy and do miracles in the name of God but do not do his will in Matthew 7:21-23, Jesus says he will declare: "I never knew you." Consider, if eternal life is knowing God (John 17:3), what does not knowing him produce?

As we discussed in chapter 1, while it is common for people to think of financial losses in risk terms, we often overlook the impacts of decisions we make in other areas of life. We don't always consider or count the cost of these choices on our well-being, the well-being of our families, those we love, and those we are called to bless, or even the eternal consequences. If we haven't by now, it is time for us to make a risk assessment of our spiritual beliefs and practices.

Ultimately, we should not constantly fear the risks and storms around us and making wrong choices. We desire to be transformed so that our choices and walk are in lockstep with God's heart for our lives. We need God's voice through the Spirit with and in us to speak and guide us. By hearing, receiving, and obeying, we find freedom, his peace rests on us, and we experience the joy of knowing him and walking in his ways.

A Revival That Lasts

Across time and in cities and regions throughout the world, there have been individuals and groups from many streams praying for healing and revival, with denominational barriers seemingly melting away for periods of time and breakthroughs happening against evil in all areas of life. Each of those revivals planted seeds in the body of Christ that, in turn, brought more fruit. In time, at least some of the love and connectedness often evaporates. What may come in like a welcome flood eventually subsides and leaves sparse evidence behind of the unity that was. Then, a new revival is needed.

What if these fires that started were to envelop the earth and keep burning brighter and brighter? What if the Spirit brought an enduring unity and mutual love, breaking down barriers, helping us appreciate one another, desire to learn from one another, and understand and share what we have? Do you believe that we have a chance to collaborate with the Spirit on a change that lasts?

What if we shared a mutual core value to know and experience God through the Holy Spirit on an ongoing basis? What if our expressed desire was to be transformed to be like Christ, bearing his love so that others see that we have been with him and are impacted by his presence within us? And what if our healing, edification, and understanding enabled the love of Christ in us to draw others into the same in-you relationship with him?

What if the Body was functioning fully in its giftings so that we could grow and mature into the temple that Paul speaks of in Ephesians 2:19-22 as true disciples of the one living Christ who makes his home in us? What might that unleash in the world?

Revivals and their seeds sown are good and a gift of God. Is it time, though, to develop such roots that revival isn't an aberration but that it is happening in the lives of individuals and communities on an ongoing basis until the return of Christ? Should it not be that whenever people enter a corporate gathering in any living church body, they encounter the presence of God and are convicted of their sin and need for him or encouraged to draw near? Is this not what Paul described in Corinth as they prophesied in the presence of unbelievers (1 Corinthians 14:24-25)? Paul wasn't talking about a unique outpouring but a regular occurrence.[167]

What Are We to Do?

For the body of Christ to truly display God's glory on all the earth, we must be united in love, not simply in deeds, actions, and doctrine. We must be drinking from the same well of life, experiencing the same presence of God within, and living in the fullness of the new covenant made possible through Christ's sacrifice. Simply having cultural diversity is not enough. Having ecumenical councils that can agree on specific doctrinal points and holding interdenominational gatherings is not enough. We must be vitally joined to the Vine, the true Source of Life, in a manner that only the Father and Son, through the Holy Spirit, can accomplish.

Have we allowed our historical doctrines to be challenged in light of the renewal of the 20th century? Have we rejected the first-century experience of the Spirit in favor of our more "mature and seasoned" religious framework?

---

167 Keener expresses a similar sentiment, noting "If God poured out the Spirit on the Day of Pentecost, then much of what we envision as "revival" is simply part of the normal Christian life." *Spirit Hermeneutics*, 53.

Do we gather and experience the movement of the Spirit as described in the New Testament? Do we spend our time and resources arguing why we should not be experiencing the same supernatural care of God for his people as was experienced in the first century?

Do we view our role as wielding power, doing signs and wonders, or knowing Christ and the Father deeply through the Spirit as our highest priority? Are we willing to humble ourselves in his presence and give up our control, yielding our most precious assets, our minds and our voices, to be filled and led by the Spirit?

As one match can cause a great fire, so one person can make a great impact. In many cases, God begins with one person in a family or community—an Abraham or Moses—so that all can see that the growth is from God. Are you willing to be, or are you already, a flame in the circle of life where you live and move, bearing God's presence among others? This is our calling.

POSTLUDE

Fruit of the Spirit and Missional Christianity

This book has focused on a single aspect of our initiation into life in Christ, Spirit baptism, and related impacts on individual and communal pursuit of a relationship with God. But the Holy Spirit in us is to produce fruit. Just as Jesus was conceived in Mary by the Holy Spirit, God conceives and births life through us by his Spirit. Paul tells us that the Spirit produces in us love, joy, peace, patience, kindness, goodness, faithfulness, gentleness, and self-control (Galatians 5:22-23). Our love relationship with God should lead us to be salt and light on the earth (Matthew 5:13-16).

Just as Jesus' mission was to seek and save the lost, heal the sick, bring recovery of sight to the blind, deliver those bound in sin or demonic oppression, and bring them into a relationship with the God who made heaven and earth, so is ours. [168] Our lives are not to be focused only on our intimacy with God, but we are to live from the place of intimacy as the source of all goodness. We are to be vessels of his presence in these jars of clay (2 Corinthians 4:7), and the world should know that we are his by his love in and through us (John 13:35).

---

168 Regarding 2 Corinthians 1:21-22, Pinnock notes that "As Jesus became Christ by being anointed by the Spirit, so it is with us. It sounds odd, but Paul's words imply that we have been anointed as "little Christs" alongside Jesus. This makes plain what the purpose of anointing is: not to excite religious affections as ends in themselves but to empower people to follow Jesus on his path. "As the Father has sent me, so I send you" (Jn 20:21)." *Flame of Love*, 188. Macchia, addressing this topic, notes "The bride does not marry her groom merely to serve him or his cause in the world. There is an intimate sharing of life and ecstatic enjoyment at the heart of that union that is not reducible to vocational or missional categories, though it can't be [understood] without them." *The Spirit-Baptized Church*, 9.

It begins in our homes, church communities, neighborhoods and workplaces, the marketplace, and wherever our feet may take us, as led by his Spirit. Just as we are to be available to him, to spend time with him and come to know him, we are to be gifts to others, to love and serve those around us, building one another up. We must make ourselves available to him and be attentive to his voice and leading. As James tells us, faith without works is dead (James 2:14-26), and as John affirms, our love is seen by our keeping his commandments, by having a listening ear to the God who leads us from within, doing as he tells us, speaking what he says, just as Christ did (John 15:8-17). Our lives are to glorify God and make his presence and glory known on the earth (John 17:22-23). What a matchless calling we have as his sons and daughters!

If you are in him, and he is in you, and his Spirit is speaking, how is he calling you to walk with him? How is the gift of his Spirit in you leading you to lay down your life for others in this world? If you don't know, ask him what he wants you to know and do. And of all things, stop and listen to what he says in response, write it down, and engage brothers and sisters in Christ as you discern his will for your life.

If You Are Considering Spirit Baptism

Jesus said: "Behold, I stand at the door and knock. If anyone hears my voice and opens the door, I will come in to him and eat with him, and he with me" (Revelation 3:20). King David implored:

> Lift up your heads, O gates! And be lifted up, O ancient doors, that the King of glory may come in. Who is this King of glory? The Lord, strong and

mighty, the Lord, mighty in battle!... The Lord of Hosts, he is the King of glory! (Psalm 24:7-8, 10)

There is no time better than now, no day better than today. If you have not yet done so, ask him to baptize you with his Holy Spirit. Don't hesitate to ask someone else to pray with you, lay hands on you (if they are so directed), and press in to take hold of that which does not perish. Do not relent until your prayer is answered. And when he is in you, continue to pursue him in love with your entire mind, heart, soul, and strength, praying in the Spirit on all occasions, building yourself up in faith, and keeping yourself in the love of God (Jude vv. 20-21). Seek out edifying relationships within the body, find a community you can grow with, and let God transform your life into a gift, bearing life for others.

If Nothing Else

If this book accomplishes nothing else but to bring the question of Spirit baptism to the consciousness, to see it more clearly for what it is or can be, to raise awareness and spur some on to dig more deeply and know God more fully, then all praise be to God. As we move forward, let not the smoldering wick go out, but let it be fanned into a flame, a fire that cannot be quenched. In many places, it is already burning.

Let us also recapture the priority of relationship, which is Jesus's primary aim: to restore our relationship with our Father through the Holy Spirit he has given us. This restoration begins with each of us, one relationship at a time.

Lastly, let us again hear and take to heart the words of our elder brother Paul as he prayed for us:

I do not cease to give thanks for you, remembering you in my prayers, that the God of our Lord Jesus Christ, the Father of glory, may give you the Spirit of wisdom and of revelation in the knowledge of him, having the eyes of your hearts enlightened, that you may know what is the hope to which he has called you, what are the riches of his glorious inheritance in the saints, and what is the immeasurable greatness of his power toward us who believe, according to the working of his great might that he worked in Christ when he raised him from the dead and seated him at his right hand in the heavenly places, far above all rule and authority and power and dominion, and above every name that is named, not only in this age but also in the one to come. (Ephesians 1:16-21)

For this reason I bow my knees before the Father, from whom every family in heaven and on earth is named, that according to the riches of his glory he may grant you to be strengthened with power through his Spirit in your inner being, so that Christ may dwell in your hearts through faith—that you, being rooted and grounded in love, may have strength to comprehend with all the saints what is the breadth and length and height and depth, and to know the love of Christ that surpasses knowledge, that you may be filled with all the fullness of God. Now to him who is able to do far more abundantly than all that we ask or think, according to the power at work within us, to him be glory in the church and in Christ Jesus throughout all generations, forever and ever. Amen. (Ephesians 3:14-21)

May God bless you, keep you, and make the light of his face shine upon you and within you. May he pour out his grace, his abundant and endless love upon you, filling you to overflowing by his Spirit within, and give you his abiding peace, an unshakable resoluteness in every storm.

May the Bride of Christ come to her full maturity, shining brightly, with an abundant supply of oil, overflowing with the goodness of God and ready for the return of her Groom.

ACKNOWLEDGMENTS

I can only begin to attempt to express my thanks to those who have most influenced me in this work. For my incredible wife Marie, for your constant encouragement and honest feedback, and my children, Audrey, Joseph, Gabrielle, Elena, Rachel, Lydia, Nathan, and Madeline, for your support to step out in faith to seek God and write, and for being my inspiration, which is to see you flourish in Christ. For Sandy Stein and your continual friendship, authorly advice and resources, prayers, and encouragement to press on. To William and Paula Turner, for the foundation of a living relationship with God you nurtured in me over my most formative years in Christ, an ever-present reminder of his love. To Brian Pritchard for your generous and insightful feedback. To John Mizerak for fanning the flame and encouraging me to let God catch me as I stepped out into the unknown. To Mike Stebbins, for teaching me to acknowledge what I don't know and how to process that in making better writing decisions. For Lorne Davidson, for your encouragement along the way, retreats with Abba, and for your helpful feedback. For Todd Westfahl, Mike Giampietro, and Eric Colton, for your steadfast prayer, brotherly love, and encouragement to persevere. To Pastor Jack Hayford, who encouraged me in the Spirit-filled life through his radio ministry and who established The King's University, which has been instrumental in helping me to see more clearly God's work in and love for the Body of Christ. For current and past scholars of the Society for Pentecostal Studies, for sharing your life's work and passion for study through your writing and inspiring me to seek truth more deeply amid diverse perspectives.

BIO

Jeff's faith journey has taken him through various streams of the body of Christ. Raised in the Roman Catholic tradition, he continued to grow among Congregational, Messianic Jewish, Baptist, Pentecostal, and independent churches, including an independent home church where he and his wife Marie spent their formative years in Christ. His risk management career of 30 years combined with ministry experience co-leading a home church and participation in prayer, teaching, and music ministry in the local church gives him a unique perspective on our walk with Christ. Jeff holds a Master's in Practical Theology from The King's University, Southlake, Texas, and loves to read and hear how others understand the Holy Spirit's work in the body of Christ and their lives. Jeff and Marie are trained classical singers who met on the opera stage in Northern Virginia. They have six daughters, two sons, and a rising count of grandchildren. Their passion is seeing the body of Christ grow to maturity in the presence, power, and love of the Holy Spirit, a united and radiant bride waiting for the visible return of her King.

Jeff would love to hear your reactions, challenges, questions, and anything that brings more insight into what is on these pages. Feel free to send comments or questions to info@fivelampspress.com.

www.ingramcontent.com/pod-product-compliance
Lightning Source LLC
Chambersburg PA
CBHW030409130626
46549CB00004B/1700